The Satiric Vision of Blas de Otero

The Satiric Vision of Blas de Otero

Geoffrey R. Barrow

University of Missouri Press
Columbia, 1988

Library of Congress Cataloging-in-Publication Data

Barrow, Geoffrey R.
   The satiric vision of Blas de Otero / Geoffrey R. Barrow.

      p. cm.
      Bibliography: p.
      Includes index.
      ISBN 0-8262-0687-5 (alk. paper)
      1. Otero, Blas de—Criticism and interpretation.   2. Satire.
I. Title.
PQ6627.T35Z618   1988   88-4877
861'.64—dc19   CIP

This book was brought to publication with the assistance of the
Program for Cultural Cooperation Between Spain's Ministry of
Culture and North American Universities.

∞™ This paper meets the minimum requirements of
the American National Standard for Permanence of Paper
for Printed Library Materials, Z39.48, 1984.

To Arleen

PREFACE

This book was conceived while teaching Humanities at Columbia University, an enterprise that brought together colleagues from many disciplines. There I soon became sharply aware of the need to interest non-Hispanists in Spanish literature and, conversely, of the need for Hispanists to profit from studies in literatures other than their own. I was also often reminded that, when looking at literary kinds, knowledge of the dangers of classification and of the practical requirement of focusing on texts saves one from much muddled abstraction.

My chief debt in forming this study of Blas de Otero is to those who have worked with satire in the past, mostly in English and Classical literatures. Also, of course, I am especially indebted to those who have written about post–Civil War Spanish poetry. However, no one who is interested in literature can for long confine his or her interest to a single literature. I hope that Hispanists are not too surprised and other specialists not too betrayed by the results of my reading.

More recently, my debt is to colleagues who have read these pages in draft form. Their comments and suggestions have constantly cleared my mind and improved my expression. At a distance and on another shore, I am grateful to those English grammar-school masters who fascinated me with the force of rhetorical figures in Dryden and Pope, and to faculty at the University of Leeds who pushed the horizon of Spanish poetry beyond Garcilaso and Bécquer. I am also indebted to mentors at Brown University who deepened my appreciation of Spanish poetry as well as encouraged comparative considerations.

For practical and material support I am grateful for library services at Ripon College and at Purdue, Columbia, and Liverpool universities, for a National Endowment for the Humanities Summer Seminar on Golden Age comedy at Duke University, and for the hospitality of the Liverpool Latin Seminar. I thank the editors of *Neophilologus* and *Hispanic Review* for allowing me to reproduce, in revised form, material that previously appeared in those journals. For permission to use Otero's writings I thank his publishers and heirs. Naturally, none of my unnamed benefactors are responsible for such errors of fact, taste, and opinion that I am sure remain.

Evident on every page is my gratitude to my family for their tolerance, fortitude, and laughter.

G. R. B.
January 1988

Contents

I

INTRODUCTION

Spanish poetry written since the Civil War is commonly examined in one of two ways, both of which tend to diminish the achievement of individual poets. The approach most common to peninsular critics is to begin with movements, pointing to magazines and anthologies to show poetic directions. There is something to be said for this method. *Garcilaso, Espadaña, Proel,* Ribes' *Antología consultada,* Castellet's *Veinte años de poesía española,* or Luis' *Poesía social* are useful if what we want is an understanding of schools and influences and the climate of a period.[1] Nevertheless, the approach has its disadvantages. Chief among them is the temptation to diminish the poems themselves and to concentrate on the perceptions of an editor so that Boscán, as it were, comes to loom larger than Garcilaso. Furthermore, the tastes of a passing decade soon grow dusty on shelf, replaced by more fashionable "promotions," as the popular marketplace nomenclature often categorizes literary movements. Poems, however, do have imaginative independence and reveal larger continuities.

A second approach directs itself to a poetic group or generation. Not Otero, Celaya, Hierro, and Nora but "social poetry," not Valente, Rodríguez, and González but "poetry of discovery," is the prime object of attention.[2] It is easy to quibble by asking, for example, whether Otero is really a member of the generation of 1936 rather than a social poet. Yet the major pitfalls of this approach are well known. The grouping becomes irreducible, so that individual writers blend indistinguishably. Epochs of Spanish poetry appear as isolated logs moving down the river, one generation following another with the critic making or denying connections between them according to personal predilections. The categories tend to become lifeless: what excites one generation becomes antiquarian in the next as the component elements are lost from sight. There are, of course, other approaches that review poetry from the standpoint of larger patterns of ideas. At their worst, such reviews present literature as incidental to a political view of Spanish history that culminates in the apotheosis of "el pueblo en marcha" with the death of Franco. The critics' attitude to poetry depends ultimately on a conception of the nature of man that enshrines social action and a political faith. Such enslavement to progressive fads characterizes a good deal of Spanish and Latin American criticism.[3]

What is lacking is an evolutionary or developmental approach that accounts for the poetry in terms of the intellectual history of Spanish liberalism, or of the persistence of Romantic modes of thought, or simply of literary kind and style. In Otero, Celaya, and Hierro, for example, the myth of the poet-rebel, the delight in attacking distinctions of aesthetic and social rank, the glorification of the people and the landscape, the elevation of poetic fragments and prose jottings, the release found in boundless and indefinite ideals, sentimentalism, the libertarian bias, all are steady currents that, with Marxian eddies, undoubtedly

I

link the surface turbulence of post–Civil War Spanish poetry with at least the nineteenth century.[4] In short, what is needed is an approach that accounts for the poems on a less topical and more long-range basis, whether in the history of ideas or in literary themes and modes. Therefore, this study addresses the poetry of a major literary figure of Francoist Spain, Blas de Otero, by placing his work within the larger pattern of experience afforded by literary satire.

Since our perceptions are mediated so naturally by literary kinds, we often entirely fail to recognize satire for what it is. Yet, as Rosalie Colie has pointed out in her seminal essays, literary kinds, sets, and patterns organize the vast body of literature to provide a set of interpretations, of forms, or of fixes on the world.[5] My attempt to transcend parochial barriers using the compass of satire is matched by a particularist concern with the special characteristics of the poems. Otero's writing can be conveniently divided into three periods: a much-studied period of religious existentialism that closes with *Ancia*; the committed writing of his major trilogy, *Pido la paz y la palabra, En castellano,* and *Que trata de España*; and a more self-consciously reflective phase that broadly extends from his return from a long stay in Cuba (1964–1967) to his death in Madrid in 1979.[6] Inevitably, he has fallen into the hands of politicizing and sociologizing commentators, evidently stimulated by the developing social and political commitment of his writing. Among British and American critics, once he adopted an overtly political stance his poetry was largely ignored, was lumped together with the so-called social poets (as useful a term as Monday poets), or was cursorily dismissed.[7] In the Spanish-speaking world, on the other hand, early recognition of Otero's talent by Dámaso Alonso led to a seminal study of rhetorical techniques in the early poetry by Emilio Alarcos, increasing critical attention and prompting a spate of reprint editions.[8] These critics believe, as do I, that the texts should be approached in their own right—here foregrounding schemes and tropes, there issues of literary kinds. The overarching literary conception most germane to Blas de Otero is satire. Satire allows the poet to measure Spain against a yardstick of peace, justice, liberty, and natural beauty and to denounce the corrupt and abominable times in which he believes he lives. Of course, the boundary between satire and political values is not hard and fast. But new light is cast on political values by emphasizing literary matters.

Political commitment has hindered the appreciation of Otero's literary art. Many poets in a prevailingly oppositionist literary milieu accepted the primary role of literature as a social document and an expression of personal protest. This can be seen from the responses to Ribes' important 1952 questionnaire circulated among writers, in disclosures in published interviews, or in a plethora of poetic testimonies.[9] Moreover, poetry gained a freedom in Francoist Spain that was denied to novel, essay, and drama. In spite of varying degrees of censorship, poetry, because of its marginality, was capable of voicing public concerns prohibited in normal channels, and thereby it received verbose and emotional appreciations. In Spain literary studies provided opportunities to express social and political concerns, no matter how obliquely.[10]

Moreover, the folding of sociopolitical concerns into nontraditional forms that are freely expressive makes literary appreciation difficult. With the European Romantic movement came a distrust of rhetoric based on the assumption that it connotes insincerity. Rhetoric was virtually synonymous with artificial discourse that lacked feeling. Otero's own rejection of his early Gongorine poetry and the presentation of himself as an ordinary Spaniard—outspoken, spontaneous, and honest—easily encourage a modern taste for sincere self-expression, although sincerity is really not a strictly literary value.[11] A legacy of Romanticism in Spain is the virtual disappearance of formal verse satire and a blurring of literary kinds. Consequently, Otero's experiments in literary form, his mingling of linguistic registers and his deliberate blurring of the distinction between art and life, challenge a literary appreciation of his art. Nevertheless, a broad view of satire accommodates the flagrant, contentious tone of the poems, the elegant concern with the common, and the topics of social change and prophecy of Spain's future.

Satire, however, is a protean term that eludes sharp and easy definition. Spanish literature lacks the generic studies of satire that abound in English or Classical literature. Greek literature has no separate categories for comedy and satire: satire is a wholly Roman invention.[12] Later, in medieval peninsular literature, as Rodrigues Lapa acknowledges, the distinction drawn between "cantigas d'escarnho e de mal dizer" (songs of scorn and slander) is a simple scholastic pretension. He recognizes, of course, the immense variety of medieval satiric poetry and draws a distinction between comic and satiric purpose: the humorist does not try to change the world in the way that the moralist does.[13] This echoes the prefatory statement to the *Cancioneiro da Biblioteca Nacional de Lisboa*, which also separates laughable from scornful intent, giggle from mockery, *escarnho* from *risadilho*.

The line is hard to draw. Indeed, Kenneth Scholberg in his studies of Spanish satire avers that satire is a state of mind rather than a literary genre, but is also an attack on somebody or something. In fact, the very name means a medley, which may account for the loose inclusion of insults, invectives, taunts, jokes, gibes, ironies, slanders, jeers, and all the other terms by which such writings are known.[14] Given such taxonomic uncertainty, it is not surprising that Scholberg and Rodrigues Lapa use the organizing principle of satiric themes, or topics of composition. Robert Jammes follows a similar procedure when studying Góngora, although he draws the line between satire and burlesque, whereas R. M. Price divides Quevedo's verse into satirical and moral.[15]

To define satire is famously difficult: "Satire is the most problematic mode to the taxonomist, since it appears never to have corresponded to any one kind."[16] Yet a broad, working definition of satire is a practical necessity. The final aim is to interpret rather than to classify: recognition of the genre permits appreciation of creative principles, of the satiric vision that informs Otero's poetry. "A poem in which wickedness or folly is censured," Samuel Johnson's timeless definition, captures the satirist's tendency to judge and reprehend. Indeed, Alastair Fowler determines that "a radical moral stance is perhaps the most striking feature of the satiric repertoire," and Geoffrey Grigson declares that "satire postulates an ideal condition of man or decency, and then despairs of it; and enjoys the despair, masochistically."[17] So, we may expect an element of polemical attack or abuse as the satirist exposes evil, incites blame, and exhorts to remedial action.[18] Insofar as he claims to envision the shape of the future, his satiric medley may be termed apocalyptic.

Vision is a deliberately loose term, suggesting both comprehensiveness and variety, for though many individual poems share features that are considered characteristic of satire, these features are not always present in every poem. Otero freely mixes complaint, invective, burlesque, cursing, parody, innuendo, diatribe, sarcasm, elegy, prophecy, epigram, irony, understatement, animal fable, ridicule, and lampoon, guided always by a vision of the good life. In this he harks back to classicists who would, of course, leave out epigram. Certainly, fullness and variety characterize Otero's poetry and give a sense of freedom from restraint. Such a varied and miscellaneous quality is the essence of satire. Classical grammarians speculating on its origins derive the word from a certain kind of sausage that was filled with many ingredients.[19] Critics influenced by Renaissance or eighteenth-century models of satire would not consider invective or denunciation appropriate. Some impose limits on satiric ingredients—"Without the joke, everything goes; and we may be left only with complaint, invective, or denunciation"—whereas others are more catholic in taste.[20] Whether from literary readings, Jesuit rhetorical training, or an ear for vituperative preaching, Otero's denunciatory poems have much in common with invective. Certainly, his satiric spectrum is uncommonly broad. The rich mixture that stuffs his collections includes both extemporaneous wit and hard attack, all spiced with casual, autobiographical revelation.

After attack and variety, a final element of this minimal working definition is a sense of moral truth and historical particularity. All is not pure rhetoric or verbosity, no matter how exaggerated and distorted the nation's rottenness may appear in his writing. The fact that Otero attacks Francoist Spain enables us to recognize his fictional distortions—and the powers of invention are what interest most. Not so for the censor: *En castellano* was prohibited; *Que trata de España* was cut in half. Although not risking imprisonment and death, Otero did run the risk of getting entangled with the law. Traditionally, much easy fame has been generated by such brushes with authority, but in fact, in Otero's poems, the historical dissolves. As Eliot suggested of eighteenth-century satire, the object satirized disappears in the poetry. What remains is the exaggerated and distorted vision of evil. Often, in counterpoint, Otero ceases to attack and begins to affirm his great apocalyptic dream of human freedom and happiness. Rhetorically, the change is from vituperation to panegyric. The result is not strictly satire, of course, but rather the other side of the coin, an appeal to those true values from which the poet believes Spain has strayed.[21] Consumed with anger and frustration, the satirist castigates wickedness and appeals to virtue: satire heals with morals what it hurts with wit. This ethical appeal gives rational purpose to Otero's arraignment of vice and, significantly, links him with Antonio Machado and pre–Civil War poetry.[22]

My approach, I hope, offers something for readers both specialist and nonspecialist alike, for readers interested in literary satire and genre theory, in the rhetorical analysis of poetry, in twentieth-century Spanish poetry, and in the literary art of Francoist Spain. I first examine satiric apologias, those ways in which a poet gains social approval for his reforming iconoclasm, in chapter 1, "The Satirist." Then I look at particular satires of religion, women, art, the times, and tyranny, offering some detailed analyses of individual poems, in chapters 2 through 6, "The Satires." Chapter 7, "A Style of Dissent," speculates on what causes literary delight in the satires. Chapter 8, "Satire and Renewal," essentially a review of poetic imagery, shows how Otero inculcates those ethical and sociopolitical norms from which Spain has gone astray. The English translations of the poems are for the benefit of the general reader. They aim at no literary merit but are simply aids to the understanding of the Spanish.

It has become clear to me in the elaboration of this study that Otero's stature as a poet can best be appreciated through a broad understanding of the satiric mode, and conversely that the satiric vein in literature is an enlightening, practical, and enjoyable focus that has provided in Otero a new master of the tradition.

2

THE SATIRIST

The temptation to identify the speaker of the poem with the poet himself is particularly strong in satire, where the poet may follow the convention of offering an apologia for his life and writings and persuade us to endorse his right to continue exposing and deriding the world. Critics, in the main, have not distinguished between fictive satirist and living poet in Otero's poetry and tend to attribute to the latter everything expressed by his literary mask. Some reject the poetry as untruthful or, an equally needless error, argue tediously for the truthfulness of its reaction to the political, social, and economic situation of Franco's Spain, as if poetic value had something to do with documentary worth. The speaker, of course, is not fully identical with the poet, any more than the impassioned lover is entirely identical with the poet of elegy or lyric.

The scarcity of biographical information on Otero, as well as repeated assertions of truth-fulness by the speaker of the poems, has tended to shift the reader's focus away from poetic invention and toward the personality of the author. Interviews with Otero are rare, and for a living poet, biographical information is remarkably flimsy. Anthologies group poems under headings such as "Vida" or "Biografía," and even the memoirs of literary associates, such as Gil de Biedma's *Diario del artista seriamente enfermo,* blur the distinction between poet and persona by confirming the impression given in the satires of a brusque, entertaining outsider: "En casa de Carlos, después, coincido con Blas de Otero y José Agustín Goytisolo. Gabriel Ferrater les llama 'el húngaro y su oso,' porque se exhiben siempre juntos y José Agustín, que tiene los ojos zíngaros, hace de impresario. Otero me ha sido bastante simpático, a pesar de su tosquedad" (In Carlos's house, later, I bump into Blas de Otero and José Agustín Goytisolo. Gabriel Ferrater calls them "the Hungarian and his bear," because they are always together and José Agustín, who has gypsy eyes, plays the impresario. Otero has been quite nice to me, in spite of his coarseness).[1] In fact, Otero abets this spurious coalescence of life and literature when he adds the epigraph from Walt Whitman to an anthology of poems that refer to real people and places: "esto no es un libro. Quien vuelve sus páginas toca un hombre" (this is not a book. Whoever turns its pages touches a man).[2] The congenial and disarming title invites expectations of sincerity and frankness, not craftsmanship. Such apparent attempts to sidetrack the Muse, like the self-consciousness Otero chooses to show in his writing, understandably beguile an audi-ence lacking a clear realization that the poet is a masterful rhetorical artist donning a mask or creating an objective character. The fact is, however, that in an interview at the close of the turbulent sixties, at the height of the fashion for so-called social poetry, Otero affirms his primary, aesthetic responsibility: "el poema es un ente estético . . . la calidad estética es insos-layable" (the poem is an aesthetic entity . . . the aesthetic quality is undeniable).[3]

By focusing attention on the poem rather than on the poet, thinking of the poetry as working on the beliefs and emotions of his audience, we develop a principled understanding of his skills of invention. Rosemond Tuve's emphasis on artistic effects, not on moral or psychological causes, when reading the English Metaphysicals, is not inappropriate to the appreciation of Otero:

Earlier theory reads as if poetry were conceived of as a relation established between a subject and a reader, though only establishable by a poet. The emphasis on poetry as interesting evidence of the relation between a subject and a particular poet is an emphasis we have learned since, and one which seems the least helpful of any to the understanding of earlier poetry.[4]

Satire, of course, is an offshoot of epideictic rhetoric, the art of praise or blame, and ancient theory considered proof deriving from the moral character of the speaker to be the most effective, provided such proof arose from the work itself and not from the private life of the author.[5] Accordingly, Otero dramatizes the role of the honorable man driven to virtuous indignation at the state of Spain, compelled to speak out with a passion for truth. The figure, like Juvenal's indignant noble wandering the streets of Rome, is a deliberate rhetorical invention designed to persuade his audience to endorse his right to go on attacking and correcting the world. Moreover, although the figure develops, or rather ages, over twenty-five years, his main features remain the same. His moral character is impeccable; he speaks out bluntly, even inartistically; and his life is a long, unresting search for luminous truth. In short, Otero creates the figure of the poet as an acceptable authority for satiric attack. It makes his audience well disposed, attentive, and tractable, so that he can then proceed to play on their passions.

The modern satirist lacks the authority and privilege of the ancient poet that derived from his magical command over preternatural forces.[6] One way in which Otero inspires trust and confidence is through his literary persona's nobility of character. In Otero's early poems, God has withdrawn and man stands alone in a desolate world, faced with the task of preventing further degeneration:

Un mundo como un árbol desgajado.
Una generación desarraigada.
Unos hombres sin más destino que
apuntalar las ruinas.[7]

(A world like a dismembered tree.
An uprooted generation.
A few men with no other fate than
propping up ruins.)

In the absence of divine and human forces for good, the poet struggles to make his own suffering immortal and fecund. The motif of sacrifice is especially sharp in the early postwar poems: in "Aren en paz," where the poet offers his life in the hope of turning swords into ploughshares and of establishing, through his loving martyrdom, a reign of peace and free-dom;[8] or in "Crecida," where the speaker wanders compulsively, his cries unanswered, though a Europe awash with blood. The bold exaggeration of these poems helps to point up two important features of the victim-hero: the sense of moral outrage and the vision of the world as a battlefield between good and evil:

Traigo una rosa en sangre entre las manos
ensangrentadas. Porque es que no hay más
que sangre,
y una horrorosa sed
dando gritos en medio de la sangre.
                    ("Crecida," *Angel,* 58)

(I bring a rose set in blood in my bloodied
hands. Because there is only
blood,

and a horrible thirst
screaming in the midst of the blood.)

The poet possesses powers of redemption here symbolized by the rose of peace and justice, made explicit in "Canto primero" by a promise of relief to those in spiritual darkness:

Yo os traigo un alba, hermanos. Surto un agua,
eterna no, parada ante la casa.
Salid a ver. Venid, bebed. Dejadme
que os unja de agua y luz, bajo la carne.
                    ("Canto primero," *Angel,* 49)[9]

(I am bringing you a dawn, brothers and sisters. I provide water
that is not everlasting, but right here in front of the house.
Come out and see. Come, drink. Let me
annoint you with water and light, under the flesh.)

This priestly figure, impregnated with asceticism and mysticism, is a lay representative of Spanish monastic tradition. In the early poems the persona makes explicit his sense of messianic purpose: "¡Ay, ese ángel fieramente humano / corre a salvaros, y no sabe cómo!" (Oh, that fiercely human angel / runs to save you, and does not know how!) ("Estos poemas," *Redoble,* 13). His noble and selfless sacrifice is metaphorically associated with that of Christ: "Calvario como el mío pocos han visto" (A Calvary like mine few have seen).[10] Moreover, even after the author's invited visits to Communist countries, his literary work expresses a longing for revolution in mainly moral and religious terms: Otero's blind subscription to the Marxian gospel has much of the character of a religious revival. The closing sestet of "Que nadie me veía" is couched in the same messianic language of utopian quest and of dependence on inner light encountered in the earlier poems:

Doy señales de vida al enemigo
y sigo halando infatigablemente,
acercando a la tierra el horizonte.

Ultima etapa que acometo y sigo,
sigo, sigo subiendo airadamente
hacia la luz suavísima del monte.[11]

(I give signs of life to the enemy
and carry on hauling tirelessly
bringing the horizon close to earth.

This is the last stage I'll undertake and I go on,
on and on, climbing angrily upward
toward the soft light of the mountain.)

This hopeful faith in a beyond, a faith that quickens passion and incites to sacrifice, gives the speaker's convictions divine authority in his own eyes and in those of others. By his moral temper, he rises above the political and social ills of Spain, her hollow religiosity, the denial of human brotherhood, and the rapacity of the rich.

A sense of duty and service underlines this heroic posture in which the fate of Spain rests on the satirist. Detachment is impossible and the poet gains inspiration by giving himself up to everyday experience and by fusing himself with what he claims to be the real situation of his contemporaries, " . . . ruando / como / un perro de la calle, / amigo de la calle, / camarada / de la calle" (. . . wandering / like / a dog of the streets, / a friend of the streets, / a comrade / of the streets).[12] The city is frequently the setting, either Madrid or native Bilbao, for there the satirist is at once conscious of his own redeeming grace and of omnipresent vice, although the boundaries between self and the mass of mankind are blurred. "Igual que vosotros" proclaims the poet's private quest for serenity to be in harmony with that of other men (*Angel*, 33–34). In contradistinction to Juan Ramón's *inmensa minoría*, "Estos poemas" speaks to and on behalf of the majority:

Es a la inmensa mayoría, fronda
de turbias frentes y sufrientes pechos,
a los que luchan contra Dios, deshechos
de un solo golpe en su tiniebla honda.

A ti, y a ti, y a ti, tapia redonda
de un sol con sed, famélicos barbechos,
a todos, oh sí, a todos van, derechos,
estos poemas hechos carne y ronda.
                    ("Estos poemas," *Redoble,* 13)

(To the great majority, to those like tender shoots
with troubled brows and heavy hearts,
to those defying God, crushed small
by a single blow in their lightless depths.

To you, you, and you, walled in
under a thirsty sun, starving, fallow fields,
to all of you, yes, to all of you, go forth
these poems made flesh and song.)

Gradually, the distinguishing feature of the *inmensa mayoría* changes from spiritual disorientation to social deprivation.[13] Influenced perhaps by fashionable populist cant, the poet adopts a bottom-dog consciousness and speaks for the excluded, the rebellious, the idealized common man:

hablo
para la inmensa mayoría, pueblo
roto y quemado bajo el sol,
hambriento, analfabeto
en su sabiduría milenaria,
"español
de pura bestia," hospitalario y bueno
como el pan que le falta
y el aire que no sabe lo que ocurre.[14]

(I speak
for the great majority, a people
broken and burned under the sun,
hungry, illiterate
in their millenarian wisdom,
"pure-blooded
Spanish," hospitable and as good
as the bread that is lacking
and the air that does not know what is happening.)

Yet throughout the poetry the idea of service to man is repeated to reinforce the role of the selfless, honorable man in such a way that virulent, critical attack appears credible and acceptable.

What provokes his burning indignation is a world so corrupt that he appears to be living at the zenith of vice. Impatient, afire, unable to endure the wickedness he denounces, the satirist presents a fantastic vision of a Spain transformed: "Aquí / no se salva ni dios. Lo asesinaron" (Here / not even God is saved. They murdered him) ("Me llamarán, nos llamarán," *Pido,* 45). Beset with lies and neglect, his countrymen are, as a virulent neologism puts it, *españahogándose,* "chokingonSpain." The situation impels him to write, and filled with a virtuous indignation, he lashes out, depicting the moral depravity of priests, prostitutes, and the powers that be, swinging his scourge without compromise. His abhorrence of vice obliges him to speak out, and never for a moment does he show the least hesitation in distinguishing between right and wrong. The portrait in "Manifiesto" insists on this moral stimulus to writing, and, incidentally, the third person calls attention to Otero's self-conscious literary dramatization:

Ha porfiado contra la fe, la desidia y la falsedad, afincándose más y más en los años incontrovertibles, el esfuerzo renovado y la verdad sin juego. Ha leído hermosas y lamentables páginas, no ha perdonado ni olvidado porque apenas si recordaba, ha dejado que hablen la envidia sin causa y el odio sin pretexto, ha escrito unas pocas líneas ineludibles y ha arrojado el periódico a los perros.[15]

(He has struggled obstinately against faith, idleness, and falsehood, trusting more and more in the indisputable years, renewed efforts, and truth without little games. He has read beautiful and pitiful pages; he has not forgiven or forgotten because he scarcely remembered; he has let senseless envy and unabashed hatred speak; he has written a few inescapable lines and has thrown the newspaper to the dogs.)

Quite traditional and straightforward, the moral character of the satirist's indignation enhances the persona of the honorable man. Moreover, by assuming righteous anger and by insisting on the strength of his convictions, selfless virtue, courage, and patriotism, he wins favor with his audience. The persona, of course, is not quite so straightforward, for the more outspoken he becomes, the more he employs an exaggerated style to express his appalled recognition of flagrant vices and, consequently, the less likely he will appear to be morally objective. The aesthetic effects are, however, persuasive and beguiling.

The speaker's repeated declarations of his compulsion to write are part of the rhetorical stock-in-trade of satire. The vigor of such poems and their continued appearance signal a deliberate literary device, and they are usually positioned at the opening or close of collections.

Mis ojos hablarían si mis labios
enmudecieran. Ciego quedaría,
y mi mano derecha seguiría
hablando, hablando, hablando.
("Mis ojos hablarían," *Pido,* 15)

(My eyes would speak if my lips
were to become mute. If I were struck blind,
my right hand would go on
speaking, speaking, speaking.)

Escribo
por
necesidad,
para
contribuir
(un poco)
a borrar
la sangre
y
la iniquidad
del mundo
(incluída
la caricaturesca españa actual).
        ("Por-para," *Parler,* 18)[16]

(I write
out of
necessity,
in order
to contribute
[a little]
to wiping out

the blood
and
the iniquity
of the world
[including
the caricature that is spain today].)

Such lines highlight the routine apology of the satirist for the pedestrian nature of his muse. Unavoidably, the satirist is impelled to write, unable to restrain himself from expressing his dissatisfaction. The intention of these repeated assertions is to establish credit as a witness so that the audience will evaluate his testimony sympathetically. Yet by stirring the emotions of his audience, inflaming them with the hatred of vice, the speaker does not aim to make them think of or dwell on the merits of his case: he aims to shock, to induce feelings of indignation, horror, disgust, pity. The satirist's compulsion to write is a topic drawn from an arsenal of devices designed to win over the reader and to soften the impact of vitriolic and vengeful sentiments.

That the satirist's determination and passion to speak is fraught with peril only enhances his moral character. Censorship is the major obstacle to free expression. The mockery and sarcasm at the close of "Impreso prisionero" present a derisive image of the trials of the writer in Francoist Spain:

¡Ira de Dios,
espanto de los siglos venideros!
Hablo
en español y entiéndese en francés.
¡Oh qué genial trabucamiento
del diablo!
¿Hablar en castellano? Se prohibe.
Buscar españa en el desierto
de diecinueve cegadores años.
Silencio.
Y mas silencio. Y voluntad de vida
a contra dictadura y contra tiempo.
("Impreso prisionero," *Que trata,* 29)[17]

(God's wrath,
the terror of centuries to come!
I speak
in Spanish and am understood in French.
Oh what a clever confusion
on the part of the devil!
Speaking plainly in Spanish? It is forbidden.
Looking for Spain in the desert
of nineteen blinding years.
Silence.
And more silence. And a will to live
against dictatorship and against time.)

The speaker tells the truth about the restrictions of censorship in Francoist Spain, but historical accuracy or authorial sincerity are of little import. What matters is the poet's truth, not
that of the historian or biographer. The bitter amusement at the situation of the writer in
Spain here and in "Nadando y escribiendo en diagonal," for example, is persuasive. One
effect is to stress the thwarted passion of a great soul for good:

Escribir en España es hablar por no callar
lo que ocurre en la calle, es decir a medias palabras
catedrales enteras de sencillas verdades
olvidadas o calladas y sufridas a fondo,
escribir es sonreír con un puñal hincado en el cuello, . . .
    ("Nadando y escribiendo en diagonal," *Que trata,* 45)

(To write in Spain is to speak for the sake of not hushing up
what happens on the street, it is to tell in half words
whole cathedrals of simple truths
forgotten, or hushed up and thoroughly suffered,
to write is to smile with a dagger stuck in your neck, . . .)

Hyperbole only emphasizes the dangers of the situation and the writer's courage elicits the
reader's admiration.

Good company and good reading are the sinews of virtue, and the poet draws attention to
himself working within a framework of noble poetic achievement via references to earlier as
well as contemporary writers. Otero's first collection, *Cántico espiritual,* shows its literary
pedigree in St. John of the Cross, and the title of the second, *Angel fieramente humano,* is
taken from Góngora. But it is not the allusions, borrowings, literary echoes, and poems
constructed around lines from other poets that concern us at this point, rather it is the effort
to salute worthy companions in the struggle against vice and depravity. The satirist follows
in the footsteps of his doughty ancestors, the Basques. "—Estos castellanotes—decían los
fieles al rey—hasta en el hablar se muestran rebeldes y a apartadizos . . . , parecen vascos . . ."
("These dyed-in-the-wool Castilians," said the faithful to the king, "even in their speech
show themselves to be rebellious and remote . . . , they seem like Basques . . .") declares the
epigraph to *En castellano,* paying tribute to the race's courage and independence. He begs
assistance from Velázquez, encouragement from the Turkish poet Nazim Hikmet, and
strength of companionship from Rafael Alberti, Eugenio de Nora, and Gabriel Celaya. His
elegies for Antonio Machado, Paul Eluard, and Miguel Hernández are preoccupied with
diagnosing the qualities that have been lost: fellowship, love of liberty, hope. Indeed,
Machado, preferred poet of Otero's generation, is frequently recalled. The choice of friends,
however, is quite catholic and, especially at the beginning of the sixties, reflects a then
fashionable political leftism:

Todos los nombres que llevé en las manos
—César, Nazim, Antonio, Vladimiro,
Paul, Gabriel, Pablo, Nicolás, Miguel,

Aragon, Rafael y Mao —, humanos
ángeles, fulgen, suenan como un tiro

único, abierto en paz sobre el papel.
("Coral a Nicolai Vapzarov," *Parler,* 134)

(All the names which I carried in my hands
—César, Nazim, Antonio, Vladimiro,
Paul, Gabriel, Pablo, Nicolás, Miguel,

Aragon, Rafael y Mao—human
angels, shine forth, ring out like a single
shot, opened in peace on paper.)

    The poet affiliates himself with universal defenders of the brotherhood of man and the common destiny of mankind. The host of literary companions and precursors justifies his own efforts by the testimony of their character and the authority of literary tradition. Thus when the satirist compels Spaniards to consider where they are heedlessly drifting, he places himself at the head of a long line of liberal thinkers. The roll call of forebears stretching back to Cadalso and Jovellanos in "Avanzando," for example, serves as a touchstone that intensifies the sense of present moral decay (*Que trata,* 142).

    The tensions and moral ambiguities in Otero's presentation of his satirist play a necessary role in the artful display of indignation. Posing as a self-styled saint who abhors vice, the character is only too concerned with the sensational, the red light district of Bilbao, extremes of poverty and degradation, a Spain asphixiated by the censor and manacled by the priest. Although for the most part he stops short of the obscene, avoids excremental and copulative imagery, and limits sordid details, he displays a marked fascination with vice and a sadistic delight in attacking his victims. For all his scorn and denunciation, his longing for freedom and escape, he longs to return from self-imposed exile and he writes lyrical evocations of his *patria chica,* or nostalgic declarations of patriotic love. Once in Bilbao, and in spite of opposition to almost every facet of contemporary Spain, the satirist stays on, threatening to leave for good next time. Bilbao maneuvers in his mind for first place as the ultimate fatherland of his spirit, but he is unable to belong to the city of his choice. "Y yo me iré" presents the ancient topic of the abandonment of the city by the satirist with the aim of engaging the listener's compassion and of persuading him that something must be done. It is worth exhibiting in full:

        otras veces voy al cine, que es como
        un río pero retratado
BILBAO. ME VOY YA PRONTO,
y no sé si volveré.

Esta vez llevo mis libros,
mis discos, y otras chanfainas
menudas. No volveré.

Te padecí hasta el ahogo,
Bilbao: tu cielo, tus casas
negras. Y tu hipocresía.

No; no volveré.

Quemaste mi juventud
como un trapo viejo. Un día,
me rebelé. Vi y volví.

No; no volveré.

Me laceraste hasta el fondo
del alma. Me arrebañaste
la ilusión: no el entusiasmo.

Insistí hasta lo inverosímil.
Eso me salvó. Rompí
la puerta, y me fui. Y volví.

No; no volveré.

Labrad, amigos.
un túmulo a mi ausencia (si
es plagio, mejor). Si muero,

dejaré el balcón abierto:
no sé si en Cuba, en Madrid,
en Moscú, en París. No sé

dónde. Pero lo que sé
seguro, es que me voy. Y
no volveré.
("Y yo me iré, *Mientras,* 147–52)

      (At other times I'll go to the cinema, which is just like
      a river except for being photographed
Bilbao. I'm off in a while,
and I don't know if I'll be back.

This time I'm taking my books,
my records, and other petty
bits and pieces. I won't come back.

I suffered you up to the gills,
Bilbao: your sky, your black
houses. And your hypocrisy.

No; I won't come back.

You burned my youth
like an old rag. One day,
I broke away. I looked around and came back.

No; I won't come back.

You cut me to the bottom

of my soul. You swallowed
my illusion: but not my enthusiasm.

I insisted until it was unreal.
That saved me. I broke down
the door, and went off. And I came back.

No; I won't come back.

Carve, friends,
a tomb for my absence [if
it's a copy, so much the better]. If I die,

I shall leave the balcony open:
I don't know if it will be in Cuba, in Madrid,
in Moscow, or in Paris. I don't know

where. But what I know
for sure, is that I'm off. And
I won't come back.)

The intrinsic antagonism between honest man and corrupt city, the despair of city life, and the pride of absolute moral judgment devoid of compassion for his victim or doubts about his own moral standing are all conventional features of the satiric mask. Yet rather than piously fleeing, the satirist stays on, horrified at the vice he sees but ever eager to seek it out and to thoroughly enjoy exercising his skills in exposing it. This tension between the paraded disgust of the honorable man and his salacious cataloging of human vice is an artful invention that engages the reader's emotions and adds color to a fairly continuous mood of outrage.

Even though unable to retire from the busy world, the speaker presents himself as a simple, honest man and draws attention to his plain, humble origins. He prides himself on his Basque roots, praising rustic virtues in "Orozco," for example, where he summons up his youth in the idyllic innocence of a Basque valley, nourished by nature's bounty, healthy exercise on the *frontón* court, and the homely staples of his grandmother's orchard (*Que trata*, 21–22).[18] This happy state, appropriately set in an elegiac mode, has long since been lost, corrupted at first by the religious hypocrisy of Bilbao. The speaker laments in a companion poem this loss of innocence and arouses the reader's indignation through an appeal to pity for an "alma niña y tierna y destrozada" (soul young, tender, and destroyed) ("Lejos," *Que trata*, 20).[19] Even if childhood purity has been sullied by the real world, the poet's simple Basque origins have endowed him with an abrupt no-nonsense style: "Vizcaíno es el hierro—el mar, cantábrico —, / corto en palabras. Ley de los poemas / míos" (Iron is Basque—the sea Cantabrian—, / scant in words. The law of my / poems) ("Gallarta," *Pido*, 29). Here, at the close of "Gallarta," the speaker calls attention to his preference for terse, plain language to express plain truths (*Parler clair: En castellano*, as a later title has it), although his literary background is only thinly disguised, since the closure of the poem is a gloss on a Tirso epigraph.[20]

The claim to humble, honest origins is reinforced by rejecting the world of books, by calling attention to a blunt, simple style, to the use of current speech idiom, and to a conversational manner, and by a romantic faith in the natural art of the folk. This pretended scorn for controlled artistic effects coincides with the decision to find his muse in the daily life of the broad masses:

Bien sabemos lo difícil que es hacerse oír de la mayoría. También aquí son muchos los llamados y pocos los escogidos. Pero comenzad por llamarlos, que seguramente la causa de tal desatención está más en la voz que en el oído.[21]

(We all well know how difficult it is to make yourself heard by the great majority. Many are called here too, and few are chosen. But begin by calling them, for the cause of such inattention surely has more to do with the voice than with the ear.)

The fifties evidence a change of style marked by the movement away from sonnet and quatrain, an increased recourse to plain style, and the diminished importance of hyperbolic images. The declining influence of Golden Age poets and the growing admiration for Machado coincide with this development. In short, the insistence on his plain no-nonsense style, although fanning distrust of literature as the mother of lies, is a conventional device: it allows the satirist to tilt at pretentious and pompous effects while suggesting that he is a down-to-earth truth-teller. The speaker skillfully and repeatedly insists on his lack of skill in speaking, his contempt for bookish verse: "porque escribir es viento fugitivo / y publicar, columna arrinconada" (because writing is fleeting wind / and publishing, an abandoned monument) ("Digo vivir," *Redoble*, 65). In a witty account of a reunion with Gabriel Celaya he sneers at dreary volumes: "Tu *Antología* / *Pequeña*, es un gran libro. (Dios nos libre / de libros grandes y de chicas feas)" (Your *Little* / *Anthology*, is a great book. [God free us / from big books and ugly girls]) ("Segunda vez con Gabriel Celaya," *Parler*, 106). Or, in the several apologias for his life and career, he proclaims contempt for his early verses, for example, in the opening to "A la inmensa mayoría":

Aquí tenéis, en canto y alma, al hombre
aquel que amó, vivió, murió por dentro
y un buen día bajó a la calle: entonces
comprendió: y rompió todos sus versos.
        ("A la inmensa mayoría," *Pido*, 9)

(Here you have, in song and soul, that man
who loved, lived, died within
and one fine day went down into the street: then
he understood: and tore up all his verses.)

Moreover, while pretending to reject formal literary qualities the satirist extols the supposedly unskilled art of the people, praising their eloquent gestures, their vivid and robust (even if ungrammatical) speech habits. Yet for all the homage to the untutored honesty of the broad masses, Otero's treatment of the folkloric is urbane, cultivated, stylized. When in the preface to *Cantares* the speaker artfully sets an epigraph from Augusto Ferrán to his own gloss of an interpolated popular song, the reader may legitimately wonder whether the satirist is indeed so innocent. Here, for all his violent outburst against the lie of literature, the homespun advice, "y si quieres vivir tranquilo, / no te contagies de libros" (and if you want to live calmly, / don't get infected with books) ("Cuando voy por la calle," *Que trata, 63*), the satirist makes no attempt to conceal his openly literary background and his highly trained poetic ability. "Lo que quiero. / Puedo hacer lo que quiero con la pluma / y el papel" (What I want. / I can do what I want with pen / and paper), he opens elsewhere in *Cantares,* and he closes with an ironically self-conscious confession of literary naiveté:

. . . vamos a coger rosas,
a escribir como dios manda,
vámonos yendo,
voz del pueblo, voz del cielo,
vamos, es un decir
florido, pero yo de eso no entiendo.
("Aquí hay verbena olorosa," *Que trata,* 81–82)[22]

(. . . let's go and pick roses,
write like god commands,
let's get going,
the voice of the people is the voice of heaven,
well, that's a flowery
saying, but I don't know anything about that.)

Once again, although the poem is a eulogy of plain, simple truth-telling, the speaker calls attention to the artful manner in which he controls his mood.

Otero assumes the character of the honest speaker, impelled by righteous wrath to speak bluntly, not to deceive but to make the most effective presentation of his points. The defense of plain speaking is but one way of characterizing the indignant Spaniard within a predictable rhetorical convention. The first of the pair of sonnets, "Y el verso se hizo hombre," is a manifesto of the poet's need for a poem that will obtain a favorable hearing on account of its ordinary, common humanity. In an appropriately brusque personification, the speaker characterizes this ideal poem as "un verso en pie—ahí está el detalle— / que hasta diese la mano y escupiese" (a verse on its feet—there's what counts— / that even shakes hands and spits). The second sonnet cleverly insists on the speaker's lack of refinement, the strength of his convictions, the attested truth of what he has to say. Not that Otero renounces art; rather, the opposite occurs, since the verbal organization of the poem is rich and complex:

Hablo de lo que he visto; de la tabla
y el vaso; del varón y sus dos muertes;
escribo a gritos, digo cosas fuertes
y se entera hasta dios. Así se habla.

Venid a ver mi verso por la calle.
Mi voz en cueros bajo la canícula.
Poetas tentempié, gente ridícula.
¡Atrás, esa bambolla! ¡Que se calle!

Hablo como en la cárcel: descarando
la lengua, con las manos en bocina:

"¡Tachia! ¡qué dices! ¡cómo! ¡dónde! ¡cuándo!"

Escribo como escupo. Contra el suelo
(Oh esos poetas cursis, con sordina,
hijos de sus papás) y contra el hielo.
    ("Y el verso se hizo hombre," *Ancia,* 123–24)

(I speak of what I have seen; of bar table
and glasses; of man and his two deaths;
I write at a shout, I tell things straight
and even god finds out. That's the way to speak.

Come and see my poem in the street.
My voice stark naked under the dog star.
Rhymsters, ridiculous people.
Away with all of that sham! Shut up!

I speak just like in jail: unleashing
my tongue, with my hands cupped:
"Tachia! What are you saying! What! Where! When!"

I write just as I spit. Against the ground
—oh, those tasteless poets, all so muted,
daddy's little boys—and against the [censor's] ice.)

Throughout the sonnet emotions run high, whether of enthusiasm or of scorn. However, in spite of the association of unexpected ideas, the rambling impromptu development, and the apparently spontaneous abuse, the speaker clearly holds himself in check. He simulates his fury and, for all his vaunted honest anger, controls his mood. Essentially, the pose of simplicity is a variant of the topic of modesty. "Escribo / hablando" (I write / while speaking), one humble disavowal of literary aspirations simply states, but the satirist's innocence only contrasts with Spain's degeneracy and aims to win his listeners to the cause of virtue and truth ("Poética," *Parler,* 24). Given a modern distrust of rhetoric, the familiar Platonic attack on poetry as the concealer of truth is alluring. Indeed, when interviewed by Antonio Núñez, Otero allows condemnation of the aims of his early poetry to attach itself to the neutral means employed, but the later poems are no less rhetorically impassioned.

The poet's serious assurance that he describes Spain as it really is and the frequency of his claims to historical truth indicate another traditional topic of the satirist. Lilliput may not be on the map but the 130-odd place names that appear in *Que trata de España* certainly are. Along with topical references to Vietnam, the United Nations, communism, agrarian reform, migrant labor, consumerism, and censorship, this has led some critics to swallow whole the satirist's claim to accuracy. It is not difficult to understand the temptation that has led commentators to eagerly praise the testimonial value of the poems, their putative realism. Apart from contemporary references and the proud boast to speak plainly, banishing fancy poetic ornament from his work, the satirist himself insists on a fearless determination to tell the truth about Spain. He reiterates his categorical contention to show the world as it actually is: "Aquí, junto al río Ebro, / digo la verdad" (Here, beside the Ebro River, / I say the truth) ("Logroño, *Parler,* 42); "Ni una palabra / brotará en mis labios / que no sea /

verdad" (Not one word / will appear on my lips / that is not / true) ("Ni una palabra," *Pido,* 62); "Testigo soy de ti, tierra en los ojos" (I am your witness, land before my eyes) ("Sobre esta piedra edificaré," *Pido,* 17–18). He implores the aid of Velázquez in forging an iron tongue on the anvil of truth ("Diego Velázquez," *Que trata,* 136). He professes to speak through "los labios de la patria" (the lips of our native land) ("Espejo de España," *Pido,* 22).[23] He seeks often to persuade us of his vigilance, his reliability as a witness, and "Cantar de amigo" is a powerful illustration of this fiduciary topic:

¿Dónde está Blas de Otero? Está dentro del sueño, con los ojos abiertos.

¿Dónde está Blas de Otero? Está en medio del viento, con los ojos abiertos.

¿Dónde está Blas de Otero? Está cerca del miedo, con los ojos abiertos.

¿Dónde está Blas de Otero? Está rodeado de fuego, con los ojos abiertos.

¿Dónde está Blas de Otero? Está en el fondo del mar, con los ojos abiertos.

¿Dónde está Blas de Otero? Está con los estudiantes y obreros, con los ojos abiertos.

¿Dónde está Blas de Otero? Está en la bahía de Cienfuegos, con los ojos abiertos.

¿Dónde está Blas de Otero? Está en el quirófano, con los ojos abiertos.

¿Dónde está Blas de Otero? Está en Vietnam del Sur, invisible entre los guerrilleros.

¿Dónde está Blas de Otero? Está echado en su lecho, con los ojos abiertos.

¿Dónde está Blas de Otero? Está muerto, con los ojos abiertos.
("Cantar de amigo," *Expresión,* 293–94)

(Where is Blas de Otero? He is inside dreams, with his eyes open.

Where is Blas de Otero? He is in the midst of the wind, with his eyes open.

Where is Blas de Otero? He is close by fear, with his eyes open.

Where is Blas de Otero? He is ringed by fire, with his eyes open.

Where is Blas de Otero? He is at the bottom of the sea, with his eyes open.

Where is Blas de Otero? He is with the students and the workers, with his eyes open.

Where is Blas de Otero? He is in the Bay of Cienfuegos, with his eyes open.

Where is Blas de Otero? He is in the operating room, with his eyes open.

Where is Blas de Otero? He is in South Vietnam, invisible amongst the guerillas.

Where is Blas de Otero? He is stretched out on his bed, with his eyes open.

Where is Blas de Otero? He is dead, with his eyes open.)

Parallelism highlights the singleness of theme, that is, the consecration of the poet's life to searching out the unknown and bearing witness to it. To take the poem literally as an explanation of Otero's whereabouts in the late sixties, as one critic has done, is to miss the point. For in spite of all these protestations, the satirist makes it abundantly clear that he delights in his fiction and savors the tension he maintains between history and poetry.

The primitive satirist was often thought to possess preternatural powers that resided in a magical union of words and rhythm, and our poet claims for himself this ancient power to shape the world at will:

Esta
es mi casa.
Propiedad
de la palabra.

Abro
si digo *rambla de cataluña sol*
la ventana.

Esta
es mi patria.
Horadar
dormida piedra, hasta encontrar españa.
("Propiedad de la palabra," *Parler,* 22)[24]

(This
is my home.
Property
of the word.

I open
if I say "Cataluña Avenue Sunshine"
the window.

This
is my native land.
Bore through
sleeping stone, until spain is found.)

Command of words is control of the things signified, so for the satirist, the process of naming establishes the actual order of things. His task is both to recover a true image of Spain and to eliminate its enemies with the lethal barbs of his ridicule. However, the pretense of realism is simply a persuasive topic designed to impress on the listener the urgency of what the satirist has to say and, ultimately, to inflame him with love of virtue and hatred of vice. In a reflective moment at the beginning of "Historias fingidas y verdaderas" the poet confesses to feigning the truth, but Otero's presentation of the fully self-conscious satirist is ironic. The balance, economy, and pacing of the sonnet, the juxtaposition of incongruous statements, and the ironic contrast of appearance and reality all serve to convey the satirist's bitterness and indignation at the folly of his beloved Spain:

un hombre recorre su historia y la
de su patria y las halló similares, difíciles de explicar
ESTAS HISTORIAS QUE SE ACERCAN TANTO
a la verdad, son puro fingimiento:
no ostentan otro firme fundamento
que la verdad que veo y toco en cuanto

escribo y finjo que soñé: vi tanto,
tanta realidad se llevó el viento,
que imaginé ya fútil aspaviento
vida, sueño, verdad, historia, espanto.

Nací en España, y en España apenas
engendra la razón sino hórreos sueños
y lo que existe, existe a duras penas.

Tal fue la historia de mi vida: imagen
real y semejanza de los sueños
de mi patria. Compruébenlo, y barajen.

("Historias fingidas y verdaderas," *Mientras*, 83–87)

(A man peruses his own and his country's history, finding them similar,
both difficult to explain
These stories that get so close
to the truth are pure pretense:
they boast no other firm foundation
than the truth I see and touch while

I write, pretending I was dreaming: I saw so much,
so much reality carried off by the wind,
that I already thought it all a trivial fuss:
life, dreams, truth, history, fear.

I was born in Spain, and in Spain reason hardly
begets anything but stored-up dreams
and what exists, exists with great difficulty.

Such was the story of my life: a true
image and likeness of the dreams
of my homeland. Sample it, and spread it about.)

If the satirist so openly displays his irony and sardonic wit, let alone his rhetorical pyrotechnics, then truthfulness walks hand in hand with exaggeration.

What is surprising is that critics have not gone to the other extreme and, instead of praising the testimonial value of the poetry, condemned Otero as an unbalanced, prurient liar. He is not a historian, for his aim of making evil appear hideous prevents a sober, balanced viewpoint. His attacks are full of drastic simplifications and wild distortions. As a witness, he ignores much of the evidence and slants the rest, and although his picture of Spain is brilliant, it is limited and superficial. Nor is he a thinker: his reactions are strong but vague; his aspirations for Spain are nebulous; his incuriosity when in Russia and China is enormous. Besides, he passes over vulnerable contemporary targets such as tourism, American military bases, the Civil Guard, individual figures of the regime, even the Generalissimo himself, to attack Aunt Sallies that were already venerable in the time of Quevedo. The point, however, is neither to praise the accuracy of the satirist nor to pick holes in his false assertions, but to see his passionate claims of truth and his simultaneous technique of exaggeration as vital tensions in his dramatic character.

Why these internal conflicts should be a necessary part of the portrayal of the indignant satirist possibly can be explained by the deeper rhythms of the genre. Satire shares with tragedy a dark view of the world, but although the tragic hero comes to a new understanding as a result of his suffering, the suffering of the satirist brings no such revaluation. The youthful poet of "Biotz-Begietan," wandering from Bilbao to Madrid and Paris and back, grows into the restless "vagamundo" of the later poems. Spain may be more prosperous than before but the scene is just as crowded with villains and fools driven by the same selfish forces of ambition and greed; and the satirist, of course, strong and steady in his belief, continues to suffer and sing, rejecting society in favor of a derisive, if poor, independence. To view the satirist as a jaundiced failure, ranting away for the sheer pleasure of denouncing others and ignoring his own faults, is to forget the convention that obliges the satirist to be scathing. Naturally, the mode of the satires varies, but the satirist's attitudes are unchanging. In the late poem "Ergo sum," the poet continues to complain of a world that has not been disturbed in the slightest by his patient efforts. The title echoes Descartes' historical scepticism, the idea that the practical lesson of history is that no one ever learns anything from history. In short, the satirist's purpose and the world in which he lives do not change:

> sin una idea preconcebida. Como
> una película de la Keystone: sin
> guión y con ganas de trabajar, entre-
> vistarme, sorprender

A LOS 52 AÑOS SIGO PENSANDO LO MISMO QUE A LOS 7.
Que las nubes son grandes, los monopolios enormes, los vietnamitas chiquitos
e invencibles.
A los 52 años sigo pensando lo mismo que Carlos Marx,
con la única diferencia de que le copio un poco pero lo digo mas bonito.
A los 52 años, me planto
en medio de los hombres y les espeto que me engañaron a los 7 años, a los 17 y casi a los 27.
A los 52 años, escribo
y no escarmiento y me dedico exclusivamente a pasear, a leer, a trasladar maletas de un país a otro, y a
conspirar.
(Esto lo digo para confundir a la policía.)
A los 52 años sigo enamorado de Carmencita, de Merche, de Carmela y de la Niña de los Peines.
A los 52 años, Málaga.
Y escribo como un autómata, corrijo como un robot, y publico lo que pienso (es un decir).
A los 52 años, ni tengo bicicleta, ni televisor, ni ganas de dormir, ni cuenta vulgar y corriente.
A los 52 años, chufas.
A los 52 años, escucho el agua de los montes, el fuego de los campos y el ruido de las batallas.
Y sigo pidiendo la paz y, de momento, me la conceden en parte; y la palabra, y me mutilan la lengua.
A los 52 años, los caramelos son de más vivos colores y la bandera, mas desteñida.
Y me dedico fundamentalmente a silbar, a deambular y a pensar que existo puesto que pienso que
existo.

("Ergo sum," *Mientras*, 115–20)[25]

(without any preconceived idea. Like
a film of the Keystone Cops: without
a script and feeling like working, inter-
viewing myself, surprising
At fifty-two I still think the same as at seven.
That clouds are big, big business huge, and the Vietnamese tiny and invincible.
At fifty-two I still think the same as Karl Marx,
the only difference being that I copy him a bit but say it better.
At fifty-two, I plant myself
among people and spring it on them that they tricked me at seven, at seventeen, and almost at
    twenty-seven.
At fifty-two, I write
and don't teach a lesson, just spend my time strolling, reading, moving suitcases from one country
    to another, conspiring.
[I'm saying this just to confuse the police.]
At fifty-two I'm still in love with Carmencita, Merche, Carmela, and the Niña de los Peines.
At fifty-two, I'm in Malaga.
And I write like an automaton, revise like a robot, and publish what I want (it's just a phrase).
At fifty-two, I don't have a bicycle, a television, the desire to go to sleep, or a common checking
    account.
At fifty-two, jibes.
At fifty-two, I listen to mountain streams, gunfire in the fields, and the din of battles.
I'm still suing for peace [they grant me some for the moment] and demanding to be heard [but they
    mutilate my tongue].
At fifty-two, caramels come in brighter colors, and the flag is a bit more faded.
And I spend most of my time just whistling, wandering about, and thinking that I exist because I
    think that I exist.)

If there is any change in the aging satirist it is that he no longer questions divine justice. Not deliverance from his loneliness and suffering but acceptance of his suffering is the lot of the innocent sufferer. Thus, satire, unlike tragedy, offers no solution to the mystery of evil except for the satirist to go on wielding his lance and whip with patient determination. This lack of development perhaps accounts for the tendency of satire to concentrate so much of its effort on creating, in the role of the satirist, a complex character whose intricate combination of attractive and repellent traits, not to mention his fresh and forceful humor, engages the reader's imagination. Certainly, it is not so odd that Otero's approach to his satirist should be fertilized by the larger pattern of experience that satire affords.

Otero's dramatization of the indignant Spaniard is a masterpiece, and I have drawn attention to the literary kind by outlining several features of the satiric mask. To fancy the poetry for accidental reasons of a biographical or political kind is to neglect invention, to confuse life and art, in short, to behave little differently from the gamekeeper in the theater balcony who shoots the villain of the play. Writers cannot be interpreted only in terms of what lies behind and around them. That is to reduce genius to the level of mediocrity and to forget that the reason we read Otero is because he is more than simply a sensitive Spaniard in Francoist Spain.

3

The Satires, Hypocrisy

The Nationalist victory in 1939 meant that democratic government would not, in the normal course of events, have the remotest chance of office in Spain for at least some years to come; and the vigorous extent of the reprisals immediately following also meant that opposition would achieve very little. This would have been bad enough if the forties had been normal times, but the struggle against fascism in Europe only sharpened the triumph of a reactionary dictatorship in the peninsula. The press was severely controlled; play, novel, and essay were censored; and a sponsored neoclassicism was proclaimed in poetry. Officially, at any rate, satire and intellectual integrity were mutually exclusive ideas. Yet it is curious that the very presence of the censor eventually heightens artistic self-consciousness and strengthens the poet's powers of bold invention.[1]

Although Otero's poetry is various, the satiric attitude is plain in the severe moralistic vein, the refusal to tolerate and the compulsion to speak out, the irresistible impulse to expose, deride, and draw attention to the gap between present human corruption and a vision of what might be. If sermon and carnival are the poles of satire, then Otero ranges from the high tradition of jeremiad through saucy burlesque. In the main, his laughter is bitter and strident, his raillery not infrequently insulting, and his violent outrage often assumes the form of caricature. There is something of the spirit of Quevedo: serious and grim comedy, realism prosaic in its lucidity amidst the wildest play of fancy, and above all an ever-present appeal to an enduring standard, kept up in spite of so much violence and exaggeration of form.[2] The questions of divine justice and the problem of evil addressed in the early poems are not abandoned. Indeed, in spite of the intrinsically miscellaneous nature of satire and the wittily expressed Marxian sympathies of the sixties, Otero is often inspired by the more spiritually conservative tendencies of Christian life, although he is by no means a Christian writer. He evades the freezing grip of the censor and distinguishes himself not only by writing biting satires but also by appealing, despite all the revolutionist posturing, to familiar moral yardsticks of greed, tyranny, injustice, and hypocrisy.

It is chiefly the life of Franco's Spain that Otero has in his mind's eye, but searching the poems for an objective witness to corruption or a truthful record of society's failings is like gathering fog in buckets. The satirist by nature exaggerates. He lives in "un tiempo / amargo como el poso / de la historia" (times / as bitter as the well / of history) ("Juntos," *Pido*, 42), and as he stirs himself to fury he presents an image of Spain that is both simplified and distorted, for all its claims to truth:

Existen todavía millones de hombres cuya soledad es un lujo. Hijos de Judas que no salieron aún de su dilatado vientre. Si hubiese que nombrarlos, yo sé sus nombres, su domicilio, su profesión y el nombre de sus queridas. Aquí los tenéis, besucones del oro, resbalosos de su inmortalidad. Entran y salen de sus ombligos, como si todos los parias de la tierra hubiesen nacido con el exclusivo objeto de abotonarles y desabrocharles su dorada desidia. Y los otros... Se han hecho un dios a su medida, ¡mirad si son soberbios! Y yo os digo que también medrosos, con mucha medrana y poca vergüenza. ("Ultimas noticias," *Parler,* 112–14)

(There still exist millions of men whose solitude is pure luxury. Sons of Judas who still have not emerged from his bloated belly. If we had to designate them, I know their names, addresses, professions, and the names of their mistresses. Here they are, fond of kissing gold, slithering with its immortality. They go in and out of their navels, as if all the pariahs on earth had been born with the exclusive purpose of buttoning and unfastening their golden indolence. And the rest...They have made a god to measure for themselves. Look if they aren't proud! And I can tell you that they're timid too, with a lot of fear and little shame.)

Otero takes delight in elaborate description of those faults against which he inveighs, and the complex and vivid imagery aims to shock and thus to reform. In the poet's album of evil, however, the omissions are glaring: there are no *ad hominem* attacks like those, say, of Unamuno in the *Romancero del destierro.* At most, Otero censures the individual through synecdoche, as in the attack on the alliance of Church and State, symbolized by the priest's sandals and the general's victory laurel, in "Biotz-Begietan":

Días de hambre, escándalos de hambre,
misteriosas sandalias
aliándose a las sombras del romero
y el laurel asesino. Escribo y callo.
    ("Biotz-Begietan," *Pido,* 55)[3]

(Days of hunger, scandals about hunger,
mysterious sandals
forming an alliance with the pilgrim's shadow
and the murderous laurel. I write and keep quiet.)

As a satirist, Otero simplifies, distorts, exaggerates; he spouts timeless moralistic reflections and usually avoids the merely ephemeral. Satire, moreover, given its constant preoccupation with the spirit of the individual and of society and its insistence on moral principles, has certain consistent topics. Otero, sharply conscious of his literary predecessors and linked through Quevedo with the ancients, is not strikingly original: his achievement lies in the power to delight with wit and to make the reader live his mood. In short, the bottles are old, but the wine is new.

The aim, for the moment, is to illustrate Otero's approach to what he considers one of the outstanding problems of his times, hypocrisy, and also to suggest the range and success of his techniques for expressing burning hatred of moral perversity. In the satires composed during the decade after the Civil War, historical effects concern the poet less than general causes. His indignation is directed, in "Que cada uno aporte lo que sepa" and "Mundo," at political and religious hypocrisy. Both poems avoid the sense of being overwhelmed by the horror of experience through the detachment irony affords. Both poems find their shape through a series of contrasts, although the incongruous elements are brought into a much closer relationship in "Mundo" than in the first poem. In both poems, sarcastic mockery of either saint or statesman is balanced by compassion for human suffering.

"Que cada uno aporte lo que sepa" unmasks the comedy of political pretension by exposing the distance between official pronouncements and daily life, the gulf between official talk and action. To deepen the irony, Otero treats a serious theme lightly in free verse that is only loosely knit together by assonance:

Acontece querer a una persona,
a un sapito, por favor, no lo piséis,
también a un continente como Europa,
continuamente,
herido, muerto, nada más que helado por la boca,
y simultáneamente, a voz en grito,
otras palabras nos estorban,
tales como "armisticio", "teatro",
"suspensión de hostilidades", "todo era una broma", y otras.

Pero la gente
lo cree así y cuelga colgaduras
y echa por la ventana banderas y una alfombra,
como si fuera verdad,
como (se suele decir) si tal cosa...

Ocurre, lo he visto con mis propios medios. Durante
veinte años la brisa iba viento en popa,
y se volvieron a ver sombreros de primavera
y parecía que iba a volar la rosa.

En 1939 llamaron a misa a los pobres hombres.
Se desinflaron unas cuantas bombas
y por la noche hubo fuegos japoneses en la bahía.
Estábamos - otra vez - en otra.

Después oí hablar en la habitación de al lado.
(Una mujer desgañitada, loca.)
Lo demás, lo aprendísteis directamente.
Sabíamos de sobra.
    ("Que cada uno aporte lo que sepa," *Redoble,* 49–50)

(It turns out that you can love a person,
a little toad, no, please don't step on him,
as well as a continent like Europe,
constantly
wounded, killed, just with its mouth frozen over
and, at the same time, yelled out,
strange words disturb us,
such as "armistice," "theater,"
"suspension of hostilities," "it was all a joke," and so on.

But people
believe it's like that and put up bunting,

hang flags and banners out of their windows,
as if it were true,
as if, they usually say, such a thing...

It happens, I've seen it with my own eyes.
For twenty years the breezes blew smoothly,
spring bonnets could be seen again,
and it looked as if the rose was going to fly.

In 1939 they called the poor men up, for mass.
They let the air out of a few live bombs
and at night there were Japanese fireworks across the bay.
We were in the middle of another one again.

Later I heard voices in the room next door.
[A woman screaming herself hoarse, crazy.]
The rest you all learned about directly.
We knew more than enough.)

A speaker whose casual understatement betrays an absence of expectation reduces the recent social and political history of Europe to simple terms. By using the detachment now afforded by the voice of an impartial narrator, Otero avoids the bathos that had marred an earlier attempt, in "Crecida," to come to imaginative grips with Europe at war. Each stanza begins with conversational nonchalance, except perhaps for the fourth, where the pun on *llamar a filas* signals a change in the poem's direction. Europe herself is casually personified in the opening tercet, linked with people and little toads as an afterthought, the last of three objects of love. However, the fanciful, frivolous tone of the opening, enhanced by the tender and prosaic instruction "por favor, no lo piséis," serves only as a foil to the image of devastation in line five, an image that is in turn juxtaposed with conventional statements of politicians. At least these statements are almost conventional, since Otero parodies the peacemakers' officialese by scornfully placing their statements beside the incongruous "todo era una broma." The dark implication that political rhetoric is nothing but an excuse for murder becomes more sinister in view of the understatement "nada más que helado por la boca." Denial of freedom of speech is dismissed ironically as being of little consequence; also, personification helps reduce the magnitude of continental events.

The irony becomes more bitter as the poem develops. The satirist selects and orders the elements of his description so that there is an imaginative progression in celebrating peace, from the simple bunting and banners of 1918 to symbolic Easter bonnets and the metaphor of imminent euphoria, "iba a volar la rosa," before the outbreak of the Second World War (ll. 10–18). All along, the speaker detaches himself from the multitude and their willing acceptance of political bunkum: first, by the dry mockery of polyptoton, "cuelga colgaduras"; then, by sarcastic asides, "como si / fuera verdad, / como (se suele decir) si tal cosa..."; finally, by the sardonic observation "Durante / veinte años la brisa iba viento en popa." The innocent witness, for all his willingness to tell what he has seen of people's ready acceptance of official sham, is not quite so innocent. His testimony of the outbreak of the Second World War is derisively casual (ll. 19–22). He colors his account with a pun ("llamaron a misa") that at once censures innocent sacrifice, suggests its ritual necessity, and burlesques the Eucharistic thanksgiving. Also, he has frequent recourse to ironic understatement ("se desinflaron," "unas cuantas bombas," "fuegos japoneses"). Indeed this lightness of the speaker's manner, his refusal to be overwhelmed by experience, characterizes the deadpan close to the central section of the poem: "Estábamos - otra vez - en otra." The control achieved here by simplicity, witty repetition, and ellipsis is as lacerating in its effect as any outburst of savage indignation. The ironist's restraint extends to the close, where his dispassionateness contrasts with an image in parentheses of the mental effects of political folly on one of its victims. The ending, like the title, associates the audience with a knowing band that, in Spain at least, needs no further example of the repercussions of governmental hypocrisy. Thus, the very failure to mention the Civil War in the poem becomes its most telling indictment.[4]

Satire is by nature reductive and unmasks the actor of hypocrisy to show his true colors. "Que cada uno" strips away the illusion of responsible political behavior in Spain and Europe; "Mundo" degrades the lofty pretensions of the Catholic Church. The joining of incompatible frames of reference is a major technique of composition in both poems. "Mundo" is an anticlerical lampoon in which the satirist deflates the sublime world of the Christian Fathers, represented by St. Augustine, by setting it against the way of the world. St. Augustine in fact does little in the poem: he pushes his pen and corrects his proofs, oblivious to the world that teems around him. At most, his presence can be felt in the mimicry of a ponderous style which, for all its comic parallelism strengthened by anaphora in the exordium and its long flowing periods and loose arrangement, leads nowhere. Otero parodies the grand manner in the fullness of its rich diction, incantatory rhythm, and grave tone, but the style is incongruous with the subject and provokes laughter:

Cuando San Agustín escribía sus *Soliloquios.*
Cuando el último soldado alemán se desmoronaba de asco y de impotencia.
Cuando las guerras púnicas
y las mujeres abofeteadas en el descansillo de una escalera,
entonces,

cuando San Agustín escribía *La Ciudad de Dios* con una mano
y con la otra tomaba notas a fin de combatir las herejías,
precisamente entonces,
cuando ser prisionero de guerra no significaba la muerte, sino la casualidad de encontrarse vivo,
cuando las pérfidas mujeres inviolables se dedicaban a reparar las constelaciones deterioradas,
y los encendedores automáticos desfallecían de póstuma ternura,

entonces, ya lo he dicho,
San Agustín andaba corrigiendo las pruebas de su *Enchiridion ad Laurentium*
y los soldados alemanes se orinaban encima de los niños recién bombardeados.

Triste, triste es el mundo,
como una muchacha huérfana de padre a quien los salteadores de abrazos sujetan contra un muro.
Muchas veces hemos pretendido que la soledad de los hombres se llenase de lágrimas.
Muchas veces, infinitas veces hemos dejado de dar la mano
y no hemos conseguido otra cosa que unas cuantas arenillas pertinazmente intercaladas entre los
    dientes.

Oh si San Agustín se hubiese enterado de que la diplomacia europea
andaba comprometida con artistas de *variétés* de muy dudosa reputación
y que el ejército norteamericano acostumbraba recibir paquetes donde la más ligera falta de ortografía
era aclamada como venturoso presagio de la libertad de los pueblos oprimidos por el endoluminismo.

Voy a llorar de tanta pierna rota
y de tanto cansancio que se advierte en los poetas menores de dieciocho años.

Nunca se ha conocido un desastre igual.
Hasta las Hermanas de la Caridad hablan de crisis
y se escriben gruesos volúmenes sobre la decadencia del jabón de afeitar entre los esquimales.

Decid adónde vamos a parar con tanta angustia
y tanto dolor de padres desconocidos entre sí.

Cuando San Agustín se entere de que los teléfonos automáticos han dejado de funcionar
y de que las tarifas contra incendios se han ocultado tímidamente en la cabellera de las muchachitas
    rubias,
ah entonces, cuando San Agustín lo sepa todo
un gran rayo descenderá sobre la tierra y en un abrir y cerrar de ojos nos volveremos todos idiotas.

("Mundo," *Redoble*, 52–54)[5]

(When St. Augustine was writing his *Soliloquies*.
When the last German soldier was collapsing from loathing and impotence.
At the time of the Punic Wars,
with women slapped around on stairway landings,
then,

when St. Augustine was writing *The City of God* with one hand
and with the other taking notes in order to combat heresies,
just then, when being a prisoner of war did not mean death but the coincidence of being alive,
when treacherous inviolable women went in for repairing damaged constellations,
and cigarette lighters were burning faintly from a feeling of posthumous tenderness,

then, as I have already said,
St. Augustine was correcting the proofs of his *Enchiridion ad Laurentium*
and German soldiers were urinating on top of recently bombed children.

The world is sad, miserable
like a fatherless girl clutched up against the wall by robbers of embraces.
Often we've wanted men's solitude to fill up with tears.
Often, so often, we've refused to shake hands
and not gained anything but a few bits of grit stuck stubbornly between our teeth.

Oh, if St. Augustine had found out that European diplomats
were involved with variety artists of very dubious reputations
and the American army was in the habit of receiving packets where the slightest spelling mistake
was hailed as a favorable omen for the liberation of peoples oppressed by endoluminism.

I am going to weep for so many broken legs
and all the exhaustion you can see in poets under eighteen.

Such a disaster has never been known.
Even the Sisters of Mercy talk about a crisis
and thick volumes are written about the decline of shaving soap among the Eskimos.

Tell me where it is going to end with so much anguish
and so much grief among parents who are strangers to each other.

When St. Augustine finds out that the automatic telephones have stopped working
and fire insurance premiums have nervously been hidden in the hair of little blond girls,
ah then, when St. Augustine knows it all,
a great thunderbolt will cover the earth and in the twinkling of an eye we shall all become idiots.)

The satirist jolts the reader's expectations by disregarding chronology, darting back and forth from the age of St. Augustine to Europe in the Second World War, from pre-Christian Punic Wars (which, of course, do have a bearing on Spain) to an imagined apocalypse. The result is a rapid dance of images aimed at deriding the seclusion and ethical neutrality of the Church. The absence of any clear sense of time in this portrait of ecclesiastical authority suggests that the Church's indifference to vice and suffering continues. Laconically, the title indicates this to be the way of the world.

The poet clearly enjoys wedding the gravely formal tone with a shifting subject in the lengthy opening but knows that the danger of unrelieved burlesque is monotony. Hence, in two interpolated passages a backdrop of despair contrasts with the foregrounded absurdity, providing a change by expressing private lament at the state of public affairs (ll. 15–19, 24–31). The first of these passages sounds a melancholy, elegiac note and is strengthened by a powerful simile, although the diminishing process of burlesque still is present at the close. The speaker's mock heroic stand against the way of the world points up the inadequacy of his means compared with the enormity of the outrage (ll. 18–19). In fact, the whole poem can be seen as progressing from mordant laughter to mere jesting. The images of inviolable women and cigarette lighters are distinctly ludicrous, and the satiric foolery is not to be blunted by pretended pathos in the interpolated sections. When Otero returns to St. Augustine he treats him familiarly and irreverently (ll. 20–23). Exclamation ("Oh si") signals an ill-managed attempt at elevated expression where the satirist reveals the trivial modern subjects that would have surprised the saint: political sex-scandals and cold war folly. In this stanza, Otero amuses by both belittling the saint through bathos and ridiculing American anticommunism through the mock-serious revelation that comes to rest on the nonsense word, *endo-luminismo.*

The lampoon becomes more extravagant and ludicrous as it progresses. In the second mock outburst of pity, comic irony develops with the help of memorable instances of zeugma (ll. 24–25), plain-style hyperbole (l. 26), and anticlimax (ll. 27–28). Otero mocks St. Augustine's learning and the wrongheaded pedantry of his spiritual heirs, the Sisters of Mercy. Like the politician's rhetoric in "Que cada uno," such cloistered penning becomes morally untenable when set against a backdrop of human suffering. The poem closes with a fantasy that trivializes the apocalypse that will occur when the saint at last discovers the vice and folly of the world (ll. 31–34). Withheld till the very end, this colloquial anticlimax consigns him to an ignominious common fate, "nos volveremos todos idiotas." Symbolically, the ecclesiastical hierarchy is overturned in this closing and the satirist enjoys the resulting chaos: an obliterating triumph of the anti-logos over the fruitless scribblings of theologians.

Of course, it is nothing new for the Church to be made a scapegoat for all the evils of the times, or for former pupils of the Jesuits to express particularly bitter resentment. In Otero, the topic of anticlericalism does occur less frequently from the sixties onward either because of liberal trends in Church social thought or through the healing of time; but, for the satirist, the Catholic Church stands always as corruptor of the young and as hypocritical defender of brotherly love. He lampoons the moral cowardice of the guardians of morality; he mocks the supposed irrelevancies of biblical exegesis and fundamental Christian truth; he pillories priests as "faldas frías" (cold skirts) and "misteriosas sandalias" (mysterious sandals) or "mendigo en faldas de eternidad" (beggars in skirts of eternity); and, in "Biotz-Begietan," autobiography becomes a satiric device that allows him to take potshots at, among other targets, education by intransigently Catholic schoolmasters:

Aquellos hombres me abrasaron, hablo
del hielo aquel de luto atormentado,
la derrota del niño y su caligrafía
triste, trémula flor desfigurada.

Madre, no me mandes más a coger miedo
y frío ante un pupitre con estampas.
            ("Biotz-Begietan," *Pido,* 54)

(Those men filled me with shame, I speak
of that ice of tormented mourning,
a disaster for the little boy and his sad
handwriting, like a quivering, deformed flower.

Mother, don't send me back anymore to catch fear
and cold at a desk full of holy pictures.)

This is straightforward denunciation, flavored with a grim humor and framed by the larger pattern of the poem, with its self-mockery and ironic refrain, "Escribo y callo" (I write and keep quiet), suggesting that the really crucial statements have been avoided.[6] In a lighter vein, the pointed close of "Amanecida" ridicules the mainsprings of pious devotion:

Las cinco
y veinticinco.

Senos de niña
llaman a misa.
("Amanecida," *Ancia,* 113)

(Twenty-five past
five.

Little girls' breasts
call people to mass.)

The second part of the epigram surprises with its unexpected incongruity and metrical control. However, no matter the mode and means of Otero's anticlerical satire, the target is most often spiritual pride and hypocrisy, the gulf between vaunted principles and actual practice.

Hypocrisy, allegiance to the letter and denial of the spirit, is also the theme of "Muy lejos," an important poem not only because it shapes an image of the satirist's native Bilbao to be reflected in the poetry for years to come, but also because it gives new life to a traditional topic through exuberant wit and wordplay:

Unas mujeres, tristes y pintadas,
sonreían a todas las carteras,
y ellos, analfabetos y magnánimos,
las miraban por dentro, hacia las medias.

Oh cuánta sed, cuánto mendigo en faldas
de eternidad. Ciudad llena de iglesias
y casas públicas, donde el hombre es harto
y el hambre se reparte a manos llenas.

Bendecida ciudad llena de manchas,
plagada de adulterios e indulgencias;
ciudad donde las almas son de barro
y el barro embarra todas las estrellas.

Laboriosa ciudad, salmo de fábricas
donde el hombre maldice, mientras rezan
los presidentes de Consejo: oh altos
hornos, infiernos hondos en la niebla.

Las tres y cinco de la madrugada.
Puertas, puertas y puertas. Y más puertas.
Junto al Nervión un hombre está meando.
Pasan dos guardias en sus bicicletas.

Y voy mirando escaparates. *Paca*
y Luz. Hijos de tal. Medias de seda.
Devocionarios. Más devocionarios.
Libros de misa. Tules. Velos. Velas.

Y novenitas de la Inmaculada.
Arriba, es el jolgorio de las piernas
trenzadas. Oh ese barrio del escándalo…
Pero duermen tranquilas las doncellas.

Y voy silbando por la calle. Nada
me importas tú, ciudad donde naciera.
Ciudad donde, muy lejos, muy lejano,
se escucha el mar, la mar de Dios, inmensa.
              ("Muy lejos," *Parler,* 64–67)[7]

(A few women, sad and made-up,
would smile at all the wallets,
while the men, illiterate and noble-hearted,
eyed them to the core, just around their stockings.

Oh how much thirst, how many beggars in skirts
of eternity. City crammed with churches
and brothels, where men have had enough
and hunger is doled out by the handful.

Blessed city stained with faults,
plagued with adulteries and indulgences,
city where souls are made of mud
and mud muddies all the stars.

Hard-working city, psalm of factories
where man curses while chairmen
of the board pray: oh tall blast
furnaces, deep hells in the fog.

Five past three in the morning.
Doorways, doorways, doorways. And more doorways.
Down by the river Nervión a man is pissing.
Two policemen pass by on bicycles.

And I go strolling along looking in the windows. *Frannie
and Lucy. So and so and Sons.* Silk stockings.
Prayerbooks: and more prayerbooks.
Missals. Shawls. Veils. Candles.

And nice little Novenas to the Immaculate Conception.
Upstairs, it's a spree of interlocking
legs. Oh that district for scandal...
But young maidens sleep in peace.

And I go whistling down the street. You don't matter
to me at all, city where I was born.
City where, a long way off, very far away,
you can hear the sea, the sea of God, immense.)

The poem opens with a compressed picture of brothel life which ridicules the prostitute-client relationship by reducing men to wallets, women to stockings. The corresponding structure of the couplets in this vignette mockingly underlines the mutual advantage of the business transaction (ll. 1–4). Moreover, the derisive pairs of adjectives and the ironic apposition suggesting that inner life starts at the stockings make plain that this opening description is not meant simply to describe but to blame. The poet then sets about discovering the truth behind false appearances: first, in a series of richly textured exclamations which confirm the initial image of corruption and extend it to town and factory (ll. 5–12); then, by the relaxed testimony of the speaker as he strolls through the red-light district late at night (ll. 17–28). Finally, the moral concern to admonish gives way to prophecy: the satirist washes his hands of Bilbao and ends with a tribute to divine hope (ll. 29–32).

A battery of spirited exclamations in the first section gives force to the satirist's denunciation of hypocrisy. He pierces his adversary with the quick, repeated thrusts of his complaint
(l. 5); then he expresses his indignation in a series of impassioned, accusatory repetitions
("Ciudad . . . Bendecida ciudad . . . ciudad . . . Laboriosa ciudad"); and in the closing
apostrophe he fulminates against the industrial world of Bilbao, epitomized by the steel-
works, and consigns all to hellfire and damnation (ll. 15–16). The insistent rhythm of this
section is sustained by corresponding structure in the periods (ciudad [llena] de . . . donde
. . . y / . . . mientras) and, to a degree, in the opening and closing apostrophes (ll. 5–6,
15–16). Within this framework, however, the force and clarity of a barrage of antitheses
heighten a fundamental moral tension between the degraded city and the ethically sensitive
satirist, antitheses that link and lock together state religion and public vice while at the same
time providing an ideal resource for the display of satirical wit. Heaven and hell are the
matching poles here, variously opposed in *iglesias/casas públicas; bendecida/llena de manchas;
adulterios/indulgencias; almas, estrellas/barro; maldice/rezan; alto/hondo* and, at a distance, *eter-
nidad/infiernos*. The simple antitheses are given more force by an arsenal of rhetorical devices.
Similarity of sound (paronomasia) puts all the emphasis on the new elements, the deflating
difference in sense: "el hombre es harto / y el hambre se reparte," "adulterios e indulgencias," "altos / hornos, infiernos hondos." Zeugma helps poison the barb of "plagada de
adulterios e indulgencias"; irony intensifies the phrasing in "el hambre se reparte a manos
llenas," "Bendecida ciudad," "salmo de fábricas," "rezan / los presidentes." Anadiplosis
braids the tails of the satirist's scourge together on the key word ("son de barro / y el
barro"), whereas polyptoton sharpens his disgust at those souls estranged from divine help
("el barro embarra"). Furthermore, the emotional force of this section is increased not only
by figures of symmetry (parison, isocolon) in which repetition of a pattern gives great
emphasis to the new elements inserted into that pattern, but also by the repeated use of
chiasmus to develop a well-knit rhythm in the climax (ll. 14–16). At the close of this section
of the poem, the inversions give prominence to public hypocrisy and a blistering power to
the satirist's denunciation. In this display of wit Otero clearly delights in the variations he
can play on a promising theme.

After this searing attack the style in the next section of the poem becomes more conversational and relaxed (ll. 17–28). Having vented his rage the satirist assumes the casual aloofness
of a strolling whistler who records his impressions of the brothel district in the small hours.
Everywhere is sealed and deserted but for a man urinating and a pair of complacent policemen; and the repetition of *puertas*, with little intervening, signals the implacable facade of
hypocrisy. Externally, at least, all is proper, and the poet piles up the details in stanza six in
ascending order of importance, without conjunctions, rising to a climax in his catalogue of
devotional materials with "novenitas de la Inmaculada." Then, in a jaunty caricature of
bordello sex, he swiftly contrasts the pandemonium within (ll. 26–27). The body of the
poem closes with an apostrophe which breaks off into telling silence, a transitional pause
before the summary reflection, ironic but with serious undertones: prostitution protects
virginity (ll. 27–28). In the closing stanza the satirist detaches himself from the scene he has
portrayed and dismisses his native city with a polished cry of rejection (ll. 29–30). Yet despite
all the dark condemnation of social evil and hollow religiosity, there is ultimate optimism,
based not on man but on God. The repetition of the phrase "ciudad donde" echoes the

satirist's earlier vituperation but heightens the new element introduced: a perception of the nature of God, transcendent and all powerful (ll. 31–32). Even if for the moment it is perceived only on the far horizon, the ending expresses the belief that God's purpose will finally triumph, bringing relief from a claustrophobic official morality. Indeed, the title of the poem and its conclusion suggest that the satirist looks on Bilbao in the light of what he knows of God and pronounces judgment on it accordingly. In the autograph copy, the separation of *in-men-sa* from the body of the poem and its syllabification give emphasis, as does the lentissimo measure afforded by apposition and caesurae in the closing couplet and, inevitably, the cumulative effect of the assonance. At once, the conclusion is hopeful and reassuring, implicitly calling Bilbao to a truer obedience to the divine will.

"Por caridad" is an equally bold but much less highly wrought and dazzling satire of religious hypocrisy. Its effects are obvious and immediate:

Laura,
paloma amedrentada,
hija del campo, qué existencia ésta,
dices, con el hijo a cuestas
desde tus veinte años,
tres años en la Maternidad
fregando los suelos,
por caridad
(por caridad, te dejan fregar el suelo),
ahora en la calle
y entre mis brazos,
Laura,
te amo directamente,
no
por caridad,
estás cansada
de todo,
de sufrir frío
de tu pequeño acordeón
entre las piernas,
del desamor,
pero no olvides
(nunca),
yo te amo directamente,
y no
por caridad.
      ("Por caridad," *Parler,* 74–75)

(Laura,
frightened dove,
daughter of the countryside, what a life this is,
you say, with your child on your shoulders
since you were twenty,
three years at the Maternity Hospital
scrubbing floors,
for charity
[for charity, they let you scrub floors],

now you are on the streets
and in my arms,
Laura,
I love you directly,
not
out of charity,
you are tired
of everything,
of suffering the cold,
of your little accordion
between your legs,
of indifference,
but do not forget
[ever],
I love you directly,
and not
out of charity.)

Subjective focusing of experience is less prominent than the deception of the national Church. The declaration of love is mostly a pretext to ridicule the Church's acquiescence in alleged social injustice, ironically, out of charity. In the maternity hospital the outward form of the prime theological virtue is preserved, but Otero presents Laura as a standing denial of its reality. The arrangement of the poem is quite simple: a binary form, with an opening apostrophe to Laura that expands into a narrative of her servitude (ll. 1–15), then a brief confirmation of her suffering (ll. 16–26). Both parts close with a repeated avowal of the speaker's love, practical and direct in contrast with church charity, and the irregular rhythmic cadence of free verse serves to emphasise the contrast (ll. 12–15, 24–26). The plain, at times colloquial, style is not without polished effects. The phrase "Por caridad," repeated, is by turns ironic, sarcastic, ludicrous; and if sarcasm be the lowest form of wit, here it is refined by the sharp force of antimetabole (ll. 7–9). The images of helpless perfection and displacement that open the poem suggest inherent nobility, as does the Petrarchan echo of Laura and the wordplay of "hijo a cuestas" (cf. *cruz a cuestas*). Movement is brisk, in the first part fired by Laura's exclamation, common enough yet poetically uncommon (l. 3), and in the second part speeded by anaphora (ll. 17–21) and by the minimum of ornament, one euphemistic metaphor (ll. 19–20). This quick rhythm, coupled with exclamation and provocative descriptive details, effectively evokes indignation, and it would be churlish to point out that the poet's immensely priggish love for Laura reflects eros rather than agape.[8]

Otero's handling of the theme of hypocrisy is varied and distinguished. Above all the satirist is a hater of shams and he often returns to the subject of his native Bilbao, "ciudad . . . / húmeda de lluvia / y ahumada de curas" (city . . . / damp with rain / and smoked up with priests) ("Bilbao," *Expresión,* 291).[9] In "Lejos" the easy sarcasm of "Por caridad" or the denser rhetoric of "Muy lejos" are rejected in favor of a more discreet approach. Whereas it has the appearance of autobiographic recollection, one purpose of the sonnet is to censure a pervasive and asphyxiating religiosity. Although the poet sounds a quiet, elegiac note in lamenting his loss of innocence, he finds no consolation in any permanent principles, as in a conventional elegy, but only contemplates with growing bitterness the tragic aspect of his life.

Cuánto Bilbao en la memoria. Días
colegiales. Atardeceres grises,
lluviosos. Reprimidas alegrías,
furtivo cine, cacahuey, anises.

Alta terraza, procesión de jueves
santo, de viernes santo, santo, santo.
Por Pagasarri las últimas nieves.
y por Archanda helechos hechos llanto.

Vieja Bilbao, antigua plaza Nueva,
Barrencalle Barrena, soportales
junto al Nervión: mi villa despiadada

y beata. (La virgen de la Cueva,
que llueva, llueva, llueva.) Barrizales
del alma niña y tierna y destrozada.
              ("Lejos," *Que trata,* 20)

(So much of Bilbao sticks in my mind. Those
schooldays. Grey late afternoons,
rainy and wet. Repressed joys,
cinema on the sly, peanuts, shots of anisette.

From the top balcony, those processions on Maundy
Thursday and holy, holy, holy Good Friday.
The last snows up on Pagasarri
and that mournful gorse over by Archanda.

Old Bilbao, with its ancient New Square,
Barrencalle Barrena, the arcades
down by the River Nervión: my merciless

and pious town [and the Virgin of the Cave,
where it rains and rains and rains]. Quagmire
of my soul, so young and tender, and destroyed.)

The appeal to pity and the pressure of personal anguish are strong, but Otero disciplines his art into a reserved style. The paucity of verbs suggests absence of movement and growth, yet a stately dance of images in the sonnet moves along within the alternately rhymed quatrains and the interlaced rhyme of the tercets. A complex underpattern based on triplets of noun phrases and of adjectives is set up in the quatrains, and this prepares for the hammering triplets of the last tercet, particularly in the final line. Thus the familiar elegiac movement away from awareness of the past toward a revelation about the nature of human life and destiny takes place, although the discovery of a crippled childhood identity is melodramatically kept back until the last word.

    The opening exclamation draws attention to the subject, then follows a steady enumeration of details: limited schoolboy pleasures (ll. 1–4), the natural and church year (ll. 5–8), and guidebook points of interest (ll. 9–11). With a blend of tension and desultoriness the images dance toward the closing revelation: a recognition and rejection of corrupting hypocrisy (ll.

12–14). "Lejos" puts Bilbao at a distance temporally, spatially, and morally. "Reprimidas" and "furtivo" introduce the tone of censure, and the repetition of "santo" in the following stanza (epizeuxis) mocks a piety that bears no fruit. This repetition parodies liturgical chant and is echoed with scornful vehemence in the parenthesis later (ll. 12–13); but in the intervening lines Otero restrains his satiric impulse, humorously crediting nature with human feeling (paronomasia, l. 8) and lightheartedly describing the old town (comic oxymoron and alliteration, ll. 9–10). The jarring paradox that stands in apposition to this description, "mi villa despiadada / y beata," made bold by the enjambment, ushers in the final denunciation of hollow godliness. Piety tends toward pietism, and its incantatory phrases, once charged with earnest force, become the stock equipment of pretentious insincerity. The satirist burlesques such pietism in the jeering parenthetical couplet, adapted from a children's song, "La virgen de la Cueva, / que llueva, llueva, llueva." Finally, the city's repressive religious ethos is held responsible, by logical implication, for the corruption of his young and tender soul.

In "Lejos" the Church is the corruptor of youth; in "Un minero" Otero scorns the Church for proclaiming a spiritual message that for the ordinary man is nugatory. Paradise, Trinity, and Eucharist have no meaning in the life of this miner:

Sentado está, sentado
sobre su propia sombra corrosiva,
a la derecha, dios, y a la izquierda, inclinado,
el hijo. Y el espíritu santo en el aire, a la deriva.
¿Quién ha puesto esta cara
cadavérica? ¿Quién comió de su hambre y ha brindado
con su sed? Ni dios le ampara.
He aquí a su hijo: sordomudo,
y a Teresa, la hija, en una casa de salud o
más crudamente, manicomio.
                              ¡Mina
de los demonios! ¡Paraíso
subterrenal de tal o cual patrono!

Su compañera, de moza, dicen que era divina.
Ahora es como un paraguas roto. No
quiere ni oír hablar del paraíso.
No oír, ni hablar. ¡Bastante
ha visto y ve lo que tiene delante!
                              ("Un minero," *Que trata*, 118)

(He is sitting, sat
right down on his own corrosive shadow,
on his right, god, on his left, with head bowed,
his son. The holy ghost in the air, adrift.
Who put on this face
like a corpse? Who ate of his hunger and took the cup
of his thirst? Not even god protects him.
Here is his son: a deaf-mute,
and Teresa, his daughter, in a state hospital or,
to put it bluntly, a madhouse.
                              Mine

of the devil! Underground
heaven of some boss or other!

His mate, as a young lass, was divine, so they say.
Now she's like a broken umbrella. No,
she doesn't even want to hear talk of paradise.
Neither hear it, nor talk of it. She has seen
enough and sees what is before her!)

"Un minero" is a rare portrait of a member of the fictive *inmensa mayoría,* but few exact
details are presented. He simplifies drastically. The portrait is grotesquely distorted: the
subject is cowed, deathly pale, starved, married to a resentful hag, father of a deaf-mute son
and of a daughter who is an inmate of a lunatic asylum. Otero is no realist, painting society
in all its myriad hues by the accumulation of small facts and minute observations: his temper
is too extravagant. The aim is rather to stir pity, to shock complacency by exaggeration or by
omitting any redeeming details. This wild censure of the miner's state cannot be accepted
entirely as truth: it is a set piece which demands the kind of impassioned public recital that
Otero himself was used to giving. As a satirist he concentrates on the dramatic credibility of
his speaker and feels no need to dwell on the logical presuppositions of his argument. Passionate indignation and provocatively vivid images persuade his audience of the injustice of
the miner's lot.

The poem works on several levels: outrage at social conditions, protest that the miner's
suffering should continue, and denunciation of the allegedly dead formulae preached by the
Church. An attack on a local phenomenon is implicitly extended into an attack on a larger
structure that includes both Church and State, represented by industrial bosses. The debat-
able premise of the poem depends on a very literal interpretation of the blessedness of poverty
and meekness as prerequisites for entering the kingdom of heaven. Otero jeers at the irrele-
vance of the social teaching of the gospels because, for all the vaunted virtues of poverty and
suffering, they bring no consolation for this miner and his family. Their suffering has overcome faith. Hence, mockery and subversion of everyday Christian symbols suggest that
Christian dogma has no bearing on daily life.

Censure takes the form of a rather slovenly sonnet, with irregular lines, an extended
second quatrain (ll. 5–9 and run on into the broken tercet), and the addition of a reinforcing
final couplet. This stems partly from an effort, characteristic of this collection, to extend the
capability of the sonnet.[10] It is also an indulgence that allows the poet to give free vent to his
indignation, erupting into irate questions (ll. 5–7), apostrophes (ll. 11–13), an aside (l. 7), a
reproachful gesture (l. 8), and amplifying the closure with repetition and exclamation (ll.
16–18). By interrupting the train of thought with rhetorical questions embellished with
anaphora for accusatory force, or by introducing the mine itself halfway through the poem
via apostrophes, the first charged with invective, the second with sarcasm, Otero articulates
his vituperation. No matter how awkward, how unbalancing to the overall structure, he
expresses thoughts and remarks as they occur by association of ideas in the course of his
argument. Indignation thus appears to burst directly from the heart, an immediate reaction
to the stimulus of the miner, yet the poet exercises restraint in his emotions, manipulates
them knowingly, feels indignation and disciplines it somewhat by his craft.

This expanded sonnet retains, nonetheless, the functional parts of its orthodox sister. The opening quartet presents the subject, framed by the Holy Trinity. Simple inversion and reiteration in the word order of the first line imparts the idea that the poem is wrung from the speaker rather than premeditated. This preface unfolds calmly except for the jarring qualifiers that halt the end-stopped lines: "corrosiva," "inclinado," "a la deriva." The second section confirms the initial state of dejection and abandonment but explodes into a more effective and impressive style of description. After the rhetorical questions, given bite through alliteration ("cara cadavérica") and through a bitter travesty of the Eucharist (ll. 6–7, with the sarcastic substitution of "brindado" for Gospel "bebido"), comes further evidence of misery, sensational for emphasis but mitigated by a simple conversational style (ll. 7–10). In the first tercet, the apostrophes mark a shift of thought which develops the subject of the poem by surprise: the mine and its anonymous bosses are denounced as the cause of the misery just observed (ll. 11–13). This exposure of the villain is the real conclusion of the poem, and the closure is anticlimactic. Allowing his seething fury to abate in the pause provided by the stanza break, the speaker extends his proof with a succinct description of the miner's wife (ll. 14–18). In part, the closure is an appeal to pity that depends on the commonplace topic of the vicissitudes of fortune, allowing the speaker to sympathize with the wife's anger at her fate. The final couplet underlines the speaker's passion and indignation with the forceful figures of emphatic repetition (with variant, ll. 16–17), exclamation, and polyptoton ("ha visto y ve").

"Un minero" depends for its power on a quick succession of scenes, dramatized by an honest satirist who is outraged and affronted by injustice. He demonstrates the repulsive state of the miner provocatively and vividly but without relying on nasty physical detail. He even apologizes politely, if ironically, for mentioning "manicomio" after the euphemism "casa de salud." Emotional force comes from rhetorical figures of contrast, striking juxtapositions, paradoxes, and oxymora which exemplify the moral tension inherent in the miner's state, for example: *sombra/dios; en el aire/a la deriva; cara cadavérica; comió /hambre; ha brindado/sed; ni dios/le ampara; casa de salud/manicomio; demonios/paraíso; paraíso subterrenal; era divina/es un paraguas roto*. The compression of this technique makes it an ideal means to display satiric wit. Moreover, the yoking of opposites shocks, implies perversion, and by putting conclusions, as it were, side by side, presses the reader to refute one of them.[11] In this manner Otero discredits Christian dogma, Trinity, Eucharist, and the Kingdom of God, as well as mines, mental health clinics, and faceless captains of industry. Here he is not concerned with things to come, even if the closing line prejudges this family's fate. He aims to agitate, to express indignation, to denounce the miner's condition, the moral hypocrisy of Church and State. The goal, as befits the art of the satirist, is to alter the listener's feelings, to arouse pity and melt indifference. It is not ostensibly an attempt to persuade the listener to act, or to reach a decision. To confuse demonstrative and deliberative rhetoric in this fashion would simply be to turn the satires into instruments of demagoguery.

Otero's satires of hypocrisy include, of course, denunciations of censorship that merit separate analysis elsewhere together with the attacks on political injustice. In the main, the target of the satires of hypocrisy is the Church, a Church allied with the Francoist State, hence allegedly a bulwark of political reaction and tyranny. The major criticism is that the Church is no more than an actor answering the Christian message with hollow practices.

The surface has been severed from the soul: religion is a common fraud. Otero avoids old chestnuts about drinking practices of the clergy, gastronomic excesses of monks, beating habits of Jesuits, roving randiness of friars, and so on. He is not ungenerous or petty-minded, yet he still pecks mostly at the surface, at the mask of the Church. "Un minero" scoffs at the paradoxical coexistence of doctrinal religion and inexplicable suffering through a grotesque caricature which mingles pathos with sentimentality. Yet it is akin to the world of the early poems, where the poet denied God because of his despair at not finding Him. There he struck out at the heavens for their refusal to explain their design; here the satirist is angry, sceptical, resentful, since he cannot divine God's purpose when faced with His seeming absence and neglect. The Catholic Church in "Un minero," "Por caridad," or "Mundo" is simply indifferent to the problem of pain, aloof, and consequently the ordinary Spaniard finds himself deserted and deceived by his spiritual guardians.

Exposure of vice depends to some degree on knowledge of virtue. Otero's satires of hypocrisy offer not just a negative and defensive reaction to what is seen as a threat to peace, freedom, and brotherly love, but assume a positive doctrine, albeit a doctrine that from "Muy lejos" onward is lacking in any divine sanction. Tacitly the satirist assumes knowledge of moral principles from which the Church strays. If the Church is a hypocrite, professing but falsely practicing the truth, then the satires call Her bluff. Thus, Otero's anticlericalism is a mirror image of Catholicism and adopts a similar morality, the result, as it were, of a Catholic conscience working without Catholic theology.[12]

4

THE SATIRES, WOMAN

It should not be necessary to apologize for light verse, since there is no divorce between occasional verse and poetry, even if it is common to malign lighter forms as if they were signs of a failure of talent. Also, it would be tedious to categorize the distinctions drawn between satirical and burlesque writing except to point out that Otero's satires of women are amusing rather than critical. He is not malicious, simply irreverent, and he makes no moral judgment. He is less interested in social reality than in extracting, from private experiences, opportunities for witty excursions. He laughs not at the follies of the flesh, the vanity of beauty, as in a bitter homily on the deceptions and wiles of Eve; rather, he exaggerates temptation and accepts sexuality with good humor as a rich part of life's comedy. Woman is triumphant in her animal vitality, accepted joyfully and not condemned.[1]

The trio of epigrams to women in *Esto no es un libro* probably dates from the same period as the brief, pungent "Parábolas y dezires" in *Ancia*. The epigrams exemplify Otero's energetic exploitation of the comic possibilities of language. The first two are printed *piropos*, simple, ingenious, and bold in execution:

BAJAS por las escaleras
maracando con los pechos
y rumbando las caderas.
    ("La Lo-La," *Esto*, 86)

(Down the stairs you come
maraca-ing your breasts
and rumba-ing your thighs.)

HE AQUI la muchachita de los pechitos hechos
con un poquito de clavel con leche.
                ("E. C.," *Esto*, 86)[2]

(Here's the little girl with her small breasts made
of a little bit of a carnation and cream.)

"E. C." is ephemeral but illustrates the importance of metaphor, alliteration, and controlling form in those pieces. Clearly, there is no attempt to pass judgment; the aim is frivolity. However, the economy of language, the pointed rhyme, and the precision of romance form in "La Lo-La" suggest the polish that can be achieved in these experimental sallies. They offer Otero the chance to demonstrate his virtuosity, his deft and elegant crafting of words.

He plays up basic physical instincts but is not cheaply erotic because he draws attention to his grace and skill, particularly in the use of nouns as verbs. "Vaivén" is no less felicitous:

CECILIA Carol,
estudiante de Filosofía y Letras.
Anselma Lucía,
taqui-meca.

Y yo, siempre andando
de la Ce-ca a la meca.
　　　　("Vaivén," *Esto*, 87)

(Cecilia Carol,
student of Philosophy and Letters.
Anselma Lucía,
steno-typist.

And myself, always going from
Cecilia to typilia.)

Once again, bite and precision stem from Otero's unexpected extension of the possibilities of language within the bounds of the closing octosyllable.

Such close work on a small surface and with the simplest means can produce fine effects, as in "Mira," where the artifice is more exacting. The sonnet is a showpiece in which ingenuity opens the gate for the precious and far-fetched. It also exhibits Otero's ability to elaborate a commonplace technique of seventeenth-century poetry, catachresis, strained or violent metaphor:

Detrás del mirabel de tu vestido,
linealmente apuntando a los claveles,
íntimas silban y a la vez crueles,
dos finas balas de marfil erguido.

Herida seda, silencioso ruido
alrededorizando curvas mieles,
al ras del mirabel, tiros donceles
detienen con un palio sostenido.

No sin temblor, sí con vaivén de vela
alada, insignemente sollozante:
brial latido de tirante tela.

Línea movida, elipse vacilante.
Intimo sismo, mirabel que ve la
alta delicia del marfil silbante.
　　　　("Mira," *Ancia*, 88)[3]

(Behind the sunflower of your dress,
aiming directly at its carnations,
intimately and cruelly are whistling,
two fine bullets of erect marble.

Wounded silk, silent noise
surrounding honeyed curves,
flush with your sunflower [dress], maiden shots
are stopped by a hanging mantle.

Not without fear, but with the movement of a winged
sail, heaving with distinction:
a robe whipped by straining cloth.

Moving line, shaking eclipse.
Intimate earthquake, sunflower that sees the
supreme delight of whistling ivory.)

This is not so much wordplay as pure affectation, but for all its spirit of caricature in exaggerating the peculiarities of a particular style for the sake of exaggeration, "Mira" presupposes Otero's coveted ideal of telling effects on a small field.

The sonnet is a playful, comic praising of unexpected, improbable subjects for poetry. The good parodist gets inside his author's skin, and Otero's best parodies are of those writers whom he most admires at this time, Góngora and Quevedo. The sonnet is framed within a rhyme scheme found in Lope's later sonnets and favored by Quevedo.[4] The first quatrain boldly sets the scene; the second develops and confirms the tension between thrusting breasts and restraining dress and returns decisively to the hidden fleshly delights. Otero is not so zealous in making his point that he overshoots the mark: form is of the essence. Despite all the baroque dynamism, restraint and control are paramount, especially when he reins in the movement at the close with measured caesurae, a trio of similarly patterned clauses, and a concluding echo of the opening stanza ("mirabel," "marfil," "silbante").

The variety Otero gives to this sonnet is a sure sign that the subject has caught his imagination and set it to work with a keen instinct for unrevealed riches. That the sonnet is the outcome of close reading of seventeenth-century poetry can also be seen from the characteristic syntactical arrangements (hyperbaton, l. 3; "No sin . . . sí con," l. 9), from the piling up of images in a kind of logical summation, strengthened by auxesis and asyndeton (ll. 12–13) and above all from the ingenious virtuosity of the imagery. The conventional metaphors ("claveles," "marfil") and the commonplace oxymoron ("silencioso ruido") are further signs of poetic pedigree. Above all, tension derives from the organic conceit of flesh battling against its restraining gown which is expressed by a series of military images in the octave: "apuntando," "silban . . . dos finas balas," "herida seda," "tiros donceles." The dress reveals rather than conceals, and Otero's title urges the reader to admire the lady's disguised charms. Self-consciously, the title perhaps also draws attention to the ingenuity of the sonnet itself.

Certainly, this sonnet is the outcome of the poet's own readings in seventeenth-century poetry. He captures and plays on the arbitrary disproportion and eruptive power of his poetic subject. A single element is not subordinated to the whole but becomes, as in baroque poetry, the central focus of the poem. Attention is on shape, movement, plasticity, rather than on harmony and proportion. Hyperbole attracts attention and grows more bold and active as the poem develops. "Balas de marfil erguido" become "curvas mieles" and finally multiply to an ascending trio of "línea movida, elipse vacilante. / Intimo sismo." Otero exploits contrast and movement as major elements of construction so that he presents the reader with a drama in miniature, an ingenious scene that is exaggerated, singularly distorted, over life-sized. The dominant note is one of display, of seeking variety and effect, of appearing clever and striking at all costs. The aim is to be piquant and impressive, and it is pursued with vigor and with mastery of all effective artifices.[5] Of course, "Mira" is as much a parody of a particular style as it is lighthearted praise of beauty, and it provides agreeable relief from the prevailing seriousness of *Ancia*. This very seriousness is in part the outcome of actual experience in dark times, but it makes these lighter human touches rarer and more precious. This gaiety and charm also provides relief from the anguished cries of despair at isolation from God and at the final solitude of human relationships which prevail in the love poetry of *Ancia*: "Suena la soledad de Dios. Sentimos / la soledad de dos" (The solitude of God rings out. We feel / the solitude of two people) ("Tántalo en fugitiva fuente de oro," *Ancia*, 92). Indeed, the shadow of an overwhelming tragedy covers the love poetry. This is the background to "Mira," as well as to "Venus," "Un momento estoy contigo," and such celebrations of pre-pubertal innocence as "Niños de trece anos" and "Ese susurro rápido." In the end, the flesh is a symbol both of captivity in matter and of a longing and desire for transcendental purity.[6] It is this serious theme that Otero rejects so playfully in "Mira."

It is tempting to exaggerate Otero's ambivalent view of woman and to trace it back to an old and established vein of clerical homily, mischievously linking it with celibate priests, guilt fostered by readings of the more virulent fathers of the church, and the cardinal figures of Eve and the Virgin Mary. However, this fails to account for Otero's literary appeal, his sheer delight in verbal style for its own sake. "E. C.," dedicated to the anonymous woman of the epigram of the same title, is arresting parody of literary conceit:

SERPIENTE azul en forma de azucena.
Ea, azucena en trance de serpiente.
Víbora y flor besándose en la frente.
Cuna de senos. Nana mía. Nena.

Sonrisa, rayo de papel, cadena
suelta. Te quiero. Anillo transparente:
cintura niña. Y, descintadamente,
tu melena melosa, tu melena.

Río de lana, nave de mi mano...
Mira... Madeja de jacinto y luna
que no sé si navego, si devano...

Ríes. Te quiero. Delirante lirio.
Víbora viva aleteante. Cuna
íntimamente unida a mi delirio.
                    ("E. C.," *Esto,* 88)

(Blue serpent in the shape of a lily.
Hey, a lily at the point of becoming a serpent.
Viper and flower kissing on your brow.
Cradle of breasts. My lullaby. My darling.

Smile, lightning on paper, loosened
chain. I love you. Transparent ring:
waist of a young girl. And, unbridled,
your sweet flowing hair, your hair.

River of wool, ship for my hand...
Look... A skein of hyacinth and moonlight
I don't know if I am sailing, or fainting...

You laugh. I love you. Delirious lily.
Live serpent fluttering. Cradle
intimately joined to my delirium.)

This is neither a defense nor a blaming of woman but an acceptance of the torments of
youthful desire with good humor. Otero touches lightly on the old moral themes of
woman's deception and vanity through the imagery of the crafty, tempting serpent, central
to Edenic iconography. However, the ingenuity by which he enriches the theme, revelling in
elaborate punning and alliterative effects, produces a jaunty tone. Even the sinuous rhythms
imitate the breathlessness of frenzied desire. Otero unsettles the balance of the opening
chiasmus with a leering interjection, "Ea," anticipating the broken rhythms to come. Meter
is freed from any taint of effort and midnight ink through the jolting caesurae, the sudden
direct address, the breaking-off unexpectedly. The poet removes the aesthetic distance
between the poem and its reader, becoming present as a physical voice. This is symptomatic,
of course, of post-*Ancia* Otero and risks producing a strident, percussive tone in order to win
attention. Here, however, the sonnet form restrains the speaker's verve. After the intricate
twists and turns of the third stanza, the final lines build to a climax and recapitulate earlier
motifs: "te quiero," "lirio," "víbora," "cuna." The pattern of rhyme in the sestet simulates
straining passion (CDC/EDE rather than the conventional CDC/DCD). Thus, such lithe
and pliant prosody inherently expresses the youthful lover's torment, and "E. C." finally
aims to poke fun at male desire, or at love's delirium, as much as at female temptation.

Unwary critics might exaggerate the polemical intention of such poems, taking them far
too seriously and ignoring their sheer spirit of fun, but this would only suggest the lingering
power of satire to hurt even in its less virulent modes.[7] "Consejo de seguridad" invites such
misguided interpretation, yet it is no more than an exercise in humiliation by ridicule in
which the speaker appears to be as ridiculous as his victims:

AHORA me toca hablar a mí.
Tema: De las mujeres, en general.
Concienzudamente documentado
tras treinta años de traspieses,
expongo lo siguiente:
Arteras, calculadoras, mentirosas,
purísimas en público,
públicas con careta
—tales o cuales, repúblicas reconocidas
por el ONU y el otru—,
tramposas,

chismosas,
cariñosas
como las gatas
       y las patas
              de las raposas;

y otras cosas
que no digo, ni desidigo, de las cuales
soy testigo,
juez
y verdugo, por enésima
vez.
("Consejo de seguridad," *Esto,* 110–11)

(Now it is my turn to speak.
My theme: Women, in general.
Conscientiously documented
after thirty years of going wrong,
I expound the following:
sly, calculating, lying,
very pure in public,
behind the mask, open to anyone
—these or those are republics recognized
by the UNO and the othero—
tricky,
gossipy,
affectionate
like cats
      and vixen's
           paws;

and other things
that I cannot say, or deny, of which
I am witness,
judge
and executioner, for the umpteenth
time.)

Partly, the title warns of advice to come; partly, it mockingly recalls august United Nations debates. Debate, in effect, frames the poem as though it were an extract from a word duel, the satirist's contribution to a competition in abuse. He simulates a formal approach which consists of setting a definite theme before his audience and establishing his credentials as a speaker (ll. 1–5); vividly affirming his own position (ll. 6–16); and feigning an appeal to the tender feelings of his audience for his ill luck (ll. 17–22). Consequently Otero parodies the oratory of the law courts, the forensic rhetoric of legal prosecution. Whatever the facts of his case, only the most flint-faced reader would believe that the speaker's ultimate concern is with justice. The opening establishes the poem to be one side of a slanging match, and as in any contest in ridicule, victory would go to the master of the art. Entertainment is the aim, not practical instruction. Besides, the speaker's thirty years of skirmishing in a battle of the sexes permit him to offer only the lessons of defeat. This self-deprecation of the speaker extends to the manner of the opening and close: he is a pedantic windbag with delusions of being a hanging judge. Bathos, in the end, holds aggressive utterance in check.

Asymmetrical, wildly unpredictable, apparently improvised and spontaneous, "Consejo de seguridad" is a good-humored exercise in diatribe.[8] In keeping with the genre, Otero amplifies the general theme by personal testimony, topical allusion, and an outrageously scurrilous character sketch. The language is prosaic, flippant, sarcastic—utterly inappropriate to the full gravity of the theme. The rhyme clatters (ll, 6, 11–13, 16–17); the debasing adjectives and animal similes tumble forth; the punning is tumultuous. However, Otero disciplines the central section to some degree by arranging his effects in trios: the freewheeling style of the monologue never becomes freely and tiresomely self-expressive. The speaker exaggerates mercilessly, and hyperbolic fantasy, like any other form of excessive utterance, is usually more preoccupied with itself than with its ostensible subject. At the end the audience stands in judgment of the art of ridicule, rather than of rights, responsibilities, and sexual justice.[9]

From *Ancia* onward Otero has published only a handful of satires on women and even less appreciable love poetry. Political zeal in *En castellano* extends at times to his view of women and degenerates into an uncritical acceptance of the shibboleths of romantic revolutionism: "Y sé que es bello combatir unidos" (And I know it is beautiful to struggle united together) ("Poema sin palabras," *Parler,* 116).[10] In *Que trata de España* the rare poem on woman focuses on social justice, such as "Yo no digo que sea la mejor del puerto," or on communist models of heroic endeavor and achievement, such as the sputnik poem to the first woman in space, "En la primera ascensión realizada por una mujer." "Mujer," in *Todos mis sonetos,* praises domestic possessions at least as much as the possessor, although the unpublished *Hojas de Madrid* might offer something.[11] Nonetheless, to speculate on why women as a topic for satire should lose their appeal is hazardous. Perhaps because Otero takes no strong moral direction in this field, preferring the rollicking and bawdy saturnalian mood of primitive satire, he finds it to be antipathetic once he decides to strengthen his public voice. His increasing attraction to invective and denunciatory poetry after *Ancia* in order to censure political folly leads him to ignore this more playful vein. The center of gravity moves away from carnival toward pulpit as he fulminates mercilessly in his major trilogy against injustice, censorship, political stagnation, and tyranny. This is not to say the satires forfeit playfulness and flippancy—the opening squibs of *En castellano* alone would deny that—but the tone becomes more sneering and sardonic. Lighthearted jesting at the human comedy becomes inconsistent with a severer moral and political intention. The satirist assumes moral ascendancy and is out to persuade his audience to despise the powers that be, to look beneath the surface of life in Francoist Spain and to condemn the underlying moral order in the name of an ideal of peace, brotherhood, and liberty. Thus, these youthful antics are out of character with the figure of the mature satirist whose blood flows along ascetic and puritanical veins, a satirist solemn and self-righteous were it not for his exuberant exploitation of the resources and potentialities of language.

5
THE SATIRES, THE WORLD OF ART

Otero's skits on women are at most saucy, not cruel or derisive; certainly they offer no glimpse of the savagery of his wit. His satires of poetry and art are much more numerous and varied. In this area it is necessary to distinguish between deliberate imitations, echoes, parodies, and truculent manifestos, and also to recognize the inappropriateness of here attempting to study the broader question of debts and influences. *Que trata de España* alone contains some five dozen instances of proper names, either of writers or literary reminiscences, although this only confirms an oft-noted tendency dating from his earliest writing to seek a poetic way guided by the example of his literary forebears, an example to be either emulated in some fashion or lampooned. Critics have not fully come to grips with Otero's very literariness, even if they do make mention of San Juan, Fray Luis, Góngora, Quevedo, Vallejo, and Machado.[1]

The satires of poets and artists can be divided into three groups: first, those directed against the literary old guard, attacking the straw man of pure poetry in the name of a popular, committed lyric (terms that have generated more heat than light); second, parodies and humorous imitations of poetry and other art forms such as music and dance; third, satires of censorship that focus on literary effects, problems of composition, restrictions on publication, and so on.

Much of Otero's independence lies in his ability to recharge old ideas with new life. This rejuvenation occurs as much with the selection of topics of invention as with words and poetic forms. The boast of novelty, of "things unattempted yet in prose or rhyme," is an age-old claim and a favorite with the poet from his earliest compositions:

Haremos una prosa,
un verso, tan distintos y no usados,
que sean mariposa
junto a rumor de arados
abriendo surcos nuevos, no escuchados.[2]

(We shall make a prose,
a verse, so distinct and not worn out,
that they might be a butterfly
by a sound of ploughs
opening up new furrows, not heard before.)

This claim means several things—new subject matter, new style, new metrical arrangements—and is often repeated. "Y el verso se hizo hombre, 1 y 2" opens with a novel personification of the ideal poem as common man:

Ando buscando un verso que supiese
parar a un hombre en medio de la calle,
un verso en pie—ahí está el detalle—
que hasta diese la mano y escupiese.
("Y el verso se hizo hombre, I" *Ancia,* 123)

(I am searching for a verse that would know how
to stop a man in the middle of the street,
a verse on its feet—there's the detail—
that would even shake hands and spit.)

Novelty lies in the breezy image of the muse as ruffian, frank, open, unafraid to speak up, "Y tan chulo, / que mire a Tachia descaradamente" (And so saucy, / that it would look at Tachia cheekily). This figure has little in common either with the dominant trends of twentieth-century Spanish poetry or with Otero's own early work. Unashamedly one of the crowd, the poet dramatizes his rejection of more private writing in favor of a public voice:

Aquí tenéis, en canto y alma, al hombre
aquel que amó, vivió, murió por dentro
y un buen día bajó a la calle: entonces
comprendió: y rompió todos sus versos.
        ("A la inmensa mayoría," *Pido,* 9)

(Here you have, in song and soul, that man
who loved, lived, and died within
and one fine day went down to the street: then
he understood: and tore up all his verses.)

The claim to present truths that others have not yet attempted is a familiar topic of the exordium, and Otero is fond of using it in extravagantly phrased prologues:

AQUI tenéis mi voz
alzada contra el cielo de los dioses absurdos,
mi voz apedreando las puertas de la muerte
con cantos que son duras verdades como puños.
            ("En castellano," *Parler,* 14)

(Here you have my voice
raised against the heaven of the absurd gods,
my voice stoning the doors of death
with songs that are hard truths like fists.)

Whereas "dioses absurdos" and "las puertas de la muerte" might recall the unseen god and that agonized questioning of *Ancia,* they refer also to the alliance of Church and State. Moreover, the belligerent stance implicitly challenges a more complacent aesthetic position. Pure poetry, an imagined adversary, pales when faced with such passionate concern for Spain and hatred for those who have defiled her.

From his first major collection Otero jibes at the Modernist aesthetic. "A la inmensa mayoría," the epigraph of *Angel fieramente humano,* puts Juan Ramón Jiménez firmly in his place, and the phrase reappears frequently with variants throughout the sixties ("hacia, con, por, en la inmensa mayoría").[3] In retrospect, literary battles lose their whiff of gunpowder, but Otero himself recalls how daring it appeared in 1949 to scorn the old literary order. Indeed, it is the figure of the poet as an all-round man, a fully equipped, oppositionist citizen rather than a pedantic recluse, that predominates during the Franco period.

This is not to say that Otero's effects are any less exquisite. Often he is oblique, if not ciphered. The standpoint, however, is radically distinct. The beautiful porcelain of Juan Ramón and his heirs in the *Generación del '27* is found wanting: it lacks the ethical imperative demanded by the times.[4] Instead, the poet writes of what is not in the newspapers, speaks for a common humanity not an individual self, and is defiantly popular in his aspirations. Otero ridicules not only the allegedly rarified sensibility of Modernism, but even his own much-acclaimed early work:

ANTES fui—dicen—existencialista.
Digo que soy coexistencialista.
          ("Dicen digo," *Parler,* 24)[5]

(Formerly I was—they say—an existentialist.
Now I say I am a coexistentialist.)

Such squibs are generally thought to be of little importance. On the contrary, they are fundamental.

It is remarkable that an argument about taste would have lasted for so long and occupied so much of Otero's attention, for this means that literary standards were pitched very high. Pure poetry is his bugaboo, and he ridicules and denounces this villain for its emphasis on the medium of verse and its indifference to content. The times prevent such pursuits:

Sabed que la belleza, eso que llaman
cielo, mínima flor, mar Amarillo,
ya lo he visto. No tengo tiempo. Antes
hay que poner los hombres en su sitio.
("Belleza que yo le visto, / ¡No te borres ya nunca!" *Que trata,* 41)

(You should know that beauty, that which they call
sky, tiny flower, Yellow Sea,
I have already seen. I don't have the time. First
we have to put men in their places.)

He is not a poet for meditating on clouds, roses, nightingales. Instead of watching waves, he would rather dredge rivers. There is no point in commenting that pure poetry is a theoretical ideal, in practice little different from the satirist's own aspirations. Both views seek to select essential properties of the poem and to discard all material judged to be nonessential. What matters is that the satirist, moved as most satirists claim to be by the pressures of their times, holds pure poetry up to ridicule. In short, he is moved by a different aim.

"Cartilla (poética)," for example, briskly exposes the shortcomings of pure poetry while contrasting the ethical imperative that moves the satirist to write:

La poesía tiene sus derechos.
Lo sé.
Soy el primero en sudar tinta
delante del papel.

La poesía crea las palabras.
Lo sé.
Esto es verdad y sigue siéndolo
diciéndola al revés.

La poesía exige ser sinceros.
Lo sé.
Le pido a Dios que me perdone
y a todo dios, excúsenme.

La poesía atañe a lo esencial
del ser.
No lo repitan tantas veces,
repito que lo sé.

Ahora viene el pero.

La poesía tiene sus deberes.
Igual que un colegial.
Entre yo y ella hay un contrato
social.

Ah las palabras más maravillosas,
"rosa", "poema", "mar",
son *m* pura y otras letras:
o, a...

Si hay un alma sincera, que se guarde
(en el almario) su cantar.
¿Cantos de vida y esperanza
serán?

Pero yo no he venido a ver el cielo,
te advierto. Lo esencial
es la existencia; la conciencia
de estar
en esta clase o en la otra.

Es un deber elemental.
("Cartilla [poética]," *Que trata*, 39–40)[6]

(Poetry has its rights.
I know.
I'm the first to slave
before paper.

Poetry creates words.
I know.
This is true and continues to be so
saying it the other way round.

Poetry demands we be sincere.
I know.
I am asking God to forgive me
and everyone else, please excuse me.

Poetry has to do with what is essential
in existence.
Don't repeat it so often,
again I say I know it.

But here comes the objection.

Poetry has its duties.
Just like a schoolboy.
Between her and me there is a social
contract.

Ah, the most wonderful words,
"rose," "poem," "sea,"
are pure *m* and other letters:
o, a...

If there is a sincere person, let him keep
[in the cupboard] his song.
Songs of life and hope
will they be?

But I have not come to see heaven,
I warn you. What matters
is existence: consciousness
of being
in this class or the other one.

It is an elementary duty.)

Quite apart from style and metrical ingeniousness, the poem has a manner characteristic of many Otero satires. The satirist is talking at somebody *in propia persona*. The language is simple, if not bare, but animated by puns and verbal games. He shies away from introspection; he exhorts, questions, prays, and orders. The moralizing is public, being directed as much at the improvement of others as at the poet.

Wearily and wittily in the first section Otero catalogues the received views on poetry, stubbornly marking his recognition. These variations on a single theme produce not only amplitude but also an illusion of cogency. His fertile humor plays on "sudar tinta," "Dios," "repito." He clowns with aesthetic dogma ("La poesía crea las palabras") and acknowledges with mild sarcasm through his repeated "lo sé" the faded tenets of an outworn poetic. This jesting subserves the need of refuting unfashionable doctrine, and the second part of the poem expands and qualifies the premises of the first. Now the tone becomes more dogmatic ("La poesía tiene sus deberes"), the humor more biting ("*m* pura y otras letras"), the denunciation more firm ("Si hay un alma sincera, que se guarde / [en el almario] su cantar"). The ethical imperative inherited from Machado is now colored a little by the language of liturgical socialism. Poetry is not simply to be the agent of moral change but the paladin of the class struggle; the poet poses as the priest not so much of the muses as of Marx.

One offshoot of such thinking, which is nourished by an essentially nineteenth-century admiration for the folk, is the poet's scorn for written literature and his praise of oral, popular song. As mentioned previously, this is part of the satirist's claim to humble, honest origins, to speaking plainly. It is also part of the heritage of Spanish liberalism, with roots in German Romanticism, which honors a sage and immaculate *pueblo*.[7] As a satirist of literature, Otero holds up popular song as a standard by which to judge recondite book poetry:

> ...he puesto unos cuantos cantares del
> pueblo..., para estar seguro al menos de
> que hay algo bueno en este libro
> > Augusto Ferrán

Cuando voy por la calle,
o bien en algún pueblo con palomas,
lomas y puente romano,
o estando yo en la ventana
oigo
> > **una voz por el aire,**
letra simple, tonada popular

> > ... una catedral bonita
> > y un hospicio con jardín,

son los labios que alabo
en la mentira de la literatura,
la palabra que habla,
canta y se calla

> > ...donde van las niñas
> > para no volver,
> > a cortar el ramo verde
> > y a divertirse con él;

y si quieres vivir tranquilo,
no te contagies de libros.
("Cuando voy por la calle," *Que trata*, 63)

> > (...I have put in a few popular
> > songs..., to be sure that at least there is
> > something good in the book.
> > > Augusto Ferrán

When I stroll down the street,
or even in some little town with doves,
hills and a Roman bridge,
or standing by the window
I can hear
            a voice in the air,
simple words, a popular tune

            "...a pretty cathedral
            and a hospice with a garden,"

they are the lips I praise
against the lie of literature,
the word that speaks,
sings, and keeps quiet

            "...where the lasses go
            to come back no more,
            to cut green branches
            and in love to explore";

and if you want to live in peace,
don't get infected with books.)

The stance recalls Abel Martín or Juan de Mairena: "Entre españoles lo esencial humano se encuentra con la mayor pureza y el más acusado relieve en el alma popular" (Among Spaniards the essentially human is found with the greatest purity and sharpest relief in the popular soul). Nevertheless, Otero is not content merely to transcribe. The primitive must not be too primitive; it requires sophisticated editing. Thus, the traditional is raw material to be worked up by a cultivated poet.[8]

Two more satiric devices reveal their pedigree in traditional poetry: the use of concise generalizing statements couched in romance form, and the piquant weaving of popular lyric into the texture of individual poems. General statements particularly suit those literary manifestos that deride implicitly the vice or folly of *literatura minoritaria*:

Que no quiero yo ser famoso,
a ver si tenéis cuidado
en la manera de hablar,
yo no quiero ser famoso
que quiero ser popular.
("Que no quiero yo ser famoso," *Que trata*, 67)

(For I do not want to be famous,
let's see if you can be careful
about the way you speak.
I do not want to be famous
I want to be popular.)

They also appear with effect as points of summary in overtly political satire:

Patria de pueblo y pan
partido injustamente.
("Torno," *Que trata,* 179)

(Native land of people and bread
unjustly divided.)

Otero's debt to traditional poetry is extensive. He borrows and breathes fresh life into old
forms, blending, for example, his modern themes with seventeenth-century *seguidilla* forms:

Pues que en esta tierra
no tengo aire,
enristré con rabia
pluma que cante.
("Pues que en esta tierra," *Pido,* 65)[9]

(Since in this land
I have no air,
I furiously armed myself
with my singing pen.)

Here the result is an effortlessly precise manifesto which explicitly denounces political and
implicitly condemns aesthetic evils.

Otero adapts and gives new life to familiar lines from well-known authors in several ways,
presenting them in compressed form or modified in a surprising way either because of the
context or because of an imaginative variant. Antonio Machado reverberates in "La primavera ha venido" (Spring has arrived) ("15 de abril," *Parler,* 24). Rubén Darío is lampooned
in "Oh juventud, divino / telegrama" (Oh youth, divine / telegram) ("Circo de los ferr-
ocarriles," *Mientras,* 75). Góngora is pressed into service for the title of *Angel fieramente
humano,* and the epigraph of this collection refutes the aesthetic of Juan Ramón: "Yo no soy
un poeta *de mayorías*; pero sé que indefectiblemente tengo que ir a ellas" (I am not a poet for
majorities; but I know that unfailingly I have to go to them). More extended examples are
the poems, "Yo soy aquel que ayer no más decía" and "Aren en paz," drawing respectively on
Darío and Juan Ramón (*Pido,* 37–38; *Redoble,* 59–60). The range of Otero's literary borrowings is vast, and these examples have simply tried to suggest, very briefly, the ways in which
he exploits Spanish poetry to denigrate Modernism in the name of a poetry of public responsibility.

There are other poems on art and artists which are scarcely more than a pretty exercise of
wit. "El bolero" imitates Ravel's rhythms in verse, "León de noche" playfully translates
musical effects into words, and "Birmania" does the same for dance (*Todos,* 96; *Pido,* 35–36;
Que trata, 173).[10] All are light pieces, since Otero quite naturally reserves serious treatment of
aesthetics for matters concerning poetry. "Su íntimo secreto" is, like Lope's Violante sonnet,
a sonnet on sonneteering:

El soneto es el rey de los decires.
Hermoso como un príncipe encantado,

como una banda azul, cuadriculado
para que dentro de él ardas, delires.

Es preciso que bogues raudo y gires
entre sus olas y su muelle alzado:
quede tu pensamiento destrozado
cuando te lances de cabeza y vires.

Yo tengo en cada mano un buen soneto,
como dos remos de marfil y oro.
Yo conozco su íntimo secreto.

Es un silencio pronunciado a coro
por un labio desnudo, blanco, inquieto
y otro labio sereno, abril, sonoro.
        ("Su íntimo secreto," *Todos*, 116)[11]

(The sonnet is the king of sayings.
As beautiful as an enchanted prince,
as a blue sash, squared
so that within it you may burn, rave.

You must row quickly and swing
between its waves and raised pier:
shattering your thoughts
when you dive overboard headfirst and come about.

I have a good sonnet in each hand,
like two oars of ivory and gold.
I know their intimate secret.

It is a silence pronounced in a chorus
by one bare, white, worried lip,
and another lip, calm, springlike, resonant.)

Notwithstanding his earlier jibes at the two-headed monster of pure poetry and Modernism, Otero falls back on Modernist touches in his choice of words ("príncipe encantado," "marfil y oro"), but the background to this poem is thirty years of practice in sonnet composition. Not unlike the poems on music and dance, it imitates in verse the aesthetic experience that the form provides. Humor lies in the witty imagery which constitutes a definition of the form. It offers freedom through its discipline, "cuadriculado / para que dentro de él ardas, delires," and demands that the reader surrender to the text, laying aside preconceptions. Lightheartedly, the poet affirms his command of the form's mystery and closes with an aphorism tightly bound with antithesis and balanced by triplets of adjectives. Otero's taste for point and epigram has no full counterpart in post–Civil War Spanish poetry.

At one level, the close of "Su íntimo secreto" suggests that the sonnet gives voice not only to the sentiments of the individual poet but also to those of the larger community. As Machado would have it, "Mi sentimiento no es, en suma, exclusivamente 'mío,' sino más bien NUESTRO. . . . mi corazón canta siempre en coro . . ." (My feeling is not, in the

end, exclusively mine, but rather OURS. . . . my heart always beats in a chorus . . .).[12]
The essential mystery of song conveyed by the oxymoron "un silencio pronunciado a coro"
requires personal and communal expression at the same time. The syntactical balance of the
last two lines mirrors an ideal relationship between the individual and the generic. In this
respect, the first stanza defines the form, the second states the conditions required for its
appreciation, and the sestet presents both a definition and a hope. The responsible poet seeks
within himself to discover a radical humanity. After so much art for art's sake, Otero and his
generation strive to bridge the alleged gulf that had arisen between the world of poetry and
the world of everyday life. Sonnets such as "Su íntimo secreto" and "Hagamos que el soneto
se extienda" (*Todos*, 133) challenge those lingering stragglers hiding in their ivory towers.
Whether or not Otero does realize his hopes for poetry is a question for literary journalists
and sociologists, and little is gained by pointing out that the bugaboo of pure or minority
poetry was hardly present in the fifties and sixties or that Otero is no less sophisticated in his
effects. Otero's intention is to compose even the most highly wrought stanzas 'for the
people,' that is, to become the property of the people and to be remembered and handed
down for generations.

It is not odd that the sonnet, hardly a popular form, should be used to champion popular
poetry. On the contrary, the appropriation of all means to achieve his goal is precisely Otero's
strength. More than new themes, it is the new style Otero adopts for the sonnet which
surprises and recalls, in its daring, Quevedo. By closing in an aggressively familiar style, he
can burlesque more straight-laced sonneteering: "y ahora suena el teléfono y me levanto y
termino" (and now the phone rings and I get up and finish) ("Hagamos que el soneto se
extienda," *Todos,* 133).[13] Above all, he extends the range of the modern Spanish sonnet so that
at one end of the scale he includes new topics of invention and at the other end he allows
various forms of colloquial usage into its stanzas. In neither way is he an innovator, for
already Quevedo in particular had composed in similar fashion, and there is, in fact, a community of style between the two poets. Otero simply goes further than his own immediate
predecessors and contemporaries.

To battle the censor, Otero drafts the sonnet. "Viene de la página 1936" sets the satirist
apart from the chorus of poetasters produced by censorship and invokes the reader's admiration for the writer's courage under conditions of hardship. He exaggerates the restrictions
and affirms his resolution to speak out at all costs, unlike the irrepressible scribblers whom he
flails with a trio of *esdrújulos*:

¿Qué voy a hacer con cinco o seis palabras,
siete todo lo más, si el martes próximo
saldré de España con españa a cuestas,
a recontar palabras? Cinco, es poco.

¿Qué voy a hacer? Contarlas cien mil veces,
hacérselas oír hasta los sordos.
(Hay muchos sordos porque hay muchos versos
afónicos, criptóricos, retóricos.)

¿Criptóricos? ¡Y mil, dos mil millones

oyen la radio, abren el periódico...!
¿Qué les diré cuando me pidan cuentas?

Les hablaré de cosas que conozco.
Les contaré la historia de mi patria,
¡a ver si continúa de otro modo!
("[Viene de la página 1936]," *Que trata,* 56)

(What am I going to do with five or six words,
seven at the most, if on Tuesday next
I shall leave Spain with spain on my back,
to retell my words? Five, it isn't much.

What am I going to do? Tell them a hundred thousand times,
make them heard even by the deaf.
[There are many deaf people because there are many
aphonical, cryptorical, rhetorical verses.]

Cryptorical? And a thousand, two thousand million people
listen to the radio, open the newspaper...!
What am I going to tell them when they call me to account?

I will tell them about the things I know.
I will tell them the history of my native land,
let's see if it continues differently!)

Question, answer, and parenthetical aside exemplify the casual, offhand manner adopted and reinforced with colloquialisms. Otero exposes the folly of nameless rimesters. He condemns irresponsible aestheticism, whether of those who fly in the face of the times or of those pedants and scribblers who turn their backs on Francoist Spain.

One of the most effective attacks on the constraints placed on writing by the censor is the second of the pair of sonnets that compose the prologue to *Que trata de España*:

Libro, perdóname. Te hice pedazos,
chocaste con mi patria, manejada
por conductores torvos: cruz y espada
frenándola, ¡gran dios, y qué frenazos!

Mutilaron tus líneas como brazos
abiertos en la página: tachada
por el hacha de un neotorquemada
¡gran dios, graves hachazos!

Libro, devuelve el mal que nos han hecho.
Ancho es el mundo. Como el arte. Largo
el porvenir. Perdona la tristeza,

libro, de darte nueva patria y techo.
Español es el verso que te encargo
airear, airear. Te escucho. Empieza.
("Libro, perdóname," *Que trata,* 12)

(Book, forgive me. I tore you to pieces,
you collided with my native land, run
by grim drivers: a cross and sword
braking her, oh my god, and what heavy brakes!

They mutilated your lines like open
arms on the page: struck out
by the axe of a neo-torquemada
oh my god, such severe axe blows!

Book, give back the evil they have done to us.
Wide is the world. Like art. Long
is the future. Excuse the sadness,

book, of giving you a new homeland and roof.
Spanish is the verse that I charge you
with airing, airing. I am listening for you. Begin.)

As prefatory poem, the sonnet focuses on the poet's duty to impart knowledge, to speak out those truths about Francoist Spain that cannot be hidden. This generosity in showing his knowledge makes the poet appear noble in contrast with the villainies of the censor. Ingenuity lies in the obliqueness of method. Instead of joy at the happy publication of his volume of poems, a usual prefatory stance, the author bewails his new book's fate, apologizes for its publication in Spain, and hopes that this foreign edition will have a happier fate.[14] Otero varies also the usual address to the reader by speaking instead to his book. There is no argumentation, no effort to persuade the reader of a position. The whole poem works dramatically toward its end.

The apology in the octave is not excusatory but is rather a device to make a scathing attack on the censor. The speaker simply accepts responsibility for the censor's mutilations and then exposes the real criminal through the image of a traffic accident. "Cruz y espada," the familiar metonymy for the union of Francoist State and Catholic Church, is as close as Otero comes to topicality. He implies that Spain has exceeded all limits, and her degeneracy is expressed in the exaggerated imagery. Moreover, the presence of the speaking voice increases rather than dissipates the energy of the opening stanza. His double exclamation, "¡gran dios, y qué frenazos!," suggests that the regime has gone beyond the rational limits of vice. This exaggeration continues into the second stanza where the collision image is exchanged for one of torture by the Inquisition. Such endured dangers enhance the character of the satirist and his book. On the sestet the sonnet turns to wish the Paris edition success and revenge. The speaker now apologizes for foreign publication, but the keynote of the closure is defiance. Confidently repeating his plea for freedom of speech and thought ("airear, airear"), the satirist dramatically becomes silent for the book to speak out.

By directly addressing the book rather than the censor, the unmasking is more effective. This gives the speaker a degree of detachment in the octet, which eases the transition to the rallying cry in the sestet. The closed rhyme of the octet reinforces an impassioned denunciation of the censor through apostrophe. However, the powerful imagery of the opening stanzas gives way to a freer, not affectedly poetical idiom in the sestet. Here, the pauses and shorter periods reproduce the lively rhythm of the spoken word. Like a captain comforting and inspiring his men, the satirist addresses his book and familiarly mixes brief, sententious reflections (ll. 10–11) with his orders ("devuelve el mal," "te encargo airear, airear," "Empieza"). The satirist has moral superiority over his victim and confident faith in his cause.

In short, the most devastatingly brilliant results of Otero's satiric sallies into the world of art are his stabs at the censor. Yet his saber-rattling at pure poetry and his parrying of the censor's restrictions show a common concern for freedom and responsibility. He is at variance with the prescriptions of Juan Ramón because they supposedly deny man's responsibility to his fellow man. He battles with the censor because the censor blocks his efforts to voice his ethical concerns. Otero, with a close eye on poetic tradition, claims the freedom to choose and to chart his own poetic way.

6

The Satires, The Times

Otero's attacks on the straw man of pure poetry stem from his ethical convictions. Fashionable writing that ignores political and social themes he censures as a product of a corrupt and degenerate society. In his own writing he exposes vice and folly but is not a doctrinaire moral reformer; neither is he obliged as a satirist to provide a detailed picture of daily life. This is surprising since he states often that his theme is real life, past and present, in all its aspects. Nonetheless, his calculated self-portraiture shows that the immediate presentation of real human experience is of little interest. "Manifiesto" affirms that he has been everywhere and seen everything:

Un hombre recorre España, caminando o en tren, sale y entra en las aldeas, villas, ciudades, acodándose en el pretil de un puente, atravesando una espaciosa avenida, escuchando la escueta habla del labriego o el tráfago inacorde de las plazas y calles populosas.

Ha visto zaguanes de fresca sombra y arenas de sol donde giraba una capa bermeja y amarilla, ha mirado las estrellas bajas del páramo o las olas fracasadas del arrecife, fingió desentenderse de los hombres y ha penetrado en todas las clases, ideologías, miseria y pugnas de su tiempo. ("Manifesto," *Historias,* 183)

(A man travels around Spain, on foot or by train, going in and out of villages, towns, cities, resting his elbows on the railing of a bridge, crossing a spacious avenue, listening to the farmworker's plain speech or the discordant bustle of crowded squares and streets.

He has seen cool, shady hallways and sunlit arenas with twirling red and yellow bullfighter's capes. He has looked at stars low over the bleak plateau or waves bursting on the reef. He pretended to wash his hands of men but has penetrated every class, ideology, wretchedness, and struggle of his time.)

However, it is clear not only that an angry satirist is no reliable critic of the society of his time, for he selects, exaggerates, and distorts, but also that there are so many rejected opportunities for biting portraits. There are no stabs at the frivolity and extravagances of the rulers, the character of high officials, no pictures of day-to-day life in Madrid, the social striving of mediocrities and sycophants, the flow of foreign tourists and imported customs. Otero strikes, of course, at political and religious hypocrisy and denounces the evils of the regime, but there is no full picture of a degenerate society. The deformed faces of depravity, greed, covetousness, ignorance, pride, and stupidity do not stare out from every nook and cranny of Otero's world. Possibly, the absence of extensive social portraits stems from the lack of ripe conditions: social satire tends to flourish in a stable society and presupposes homogeneous moral standards. Certainly, the censor is no real obstacle and, as Otero so ably shows, can be circumvented by simply publishing abroad.[1]

Otero's disgust with society reflects the familiar self-presentation of the satirist as an outsider, and from *Que trata de España* onward it focuses on Spain's increasing affluence and the consequent vices of the consumer society. He prefers to rage against covetousness, which shuts up the gates of charity, and against hatred, symbolized by the shadow of Cain and Abel. Indeed, he appeals to traditional Christian and, to a lesser extent, Marxian precepts: "A los 52 años sigo pensando lo mismo que Carlos Marx, / con la única diferencia de que le copio un poco pero lo digo mas bonito" (At fifty-two I still think the same as Karl Marx, / the only difference being that I copy him a bit but say it better) ("Ergo sum," *Mientras,* 115–20). However, it is difficult to disentangle the traditional from the personal and immediate in Otero's tirades against luxury and greed, for he mixes standard commonplaces of the tradition of satire and complaint with contemporary notions of social and political goodness. Furthermore, he abandons ephemeral topics in his later moral sonnets to reflect on human mutability, death, and the final vanity of his days.

The main target of Otero's social satire is the conditions of city life. He is disgusted with the bustle, traffic, fashions, and advertising of Madrid. "Túmulo de gasoil" looks back longingly if unrealistically to the Madrid of Lope, Galdós, and Quevedo, as the poet faces glaring lights, raucous yelling, "el gasoil, los yanquis y la sociedad de consumo" (diesel oil, the Yanks, and consumer society). Pessimistically, Otero denounces the finery of modern Spanish woman. In medieval manner, woman is a victim of fashion, displaying and presenting her body as a weapon of evil attraction. A comic image lightens the diatribe: "y sus mamás ostentan senos de Honolulú, y pasan muchachas con sus ropas chapadas, / faldas en microsurco, y manillas brillantes y sandalias de purpurina..." (and their mums flaunt Honolulu breasts, and girls go by with their veneer of clothes, / microgroove skirts, and shiny bracelets and purple sandals...). The satirist reflects on the vanity of modern city life and ironically concludes that modern thermoplastic technology affords a solution: "ciudad donde Jorge Manrique acabaría por jodernos / a todos, a no ser porque la vida está cosida con grapas / de plástico y sus hojas perduran inarrancablemente bajo / el rocío de los prados..." (city where Jorge Manrique would end up fucking / us all, if it were not for life being sewn up / with plastic staples and his pages enduring, impossible to pull up beneath the dew of the meadows...). In the end, political apathy is the cause of the present state of Madrid, "ahumado por unos cuántos años de quietismo" (smoked up by a few years of quietism) ("Túmulo de gasoil," *Expresión,* 289–90).[2] Yet Madrid is described only in the most selective and generalized terms. The free form of "Túmulo de gasoil" does not produce any detailed social complaint; neither is there any vivid picture in "Francisco de Quevedo," an appeal to a brother satirist from the depths of a Madrid night. Here the indictment is aphoristic and concise. The times are evil: "La mala leche corre por la vida" (Wicked bile runs through life). Once again, the final cause is political: "En Palacio hace frío y luto y miedo" (In the Palace there is fear, cold, and mourning).[3]

With all the neopuritanism of one who has flirted with Marxism, Otero hits out at the frantic scrambling for stupid luxuries in consumer society. Several late sonnets take potshots at the boundless rapacity of his countrymen stimulated by slogans, posters, and television advertising. "El castillo," "Contesten," and "Compre, o le mato" strike at a Spain prospering from industry and tourism but destined, in the satirist's view, to collapse from its own prosperity. The theme is an old Catholic one: money, the power of avarice, the evil of the pursuit of riches and this world's goods. However, there is a distinction to be drawn between these and earlier deridings of the multiplication of luxuries. In "Ultimas noticias," for example, there was the sense that the indecent display and amassing of riches is an insult to poverty (*Parler*, 112–15). Otero is not simply repeating platitudes on wealth. His satire is calculated to claim better conditions of life for the majority. Here, however, there are no social distinctions but simply a blanket criticism, a shot at the Aunt Sallies of modern times, although some might argue earnestly that advertising and consumers are a peculiarly capitalist evil.

"El castillo" illustrates the folly and final emptiness of a visit to a castle of consumerism:

> a nadie se lo digas porque no van a
> atender y mucho menos a entenderte

LOS GRANDES ALMACENES. LA ESCALERA
corrediza. Las luces. Los colores.
Telas. Alfombras voladoras. Flores.
Una muchacha tiende el brazo. (Fuera,

los raudos coches, los rostros de cera,
semikafkianos.) Tiendo el cuello: ¿*Tienen*
sombrillas? ...Vienen van y vienen,
roces de estrías rosas y madera.

Voy a gritar. Pregunto. Toco. Digo
lo mismo siempre. No comprenden. Sigo,
vuelvo, pregunto, no comprenden. ¿*Tienen*

antinas? ¡Eh, Gregorio! Sigo,
vuelvo. Demonio, no comprenden.¡Digo
antinas! ¡...*tines!*
> Vienen van y vienen...
>   ("El castillo," *Mientras,* 89–93)[4]

> (don't tell anyone because they're not going to pay
> attention, never mind understand you

The huge department stores. Escalator.
Spotlights. Colors.
Fabrics. Flying carpets. Flowers.
A salesgirl points her arm. [Outside,

screeching cars, wax faces,
semi-kafkaesque.] I stretch my neck: "Do you have
sunshades?" ...They come, go, and come again,
jostling pink fluting and wood.

I'm going to scream. I keep asking, prodding, saying
the same thing. They do not understand. I keep going,

back and forth, asking, but they do not understand. "Do
    you have any

anjars?" Hey, Greg! I keep going
back and forth. Hell, they do not understand. I say
"anjars!   ...jars!"
          They keep coming, going, coming back again...)

The whole world of the sonnet rushes toward a distant goal of wealth and luxury, but this
race is the cause of social confusion and decay which results in personal unhappiness and
defeat for the poet. The plight of the poet, unable to communicate and adrift in a Madrid
department store, is depicted in a rapid sketch in which disjointed syntax imitates a general
aimlessness. In the opening lines, a scene is set by listing observed elements without intervening conjunctions. "Alfombras voladoras" stands out, humorously symbolizing the il-
lusory world of consumer goods. Customers are anonymous, characterized only by their
lack of understanding and constant bustle, reduced to "roces de estrías rosas y madera" as
they pass by. Their children are both captivated and ignored. Man's predicament is to con-
front an incomprehensible state of existence, and the poet is not exempt: he too has no power
to resolve or control the situation. Indeed, he participates. In one way, the sonnet displays the
same negative vision as the religious sonnets of *Ancia*. It shows man adrift, lacking divine
assurance that the world is created for hopeful human contact. From another point of view,
the poem might seem to show the corruption of human social relations by the capitalist
ethic. The oppressive, exaggerated, nightmare world is conveyed by the repetitions and the
obsessive references to similar kinds of experience. Yet although Otero repeats his indictment
of consumer society elsewhere, it is noteworthy that here he too is a consumer, helpless,
isolated, and also guilty of the folly of false values. This explains, perhaps, why his approach
in "El castillo" is presentational rather than admonitory, although the corruption of an ideal
of human conduct is implicit.

    "Compre, o le mato" conveys a definite admonition: helplessness and isolation are the
consequences of foolishly seeking the material benefits of consumer society. If satire is essentially an exposure of evil, the poem presents the objective effects of vice and of the punishment of the innocent. The focus is on the crime, not the criminal, and the scene is kept at a
distance by the caricature of an advertising slogan that serves as a title:

Hay una casa y un anuncio enfrente.
La fachada es azul y giratoria.
Las letras andan sueltas por la historia,
más bien loca y cruel, del siglo XX.

Los transeúntes tropiezan de repente
igual que un muerto sin pena ni gloria.
Periódicos, gasoil, inflamatoria
atmósfera del diablo decadente.

Un niño sale de la casa. Mira
el anuncio falaz. No entiende, estira
el cuello y llora largamente y chilla.

Los hombres pasan con el gas al cuello.
El mundo es horroroso, pero bello
como un slogan en letra amarilla.
　　("Compre, o le mato," *Todos,* 123)

(Opposite there is a house and an advertisement.
The signboard is blue and revolves.
The letters appear unhampered through the history,
rather mad and cruel, of the twentieth century.

The passers-by often stumble
just like a dead man without punishment or glory.
Newspapers, gas stations, inflammatory
atmosphere of the decadent devil.

A little boy leaves home. He looks
at the deceptive advertisement. He does not understand,
　　　sticks out
his neck, cries for a long time, and shrieks.

Men go by up to their ears in debt.
The world is horrifying, but beautiful
like a slogan with yellow lettering.)

The objective presentation in the opening lines of a revolving advertisement for gasoline expands into a general indictment of modern times in the first stanza. In the second stanza a quick transition to the people in the scene reiterates this blanket condemnation with deepening intensity. The moralizing emphasis is simple, clear, not only in the choice of simile and epithet but also in the contemptuous alliteration. Yet there is no attempt at any real representation of popular life in the octet. Furthermore, the brief drama of the little boy in stanza three is exaggerated and grotesque for all the bare plainness of the language. In effect, this symbolic action conveys the central meaning of the poem, which is that the experience of the times is so discomforting as to appear monstrous. The world into which the innocent child enters defeats him inexorably, and he is free in later life only to accept, not throw off, its burden: "Los hombres pasan con el gas al cuello." The concluding reflection would be banal and sentimental except that the ironic simile points up the perverse fascination that evil holds.

　　Otero's criticism is entirely abstract and moralistic. See, for example, his selection of adjectives: "loca y cruel," "decadente," "falaz," "horroroso." Naturally, his aggressive exaggeration is polemical and might be taken as an attack on Spain's closer contact with American and European marketing techniques. However, he consistently avoids any penetrating criticism of the social or economic aspects of the milieu in which his figures move. Moral realism is Otero's concern. Moreover, the moral stance is quite pessimistic, since it admits of no possibility of redemption, although a companion piece, "Contesten," is a clarion call to proclaim a moral vision of human community in the face of "un montón de escombros alineados; / televisión, anuncios, *flash,* periódicos" (a heap of rubbish lined up; / television, commercials, news flashes, newspapers) ("Contesten," *Todos,* 124). It is in this respect that Otero's satire can be said to be social. His poems can be seen as moral statements that implicitly or explicitly call on his listeners to change their life, and to change particularly the manner in which their actions impinge on those of their fellows.

Otero does not dwell with too intense a gaze on the remedies for moral decline. There is a call to abjure the temptations of the world of consumerism, and he points to the moral superiority of a life not cluttered by unnecessary goods. Indeed, Otero's social poetry is deeply rooted in familiar sermon topics, such as a belief that greed for wealth is the main factor in the moral decline of his time, or a belief in the value of detecting the vanity and false appearances of the world about him.[5] In the end, this is trite and commonplace, and these ideas bear fruit only when they are explored imaginatively. To sneer at the hackneyed moralizing is as much a disservice to the poetry as to credit it with a host of politically relevant beliefs. The best poems are built from impressions precipitated by the general idea, which may itself remain in the background, stated, if at all, only obliquely. Ethical truth and sincerity are dubious criteria, of course, for the judging of poetry. They can be disastrous when applied to general concepts that have been abstracted from their contexts. What matters is the power of the particular concept, in its specific context and form of expression, to create and convey a mood that unifies the poem or gives it a starting point and direction. The topics of greed and of the extravagance of the times are part of a larger chorus which includes a bleakly pessimistic note on the vanity and transience of human life. Thus warnings of the silent passage of time accompany calls to abjure the material temptations of Franco's Spain. This is a traditional, cynical theme: the folly of the high hopes of man for whom the worm waits.

Approaching sixty, Otero becomes more aware of the brevity of human life and the sly, rapid passing of time. He awakens to the realization of the approach of his own death. "Cantar de amigo" insists on his power to avoid deceptive appearances, to see each unseen nook and cranny of life. The poem closes with a striking variant of its parallelistic form: "¿Dónde está Blas de Otero? Está muerto con los ojos abiertos" (Where is Blas de Otero? He is dead with his eyes open) (*Expresión,* 294).[6] He has borne witness to his times, although in "Penúltima palabra" he suggests that for all his high hopes his generation has not fully translated his vision into action. That task he leaves to his survivors whose world, if they have the will, will be different:

DENTRO DE POCO MORIRÉ.
El zafarrancho de mi vida
toca a su fin...
. . . .

Esto fue todo. No me quejo.
Sé que he vivido intensamente.
(Demasiado intensamente.) Enfrente
está el futuro: es todo lo que os dejo.
("Penultima palabra," *Mientras,* 157–58)

(In a little while I shall die.
The call to action stations of my life
is coming to an end...

This was everything. I am not complaining.
I know that I have lived intensely.
[Too intensely.] Before us
is the future: it is all I am leaving you.)

The penitential note dissolves into a hope that the wisdom he has gained in living will enable others to counter the deceits of life. This stoic vein of thought is coupled with a laconic anticlericalism in the epigraph: "nada de cajitas, pastillas de plástico, la cama, la pared, la tos del cura" (no more capsules, plastic tablets, bed, wall, priest's coughing). Denying himself any possibility of Christian hope, the aging satirist faces this closeness to death trusting confidently in his moral vision and in bold, if inevitably circumscribed, endurance.

Otero's sonnets on time and mortality spring from reflection on his times. They give new life to the perennial topics of *ubi sunt* and *vita brevis* which he has encountered in Quevedo and, demonstrably, in Jorge Manrique. The reason for examining them is to place the satires of the times in a larger perspective of moral poetry. "Libro de memorias" and "Que es el morir" find their inspiration in the theme of time and death as executors of the laws of human mortality. All, including the satirist, must die, and although he triumphs briefly, he finds no deeper consolation. In contrast with Manrique, who sees the limitless horizon of eternity beyond the merely temporal, Otero is resigned to death as a breach of life. There is no sense that death is an estuary where the river of time widens silently into the sea of eternity.

"Libro de memorias" treats the idea that all must die as material for poetic composition, subject to the ordinances of imagination and pithy humor. The tone is that of meditation, of playing with an idea, not of sermonizing:

El tiempo come mucho, es una fiera
con brazos, ilusiones en los dientes,
ropas chapadas, lluvia y sol, pendientes
de sus labios de rauda cremallera.

Pasan los días y pasamos: era
un caballito de cartón, fluyentes
ayeres y hoyes ya desvanecientes,
en mortal, rapidísima carrera.

¿Y qué? O como dice aquél: ¿Qué pasa?
Aquí no canta nadie lo perdido,
desvanecido, ido... Tabla rasa.

El tiempo es bueno, como hay dios. Hay días
en que no se ve a nadie. Es que se han ido
entre memorias y neblinas frías...
                    ("Libro de memorias," *Todos,* 103)

(Time eats a lot, it is a wild animal
with arms, illusions in its teeth,

studded clothes, rain and sunshine hanging
from the swift zipper of its lips.

The days pass and we pass on: it was
a little cardboard horse, flowing
yesterdays and todays already fading,
in a fatal, swift race.

And so what? Or as that fellow says: What's happening?
Here nobody sings of what is lost,
disappeared, gone... A clean slate.

Times are good, as God would have it. There are days
when you don't see anyone. That's because they have gone
off among memories, and cold mists...)

This opens with a fine bundle of images that provides a concrete and vivid setting for a reflection, in the sestet, on invisible things. Metaphor here is a mode of apprehension, a way of visualizing the subject of the poet's reflections on the devastating force of time. The images tumble over one another in the opening stanza, yet the effect is not one of confusion but of swift and sharpening illumination. Personification ("brazos," "dientes," "ropas," "labios") knits all together. The final metaphor, "pendientes / de sus labios de rauda cremallera," is strong and novel, delayed and extended by the run-on line.[7]

"Pasan los días y pasamos" anticipates the conclusions of the sestet. The colloquial diction of this *obiter dictum* is heightened by repetition and a shift of meaning, since *pasamos* also carries the sense of dying. However, the imagery now is less condensed and emphasizes the instability of appearances. Life's insubstantiality is suggested by the adjectives, "de cartón," "fluyentes," "desvanecientes," "mortal," "rapidísima," and by the shift to imperfect tense. Unlike that of the first stanza, the rhythm here is more fluid, aided by alliteration heightened by an uncommon plural, "hoyes." Sound underscores sense as Otero implacably strips away any hope man may have had for permanence.

The sudden colloquial questions apply the poet's powers of understanding to the subject evoked in the octet: "¿Y qué? ¿Qué pasa?" Here the connection with the first section is sharp and strong: the first tercet confirms time's obliterating power through the repeated past participles. Then the general proposition is summed up, after a breathing space, by the terse mental image, "Tabla rasa." Rhyme gives musical climax to the tercet, rounding off things neatly and giving to Otero's perception a sense of finality. The second tercet opens with a convincing, if ironic, generalization, then shifts to a simple and brief recapitulation, bringing poem and title into focus on the theme of absent friends. In the final line, the alliteration closes on "frías," indirectly providing a cover for simplicity of diction. What would seem nakedly banal by itself gains force when clothed with rhyme and music. At the mention of cold death the sonnet falls into silence.

If "Libro de memorias" presents a bleak view of life, it is because the poem entails no decision to act on the basis of what has been imaginatively apprehended. "Qué es el morir" accepts death's finality, but the poet makes a heroic and defiant stand in the face of his very transitoriness. Like the previous sonnet, it depends less on truism than on metaphor and musicality for its effects:

El tiempo, el tiempo pasa como un río.
No. Yo soy una barca pasadera
a lo largo del río. (Blanda cera
consumiéndose a fuego lento y frío.)

El tiempo, el tiempo es siempre y nunca mío
como una secuencia que fluyera
en negro y blanco, un raudo film que fuera
borrándome la estela del navío...

El árbol. Permanece. A contra viento.
Junto al río, escuchando el movimiento
de las piedras del fondo removidas.

Yo soy. Un árbol. Arraigado. Firme.
Aunque, en el fondo, bien sé que he de irme
en el río que arrastra nuestras vidas.
                ("Qué es el morir," *Todos,* 129)

(Time, time passes like a river.
No. I am a passing ship
along the river. [Soft wax
burning away in a slow, cold fire.]

Time, time is always and never mine
like a sequence that was running
in black and white, a rapid film that
was erasing the ship's wake on me...

The tree. It remains. Facing the wind.
Beside the river, listening to the movement
of the shifting bottom pebbles.

I am. A tree. Rooted. Firm.
Although, deep down, I well know that I must go off
in the river that drags away our lives.)

A one-line maxim is followed by a pair of images in the first quartet and by an extended simile in the second. In both stanzas the degree of formalism is high; yet two almost opposite literary effects appear at the same time. The sonnet opens hesitantly when the repetition "El tiempo, el tiempo" removes any sense of premeditation and suggests that thought breaks through unbidden. Then Otero firmly rejects the ordinary, traditional simile of time as a river and makes a fresh start with a more novel nautical metaphor. Something of the same effect is created by parenthesis, as if a sudden qualification of his thought had occurred to him on the spur of the moment. This aside is calculatedly impromptu and gives a sense of the poet commenting on his own words. The second stanza repeats the repetition of the first, then surprises with a compressed sequence of conceptual images. The second simile of the sonnet is intricately linked with what had gone before but excitingly sharp and developed. A Machadian echo in the image of the ship's wake leads back to the previous ship image as well as connects with the first segment of the simile, "una secuencia que fluyera." In such images Otero finds expression for visions precisely observed with detachment, remote enough for the common points of reference to surprise and stimulate the imagination.[8] Also, by using oxymoron twice ("fuego . . . frío"; "siempre y nunca"), Otero knits together sections differing in sense but common in style. The effect of repeated attempts to reflect on man's place in time is to create a sense of informality, of impromptu composition, of tentativeness, and of some inadequacy of means to end.

The rhythm changes in the tercets and introduces a new image, a hope for permanence, a protest against the ravages of the tides. Caesura obtrusively stops the flow of the sonnet in both opening lines here, imitating the new turn of thought, but it cannot stem the fluid movement of the poem which, like time itself, presses onward. "A contra viento" recalls the willed, stoical optimism at the close of "Impreso prisionero": "Y voluntad de vida / a contradictadura y contratiempo" (And with a will to live / against dictatorship and against time). Now, however, the poet disillusions himself of such confident determination. The last two lines of each tercet bring the poem round in a circle to the idea once again of the inexorable, irreversible flight of time. First, the pebbles rattling along the riverbed are a reminder that no human endeavour, however great, can withstand the onslaught of time. Then Otero shows himself to be aware of the ultimate futility of glorifying his accomplishment in living. "Aunque" marks a pause and a change of tone which suitably introduces a concluding distich that, in an epigrammatic way, looks back over the whole sonnet. Now he discredits the ephemeral thought that will last forever, a thought that is not consonant either in sound or sense, with the predominant picture of life's evanescence. Even the rhyme of the couplets links willed endurance with inexorable change. Thus, although Manrique has provided Otero with a rich source for the idea of the sonnet, "Nuestras vidas son los ríos / que van a dar en la mar / que es el morir" (Our lives are rivers / which flow to the sea / which is death) is adapted and developed so that the reality of death, not the reality of eternity, becomes the focus. Life is not a peaceful and serene flowing through a channel. The title as well as the choice of *arrastra* underscores Otero's reluctant and fatalistic acceptance of death's finality. The play on *fondo,* however, prevents morbidness.

As a satirist Otero strives to recognize error and to mend errant ways. On the one hand, he exposes the error of greed, the vanity of consumerism; on the other, he reveals the error in man's apprehension of the temporal and material. These are, of course, traditional commonplaces, and they fail to account fully for the poems. They acquire significance only when used as organizing principles, when the poet sees suddenly, as in a vision, a series of unconnected images come together in unexpected focus. To state the general proposition that capitalist consumption is evil, and that Otero tries to persuade his readers of this, is meaningless and deadens appreciation of the poetry. In fact, the assertion that this is a deep belief of Otero's is a concealed assertion that the poems in which it is expressed are good. Literarily they are good because they hold together musically and imaginatively, not because they contain good political or social messages. Otero insists: "La poesía es un ente estético y eso jamás debe olvidarlo el poeta" (Poetry is an aesthetic entity, and the poet should never forget that).[9] The notions of literary and political goodness are not totally incompatible, of course, but the literary value of general ideas is that they act as organizing factors; they serve to unify a whole series of impressions that can crystallize and take shape around them. Otero explores imaginatively his impressions of his times, playing in his mind about many ideas, interweaving them with such swiftness and dexterity that many aspects of life appear from as many different points of view. Certainly, however much representation may be involved, the generic end is rhetorical: to expose folly. After all, the secret rules of the genre do not oblige the satirist to present a true and complete view of the world beyond his imagination.

7

THE SATIRES, TYRANNY

To digress on the metaphysics of the relationship between what Spain is and what she is known as by the satirist would be merry and mischievous. In Otero's satire of the Franco regime this is an especially tantalizing temptation, since the poet constantly measures and sizes Spain, shifting the lighting to make the big look little, the little big. He forever insists that there is more in things than meets the eye, that we need always to adjust our first impressions lest we miss the view completely. Otero is so variable and nimble that, ethical considerations apart, his satirical production has a zest that stimulates the mental appetite and opens the mind to the simple wonder of poetic creation. If we are not alive and responsive now to a light stab at the working conditions of a poor Andalusian girl, now to a grim sneer at tyranny, now to a spoof on Yankee greed, now to a gibe at Falangists and priests, now to a poignant lament for a divided land, that is, if we do not read responsively, we are not likely to interpret the political satires faithfully. Satire is the daughter of Themis, goddess of law and justice, and Otero calls for her sword to slay deaf, blind, and dumb stupidity wherever he perceives it in the social and political fabric of Francoist Spain. Also, satire is the daughter of Pan, and his tricks and goat-footed swiftness accompany Otero's victims to their death.[1]

Otero scarcely concerns himself with the presentation of precise political events, and there is little that is immediately factual that interests him. He does not assail contemporaries by name: there are no proper names from the political arena, even disguised, like Dryden's Zimri. Certainly, he does condemn post–Civil War Spain hook, line, and sinker in "MXCLV":

Se ha parado el aire.

En seco,
el Ebro. El pulso.
El Dauro.

Oremus. El aire lleva
dieciseis años parados.
("MXCLV," Parler, 38–39)[2]

(The wind has ceased.

The Ebo,
dried up. The pulse.

73

The river Dauro.

Let us pray. Fresh winds
have ceased for sixteen years.)

Or he condemns, equally melodramatically, at the close of "Impreso prisionero":

¿Hablar en castellano? Se prohibe.
Buscar españa en el desierto
de diecinueve cegadores años.
Silencio.
Y más silencio. Y voluntad de vida
a contra dictadura y contra tiempo.
("Impreso prisionero," *Que trata,* 29)[3]

(Speak Castilian Spanish? It is prohibited.
Search for Spain in the desert
of nineteen blinding years.
Silence.
And more silence. And with a will to live
against dictatorship and against time.)

Yet the particular expands for the most part into a general attack on Spanish vice and folly extending backward to the sixteenth century, the familiar *Black Legend.* It is silly to say that searching references to contemporary politics and administration are not to be expected from a writer living in times of felt tyranny: Otero publishes freely abroad. Deliberately he strips his picture of the film of day-to-day familiarity. He chooses to avoid the merely ephemeral, and his satiric power lies in the bite, the urgency, and a certain scurrilousness he achieves without concrete reference to the sundry failings of the body politic. Yes, there is some impromptu, rambling, and hit-and-miss verse, rough and hard-hitting. There are oblique cross-references, allusions, and not-so-careful hints; but Otero finally does not depend on vagaries of time and place for the success of his political satire. He appeals less to quarrels of sect or faction than to larger and more enduring issues of freedom, progress, brotherhood, and justice.

Otero usually does not so much make specific attacks as present exempla, pegs on which to hang a moral generalization. Indeed, the prefatory sonnet to *Que trata de España* envisions the censor as *neotorquemada.* The Franco regime is simply the end product of a condition that stretches back through Spanish history and that began with Cain and Abel. Quevedo, Larra, and Machado attack similar moral flaws at the heart of Spain. The central problem of injustice remains unchanged except that the relentless persistence of political depravity makes the present seem cumulatively more outrageous. Only compare the dull topicality of so many Civil War ballads to see how Otero transcends the ephemeral and, at the same time, by seeing the Franco government *sub specie aeternitatis,* how he makes his attack more telling. He dwells on principles, not personalities.

Many Otero satires of tyranny are political jests in poetic form. The basis of the humor lies in a funny and sobering identification of Spain as a prison, a gas chamber, a state under martial law subject to constant and unwarranted reprisals, a paper-laden bureaucracy darkened by "la sombra de la tiranía" (the shadow of tyranny), where man lies "atado de pies a cabeza" (tied up from head to foot) ("Palabras sin sentido," "El aeroplano de papel," *Todos,*

101, 111). This technique is metaphoric, based as it is on extravagant and degrading likenesses. When taken to extremes Spain appears to be monstrous; when handled judiciously she is simply ridiculous.

"Me llamarán, nos llamarán a todos" presents a ferocious caricature of the Francoist State as being nothing more than a political pogrom.

> ...porque la mayor locura que puede hacer un
> hombre en esta vida es de jarse morir, sin
> más ni más...
> > Sancho.
> > > (*Quijote*, II, cap. 74)

I

Me llamarán, nos llamarán a todos.
Tú, y tú, y yo, nos turnaremos,
en tornos de cristal, ante la muerte.
Y te expondrán, nos expondremos todos
a ser trizados ¡zas! por una bala.

Bien lo sabéis. Vendrán
por ti, por ti, por mi, por todos.
Y también
por ti.

(Aquí
no se salva ni dios. Lo asesinaron.)

Escrito está. Tu nombre está ya listo,
te/pmblando en un papel. Aquél que dice:
abel, abel, abel...o yo, tú, él...

2

Pero tú, Sancho Pueblo,
pronuncias anchas sílabas,
permanentes palabras que no lleva el viento...
> ("Me llamarán," *Pido*, 44–46)[4]

> ("...for the greatest madness that a
> man can be guilty of in this life is to die without good reason,
> without more ado..."
> > Sancho
> > *Don Quixote*, II, chap. 74

I

They will call me, we'll all be called.
You, and you, and I, we'll all take it in turns,
like revolving glass doors, in the face of death.
And you'll run the risk, we'll all run the risk
of being smashed to bits—bang!—by a bullet.

You know as much. They'll come

for you, for you, for me, for all of us.
And also
for you there.

[Here
not even God escapes. He was assassinated.]

It's written down. Your name is already set,
shaking on a piece of paper. The one that says:
abel, abel, abel... or me, you, him...

                          2
But you, Sancho of the People,
utter spacious syllables,
permanent words that the wind does not carry off...)

This vignette is patently untrue but is based on the supposed truth that the State is repressive. Amusement depends on the absurdity of the exaggeration: how unlike Spain this land of systematic political extermination is. However, the likeness, the perception of injustice, teases. The satirist lampoons Spain mercilessly. He also offers a remedy, since he is not only angry but also, in the end, optimistic.

The Cervantine epigraph stands before the poem like a holy text with chapter and verse. Implicitly, it calls for courage to demand freedom and dignity in the face of impossible odds (the quixotification of Sancho Pueblo). The poem itself is straightforward. Part one insists we shall all be executed by a nameless oppressor; part two offers consolation. The epigraph-refrain affirms that resignation is madness. The diction is plain but saved from sparseness by pun (l. 10–11), colloquialism (l. 5), and vivid image of a mass call-up for execution (ll. 2–3). Tension comes from pronouns and verb endings that dramatically stress communal extinction ("Me . . . nos," l. 1; "Tú, y tú, y yo, nos," l. 2; "te . . . nos," l. 4; "por ti, por ti, por mi, por todos," l. 7; graphically, "Y también / por ti, ll. 8–9; "Tu nombre," l. 12; and darkly, "*abel, abel, abel... o yo, tú, él...*," l. 14). By dint of repetition this caricature gathers force. Moreover, not only are all reduced to sacrificial political victims, but also the tyrant is a violently anonymous third party ("llamarán," "expondrán," "vendrán"). Strophes and sentences are tersely, almost comically ("por ti"), brief. The only development is from informal announcement ("Me llamarán"), through audience participation ("Bien lo sabéis"), through edict ("Escrito está"), to myth ("abel, abel, abel"). The closure of the first part reveals the dark identity of the oppressor: it is Cain.[5] The second part points optimistically to both the epigraph and the common wisdom and courage of the Spanish people. This hopeful ending, together with the restrained style, ensures that the reader reacts not against the rage and disgust of the satirist (an ever-possible weakness of satire), but against the target he invites us to loathe. The tide of denunciation, arrest, and execution will be turned by the enduring words of Sancho Pueblo.

The close of "En esta tierra" involves reversal and discovery of a different sort:

A mí
lo que me duele
es el pecho.

(El pecho
tiene forma
de españa.)

El médico me ha dicho: —Mucho aire,
mucho ai...

—Como no lo pinte.
     ("En esta tierra," *Parler*, 92–93)

(For me
what hurts
is my chest

[My chest
is the shape
of spain.]

The doctor has told me: "Lots of fresh air,
lots of fre..."

"But I can't even imagine it.")

This short piece moves rapidly and carries a range of effects disproportionate to its diminutive size. The opening lines are quite neutral, although the title suggests a relationship between the content of the poem and the condition of Spain. However, the speaker's ailing chest becomes (parenthetically) a caricature of Spain herself. Quickly the doctor prescribes but ironically is unable to complete his prescription since he also suffers from the disease. Political freedom, symbolized by fresh air, is not to be found, and the final line clinches the attack by jibing at the impracticality of the doctor's advice which he himself cannot follow.[6]

    "Biotz-Begietan" takes another tack to convince the audience that tyranny and injustice are rife in Spain. There is the same persuasive end, the same techniques of careful selection and exaggeration, but the approach is quite different. The satirist knows that even the self-inflicted wound can be a clever means of attack. The title, drawn from the Basque poet Lizardi, suggests that Spain is in the poet's heart and before his eyes, although the refrain, "escribo y callo," implies that crucial statements have been avoided.

Ahora
voy a contar la historia de mi vida
en un abecedario ceniciento.
El país de los ricos rodeando mi cintura

y todo lo demás. Escribo y callo.
Yo nací de repente, no recuerdo
si era sol o era lluvia o era jueves.
Manos de lana me enredaran, madre.

Madeja arrebatada de tus brazos
blancos, hoy me contemplo como un ciego,
oigo tus pasos en la niebla, vienen
a enhebrarme la vida destrozada.

Aquellos hombres me abrasaron, hablo
del hielo aquel de luto atormentado,
la derrota del niño y su caligrafía
triste, trémula flor desfigurada.

Madre, no me mandes más a coger miedo
y frío ante un pupitre con estampas.
Tú enciendes la verdad como una lágrima,
dame la mano, guárdame
en tu armario de luna y de manteles.

Esto es Madrid, me han dicho unas mujeres
arrodilladas en sus delantales,
éste es el sitio
donde enterraron un gran ramo verde
y donde está mi sangre reclinada.

Días de hambre, escándalos de hambre,
misteriosas sandalias
aliándose a las sombras del romero
y el laurel asesino. Escribo y callo.

Aquí junté la letra a la palabra,
la palabra al papel.
                    Y esto es París,
me dijeron los ángeles, la gente
lo repetía, esto es París. Peut-être,
allí sufrí las iras del espíritu

y tomé ejemplo de la torre Eiffel.

Esta es la historia de mi vida,
dije, y tampoco era. Escribo y callo.
                    ("Biotz-Begietan," *Pido*, 53–55)

(Now
I am going to tell the story of my life
in an alphabet of ashes.
The land of the rich around my waist

and all the rest. I write and keep quiet.
I was born unexpectedly, I don't remember
if it was sunny, or rainy, or Thursday.
Your hands of wool ensnared me, mother.

A skein snatched from your white
arms, I look at myself today like a blind man,

I can hear your footsteps in the mist, coming
to mend for me my destroyed life.

I was burned by those men, I'm talking
about that ice of torturous mourning,
a disaster for the child and his sad
handwriting, like a trembling, deformed flower.

Mother, don't send me back again
to catch cold and fear at a desk full of holy pictures.
You light up truth like a teardrop:
give me your hand, put me away with the linens
in that huge mirrored wardrobe.

This is Madrid, so I am told by some women,
in aprons, kneeling;
this is the place
where they buried a fine green olive branch,
and where my blood is resting.

Days of hunger, scandals about hunger,
mysterious sandals
joining shadowy pilgrims,
and those murderous laurels of victory. I keep on writing and say nothing.

Here I joined each letter to its word,
each word to a sheet of paper.
                    And this is Paris,
the angels told me, and people
repeated, this is Paris. *Peut être,*
there I suffered furies of the spirit

and took the Eiffel Tower as an example.

This is the story of my life,
I said, and it wasn't really. I keep on writing and hush it all up.)

"Biotz-Begietan" appears at the beginning of a hopeful, assertive sequence of poems that closes *Pido la paz la palabra.* It seems odd at first to place a restrained autobiographical piece, recounting personal misfortunes in a seemingly penitential vein ("un abecedario ceniciento"), among such affirmative poems as "Vencer juntos," "Pido la paz y la palabra," or "Fidelidad." However, autobiographical reminiscence turns into an opportunity to censure Spain, her covetousness, her religiosity, and her unjust dictatorship. The warrant for credibility of these judgments is the character of the poet. His quiet and noble suffering arouses pity, and by deliberately leaving unsaid what ought to be said he moves the listener to righteous indignation. The techniques of persuasion are similar to those in "En esta tierra," since Otero both alludes and eludes at the same time.

Innuendo is of course the tactic of the dishonest debater, but rhetorical acumen moves Otero to cast his attack in this form. The prologue (ll. 1–5) encapsulates the satirist's strategy. He claims to be telling his life story but prefaces his claim with an opening that might be intoned as an exclamation of rebuke ("Ahora" followed by a pause, l. 1). Then the image of an alphabet of ashes recalls Job's final words: "Por eso me retracto y hago penitencia sobre polvo y ceniza" (Wherefore I abhor myself and repent in dust and ashes).[7] That is, the knowledge that has come to him is that his suffering was finally an enrichment, since it has strengthened his faith; and, like Job, the satirist will be acquitted and his fortunes restored. Confident that he will be vindicated, the speaker points to the circumstances of his life, though not to his personal life as might be expected from the confessional opening. The abrupt run-on line has positive meaning, as if it were a pause for things left unsaid. For the first time the refrain appears, "Escribo y callo," paraphrased by Emilio Alarcos as "aludo y eludo" (I allude and elude).[8] Indeed, the whole poem later comes to rest on this refrain, a combination of paraleipsis (pretending to pass over while actually hinting at something) and aposiopesis (becoming silent). Autobiography allows him to avoid direct vituperation and simply to show himself behaving virtuously, the innocent victim of injustice. Hence the character of the speaker encourages the audience to accept things not fully demonstrated.

Although the body of the poem outlines the speaker's growth from childhood to maturity, it is a drastically simplified account, comprised of childhood and education (ll. 6–21), impressions of Madrid (ll. 22–32), and reactions to Paris (ll. 33–37). The closure is swift (ll. 38–39), as if the satirist were too angry to continue. In any case, the technique is to pass over, with vague hints, matters already known to his readers and too ugly to recount. Otero is feinting, since he pretends to say nothing but gives full expression to his anticlericalism and resistance to the Franco government.

The body of the poem begins with a lighthearted presentation of birth with a deliberate anticlimactic letdown: "no recuerdo / si era sol o era lluvia o era jueves" (ll. 6–7). Childhood evokes an image of the writer's mother. She is both symbol of security and the protector of the poet-child from the assaults of a world of oppressive schoolmasters and religious indoctrination. This world has already been suggested in the preface: "El país de los ricos rodeando mi cintura / y todo lo demás." Now, Otero surprises with a flurry of vituperation (ll. 13–14). Personal details provide evidence of injustice: "la vida destrozada"; "la derrota del niño." Pun (abrazar/abrasar), wordplay (abrasaron/hielo), and exaggerated metonymy ("luto atormentado" for priest's black cassock) poke fun at church education. The topic is familiar, and the malicious jolting of expectations is typically Oterian.[9]

Irony colors the picture of Madrid. Kneeling women unheroically herald the seat of victory, and the poet laments the burial of new life. The city of heroes is the city of hunger, and the poem reaches a climax of vehement denunciation (ll. 22–30). The world is turned upside down: priests are reduced by synecdoche to "misteriosas sandalias," victorious generals by metonymy to "el laurel asesino." Born into an uncertain time ("no recuerdo / si era sol o era lluvia o era jueves"), the satirist is now hemmed in by a secret alliance of evil.

In Madrid he begins to write, and the poem turns toward its closure. The satirist recalls how, in the teeth of the city's rampant corruption, he took up his pen of resistance. Terse phrasing and surprise preterite ("Aquí junté la letra a la palabra, / la palabra al papel") make his opposition appear resolute. The symmetrical vowel pattern and anadiplosis here underline this new and unexpected development, emphasizing that poems grow solidly out of patient and deliberate effort (ll. 31–32). Yet this passage is finally ironical, since the laconic refrain, "escribo y callo," precedes the stanza, and Madrid is suddenly passed over despite all its promise for poetic composition. The focus shifts to Paris (ll. 33–37), an anticlimactic episode at first, tinged with mildly comic Francophobia. The city, proverbially gay, tranquil, allegedly angelic, has its opposite effect on the exiled satirist. However, there is no appeal to pity, as in his earlier trials. On the contrary, the ersatz French, contrived pun (*París/iras*), and sound effects ("París . . . allí sufrí las iras") all amuse. Moreover, the Eiffel tower is a jaunty, if outdated, symbol of hope.[10]

Otero's emphasis ensures that distracting facts do not appear to mar or blur the desired picture. "Biotz-Begietan" becomes more and more restrained as it progresses, so that the topic of teeth-gritting resistance does not overshadow the overriding sense of restriction and injustice. The closing couplet exploits antithesis and, in placing phrases of opposite meaning side by side, presses the reader to refute one or the other. Thus, unspoken and perhaps unspeakable events testify in silence to the hypocrisy and injustice of Francoist Spain.

In "Biotz-Begietan," the seeming retreat from public matters to private concerns enhances Otero's attack. In "Torno," a personal and emotive summoning up of Spain's physical beauty, Otero also attempts to demonstrate the sincerity of his public voice by showing that he is involved in what he says as a private individual. The major part of the poem is a lyric geography that recalls Machado and Unamuno's poetic toponomies, or Aragon's *Crève-coeur*, but it ends with a curt apothegm. The admonitory tone of the closing couplet is all the sharper for being so unexpected.

Torno
los ojos a mi patria.
Meseta de Castilla
la Vieja, hermosa Málaga,
Córdoba doblando la
cintura, mi Vizcaya
de robles y nogales,
pinos y añosas hayas,
clara Cataluña, puro
León, lenta Granada,
Segovia de oro viejo,
Jaén ajazminada,
Moncayo azul, altivos
Gredos y Guadarrama,
blanca Vinaroz,
Extremadura grávida,
patria de pueblo y pan
partido injustamente.
("Torno," *Que trata,* 179)[11]

(I turn
my eyes to my native land.
The tablelands of Old
Castille, handsome Malaga,
Cordova bending
her waist, my Viscaya
with oaks and walnut trees,
pines and ancient beeches,
bright Catalonia, pure

Leon, slow Granada,
Segovia of old gold,
jasmined Jaen,
blue Moncayo, haughty
Gredos and Guadarrama,
white Vinaroz,
pregnant Extremadura,
land of people and bread
unjustly divided.)

Measuring, weighing how far Spain is off course, preoccupies Otero. *Torno* is the main verb in the poem and establishes a mood of reflection. The speaker casts his eyes on Spain but delays judgment until the final line, if not the final word. It is as if he has telescopic vision and at the last moment looks through the wrong end of the telescope. The panegyric of Spain's physical beauty (ll. 3–16) contradicts the sobering sociopolitical reality of the close. Clearly, Otero has a flair for disciplined structural design.

A pleasure in placing and caressing proper names inspires the poem, rather than a desire to evoke in detail the place where the names are to be found.[12] The lyric itinerary relies for its effect on the sensuous resonance of place-names and compound, interlaced alliteration. There are no inhabitants, only an idealized sense of place, far distant from sordid, present realities. Otero cherishes a great affection for Spain, of course, but this is a sublime, not a realistic portrayal. Place-names and descriptions convey respect for a noble tradition of beauty. The speaker hops back and forth, not rising systematically to a climax of his journey but merely setting city or province side by side for cumulative effect. All Spain is an earthly paradise, or could be so, a symbolic landscape far removed from the quarrels and acrimony of Francoist Spain.

Otero's ear for nuances of vowel sound and consonant pattern is acute, but the lulling charm developed in the body of the poem is broken by the closing couplet. The assonantal pattern is ruptured, replaced by a jabbing, alliterative effect. The adverb is bitterly out of place in both sound and sense within the landscape just evoked. *Partido* is not strictly coordinate with each preceding noun, but the allusive economy is intended to suggest strong emotion. Here, then, the surprise turn and moral judgment express an implicit plea for harmony, a yearning for unity, peace, and justice appropriate to Spain's idealized land. Thus, the climax of "Torno" comes with the general statement on injustice, a neat and totally final comment on the particular case, the more telling because of the absence of any explicit transition from the roll call of places. The whole is one long periodic sentence. Moral judgment is an organic part of a larger poetic vision, not a conventional ornament tacked on for decoration.[13]

The Spain of Otero's poems eschews justice and denies freedom to her citizens. Characteristically, the satirist's picture is exaggerated and distorted: his homeland is a prison where he struggles to write, "contra la sombra de la tiranía / que se arrastra por todos los rincones" (against the shadow of tyranny / which creeps into every corner) ("Palabras sin sentido," *Todos,* 101). The Spaniard sues for peace and freedom, "y le rompen la boca" (and they smash his mouth) ("Con la espalda," *Todos,* 118). Such simplification is characteristic of satire, and for all the hullabaloo about censorship, it must be remembered that Otero had little trouble publishing his poems. There has been no flood of prohibited manuscripts with the easing of censorship and the death of Franco. Persecution only fostered his influence.

Otero greatly exaggerates the tyranny of the Franco regime, and his fury over the vices of the State is unfeigned. However, if the context of the poems makes them an implicit indictment of post–Civil War Spain, Otero moves well beyond individuals and institutions, toward a sweeping overview of Spain, the Spain of reaction, of the Counter-Reformation, of the Holy Office.[14] Otero is not interested in petty immediacy: the setting is usually unspecified even when people and places are mentioned to give local color. Such treatment can be more evocative than a representational description of the mundane details of particular acts of repression. The poetic artifact matters more than humdrum details of daily life, and the satirist is influenced mostly by his taste for memorable phrase, imaginative wit, and pointed hyperbole. Indeed, Otero is much less a social reformer than a liberal humanitarian angered by nothing less than the desecration of an ideal of peace, justice, and freedom. Repeatedly, Spain is simply represented as a prison.

Otero's satire of censorship as a symbol of tyranny has a clear basis in historical fact, although historical and poetic plausibility coalesce. His own tribulations with the censor are the inspiration for "Impreso prisionero," where an autobiography of literary outspokenness combines with imaginative attack on official decrees of silence (*Que trata,* 28–29).[15] "Cartas y poemas a Nazim Hikmet (1958…)" is from the same date; in contrast the speaker's attitude is supplicant, not defiant:

Puesto que tú me has conmovido,
en este tiempo en que es tan difícil la ternura,
y tu palabra se abre como la puerta de tu celda
frente al Mármara,

rasgo el papel y, de hermano a hermano, hablo contigo
(*acaban de sonar*
                las nueve de la noche)
de cosas que no existen: Dios
está escuchando detrás de la puerta
de tu celda,
cedida por amor al hombre: Nazim Hikmet,
quédate con nosotros.

Que tu palabra entre entre las rejas de esta vieja cárcel
alzada sobre el Cantábrico,
que golpee en España
como una espada en el campo de Dumlupinar,
que los ríos la rueden hacia Levante y por Andalucía se extienda
como un mantel de tela pobre y cálida,
sobre la mesa de la miseria madre.

Te ruego te quedes con nosotros,
es todo lo que podemos ofrecerte: diecinueve años
perdidos,
peor que perdidos, gastados,
más que gastados, rotos
dentro del alma:

ten
misericordia de mi espúrea España.

Nunca oiste mi nombre ni lo has de oír, acaso,
estamos separados por mares, por montañas, por mi maldito encierro,
voluntario a fuerza de amor,
soy sólo poeta, pero en serio,
sufrí como cualquiera, menos
que muchos que no escriben porque no saben, otros
que no hablan porque no pueden, muertos
de miedo o de hambre
(aquí decimos *A falta de pan, buenas son tortas,* se cumplió)

pero habla, escribe tú, Nazim Hikmet,
cuenta por ahí lo que te he dicho, háblanos
del viento del Este y la verdad del día,
aquí entre sombras te suplico, escúchanos.
                ("Cartas y poemas a Nazim Hikmet [1958...]," *Parler,* 98–101)

(Since you have moved me
at this time when tenderness is so difficult
and your word opens up like the door of your cell
facing the Marmara River,

I tear the notepaper to pieces and, brother to brother,
speak to you
[*it has just struck*
                nine in the evening]
about things that do not exist: God
is listening behind the door
of your cell,
given for love of mankind: Nazim Hikmet,
be with us.

Let your word come through the bars of this old prison
set above the Bay of Biscay,
let it strike in Spain
like a sword on the field of Dumlupinar,
let the rivers roll it toward the South-east coast and let it spread across Andalusia
like a warm and humble tablecloth
over mother misery's table.

I pray for you to stay with us,
but all we can offer you are nineteen
lost years,
worse than lost, wasted,
more than wasted, shattered
within the soul:
have
mercy on my spurious Spain.

You have never heard my name nor, perhaps, will you ever hear it,

we are separated by seas, by mountains, by my accursed confinement,
voluntary by force of love,
I am only a poet, but seriously,
I suffered like anyone else, less
than many who do not write because they don't know how, less than others
who don't speak because they cannot, being dead
from fear or hunger
[here we say "When there is no bread, the cudgel of life will do," and it's true]

but speak out, you write, Nazim Hikmet,
tell over there what I have told you, speak to us
about the wind from the East and up-to-date truth,
here, among the shadows, I implore you, hear our prayer.)

Everything is larger than life. Hikmet, an imprisoned Turkish poet, is Spain's redeemer. Spain is an ancient prison, the satirist locked up. Hunger, fear, and brutality are rife. The Franco regime has accomplished absolutely nothing in nineteen years. Otero draws attention to his hyperbole, and nothing is gained by trying to determine from the poem the exact number of times it is larger than life.

The hybrid title allows for diversity within an epistolary framework, an improvised blending of invective within a miscellany of contents. In the opening salutation, tactful sympathy, friendly banter, delight in the attributes that mark Hikmet off from other men, set the tone. Yet only later in the poem does it become clear that the Turk is a comparative stranger, spiritually close but geographically remote. The section ends with an unexpected petitionary prayer modelled on the liturgy, "quédate con nosotros." In the body of the poem, petition shifts to intercession. Now the bonds of friendship are clear: at a distance, both poets share prison cells as well as a high degree of moral involvement with their countries. The style rises to a level of tragic dignity to express a mixture of pathos and disgust. Furthermore, the perspective changes from the general to the particular, and an emotive crescendo of repetitions leads up to a final incantatory plea: "ten / misericordia de mi espúrea España."

Some generic features of literary epistle reappear in the closing section: a colloquial tone ("pero en serio," "pero habla," "cuenta por ahí lo que te he dicho"), the suggestion of colloquy, the speaker's self-reference, a hint of the inconsequence of talk. The aim is to pepper the target from a different angle. If oppressed, the poet speaks nobly on behalf of those even less fortunate, although a wryly quoted proverb keeps the facts at a distance. Spain is shut tight by her jailors, and the envoi, while offering a suggestion of communist hope, appeals to the reader's pity.

The image of the prison, symbol of tyranny and hyperbole for Spain, also informs "Aire libre."

Si algo me gusta, es vivir.
Ver mi cuerpo en la calle,
hablar contigo como un camarada,
mirar escaparates
y, sobre todo, sonreír de lejos
a los árboles…

También me gustan los camiones grises
y muchísimo más los elefantes.
Besar tus pechos,
echarme en tu regazo y despeinarte,
tragar agua de mar como cerveza
amarga, espumeante.

Todo lo que sea salir
de casa, estornudar de tarde en tarde,
escupir contra el cielo de los tundras
y las medallas de los similares,
salir
de esta espaciosa y triste cárcel,
aligerar los ríos y los soles,
salir, salir al aire libre, al aire.
                    ("Aire libre," *Parler,* 68–69)[16]

(If there is anything I like, it's living.
Seeing my body out in the street,
talking with you like a comrade,
looking in shop windows
and, most of all, smiling from a long way off
at the trees...

I also like grey trucks
and, much more, elephants.
Kissing your breasts,
flinging myself into your lap and letting your hair down,
swallowing seawater down like beer,
bitter, foaming.

Anything that means leaving
the house, sneezing from one afternoon to the next,
spitting against the heaven of the tundras
and the medals of the [military] robots,
leaving
this spacious and miserable jail,
quickening rivers and suns,
going out, going out into the open air, into the air.)

Treatment of the theme here differs markedly from that in the previous poem. Loosely assonantal, the structure is planned as a unity; Otero has a craftsman's eye for overall coherence. The first two stanzas expand by multiplying synonyms for the joy of living. Examples of simple, everyday pleasures become, as the poem gathers momentum, capricious and varied enthusiasms. Suddenly the poem changes direction: Otero approaches the core of his thoughts circuitously. Hedonism, the third stanza shows, is nothing more than an escape from intolerable reality. Thus, when the satirist concentrates on mundane pleasures and ignores the political situation that causes him to so eagerly seek them, he is a master of irony. Whimsical, bubbling images of joy serve only to dramatize the serious if not desperate situation in which he finds himself.

Contrast of verb and image set the last stanza apart: *ver, hablar, mirar, sonreír, besar, echarme, despeinarte, tragar,* as against *salir, estornudar, escupir;* and *calle, camarada, escaparates, árboles, camiones, elefantes, pechos, agua de mar,* as against *tundras, medallas, cárcel.* Spain is reduced to a prison controlled by priest and soldier, and, having reached the climax, Otero sums up his efforts to keep a humane ethic alive against monstrous odds. In the closing lines, anaphora, antithesis, and emphatic repetitions buttress prosaic images of hope. At the very end, "aire libre," a straightforward metaphor for freedom, recalls the conventional iconography of the Holy Spirit, the traditional agent of spiritual deliverance.

If the closing imagery of "Aire libre" is conventional, that of "Pato" is original. A people's freedom under tyranny is measured against the unlikely standard of a duck and is found wanting. In fact, the beast fable is a familiar element in satire, often used in diatribe to enforce a moral lesson. Once birds are given personality and are credited with human values in the piece, the satiric vein becomes clear.

Quién fuera pato
para nadar, nadar por todo el mundo,
pato para viajar sin pasaporte
y repasar, pasar, pasar fronteras,
como quien pasa el rato.
Pato.
Patito vagabundo.
Plata del norte.
Oro del sur. Patito danzaderas.

Permitidme, Dios mío, que sea pato.
¿Para qué tanto lío,
tanto papel,
ni tanta pamplina?
Pato.

Mira, como aquél
que va por el río
tocando la bocina...
("Pato," *Parler,* 90–91)

(Just to be a duck
to swim, to swim about the whole world,
a duck to travel without a passport
and to cross, to pass through frontiers,
like someone passing the time.
A duck.
A little wandering duck.
Silver from the north.
Gold from the south. A tiny frolicking duck.

Allow me, my god, to be a duck.
Why so much mess,
so much paper,

so much nonsense?
A duck.

Look, like that one
swimming down the river
sounding its klaxon...)

The poem develops with an ease that disguises the subtlety of its organization. Otero begins with a rolling period to invoke his metaphor of liberty (ll. 1–5); chants a brief paean to liberty (ll. 6–9); expresses longing for independence from bureaucratic controls (ll. 10–14); and ends by pointing to the duck quacking along the river (ll. 15–17). Liberty is evidently an attainable and imminent ideal.

Otero's lines are usually less spontaneous than they pretend, and once again simple diction goes hand in hand with rhetorical procedures. "Pato" is an instance of allegory, confirmed by "viajar sin pasaporte, . . . pasar fronteras." Other details also suit the metaphor: "lío," "papel," and "pamplina" suggest personal and political innuendos, a specific impulse to poetic composition. But little can be gained by looking for hidden meanings on every side: the development of detail is of no more importance than in an extended simile. Deliberately, the tone is naive and conventional, enlivened by exclamation, question, apostrophe, childlike diminutives. The glories of freely wandering find plain and simple expression: "Plata del norte / Oro del sur." "Pato" is an accomplished little piece, and the ending breaks away from the obvious to give a sense of immediacy and personal participation as a writer. *Bocina* suggests both a beak and the poet's longing for uncensored speech. The close of an earlier manifesto includes a snatch of this motif: "Hablo como en la cárcel, descarando / la lengua, con las manos en bocina" (I speak just like in jail, unleashing / my tongue, with my hands cupped) ("Y el verso se hizo hombre," *Ancia,* 123–24). "Pato" is not intended to be subtle, but it is carefully calculated. Certainly, Otero knows the debunking power of unheroic animal comparison.

The language is well managed in the poem. As always, the devices of rhyme, alliteration, and repetition create an impact on the ear. More for its differences than its resemblances, the rhyme scheme recalls a sonnet: ABCD / ABCD / (A)EFG / (A)FEG. Compound effects play on the sound of *pato*: amplification and anaphora ("pato / para nadar"; "pato para viajar"); polyptoton and anadiplosis ("repasar, pasar, pasar"); epistrophe (ll. 1, 6, 10, 14); alliteration with paronomasia ("pasa el rato"), or with polyptoton ("Pato. Patito . . . Plata . . . Patito"), or alone ("papel . . . pamplina . . . Pato"). Such features create an ingenious resonance but do not subordinate precision of statement to auditory effect. Deliberately, this extended play of sound disappears from the final tercet to make the appeal for freedom more memorable.

The ingenuous pose in "Pato" enhances the speaker's credibility. Historical references are submerged, showing their presence only by indirection and allusion. Yet under the apparent blandness, with no direct commentary on the affairs of his day, Otero mocks a Spain of centralized and absolute authority. Paper and passports symbolize the bureaucracy that carries the rulers of the Francoist State, but the poet's distance makes his criticism of Francoist Spain universal.[17]

If the satirist attacks tyranny, he also attacks bondage: he opposes both to the cardinal value of liberty. "Yo no digo que sea la mejor del puerto" is a panegyric turned upside down. It sketches, with a light touch, the inexorable dissolution of an Andalusian girl, Spain's relentless conquest and annihilation of hopes for genuine human freedom. Its very plainness commends.

María del Coro Fernández Camino,
nacida en Jaén,
destrozada en Huelva,
bonita en Madrid
y mujer a la deriva en Gijón,
ave maría purísima
buscando el amor y la libertad,
en Jaén,
tres pesetas doce horas
acumbrando las olivas,
para quién
y cuando salió de Huelva
volvió la cara y maldijo
la tierra que la pariera.
("Yo no digo que sea la mejor del puerto," *Que trata,* 68)

(María del Coro Fernández Camino,
born in Jaen,
ruined in Huelva,
pretty in Madrid,
and a drifter in Gijon,
hail Mary most pure
looking for love and liberty
in Jaen,
three pesetas for twelve hours
picking olives,
for whom
and when she left Huelva
she turned her head to curse
the land where she was born.)

Indirection and ellipsis in the title give the speaker an air of amused detachment. Here the speaker consciously separates himself from his subject, withholding expressions of sympathy, although in a companion poem he celebrates the girl's sensuality and offers consolation for the deceptions she has suffered at the hands of fate. Her surname announces her typicality and inherent wandering. *María* adds also an intimation of divinity. The poem is a compressed history of disillusionment. After the opening vocative the poem falls roughly into two sections: a taut biography in apposition to the name (ll. 2–5), then expansion, in however clipped a way, on consecutive events. Directly avoiding mention of her final rise to ruin, the ending glosses over her fall in Huelva with a parody of an Andalusian song:

Cuando salí de Huelva,
volví la cara llorando,
porque lo que más quería
atrás se iba quedando.[18]

(When I left Huelva,
I looked back weeping,
because what I most loved
was dropping away behind me.)

The adaptation of this song, given point by assonance and a trio of the only verbs in the period, gives bite to denunciation. Stylistically, "Yo no digo" presents a sequence of antithetic parallelisms: *nacida/destrozada; bonita/a la deriva; buscando el amor y la libertad/acumbrando las olivas.* This pattern of simple contrasts is punctuated by punning apostrophe (l. 6) and indignant rhetorical question (emphasized metrically, ll. 8, 11). The whole moves with ease to the concluding flourish: Spain breeds angry disillusionment.

Otero inverts the conventional features of a panegyric or, perhaps more precisely, a poem of welcome. The praise of the addressee is ironic. Her travel has achieved less and less. She endures troubles but is granted no deliverance. She seeks liberty and gains servitude. She finds no safe welcome, only sufferings undergone. She is denied divine assistance. The poem, of course, mirrors the reality of Andalusian migration and the control of the marketplace by a financially powerful minority. Nevertheless, originality and ingenuity lie in the novel form and the deftly universal application.[19]

The motive of satire is the censure of wickedness or folly; its function is to sting and amuse. Once the humor diminishes, Otero moves toward invective, although his invective is never plain. Sheer wit or novelty of form mark even his most savage moments. In a lighter mood, amusement prevails: outspoken condemnation gives way to clownish jeering. In fact, the variety of means he employs—irony, burlesque, parody, autobiographical narrative, fable, literary criticism, diatribe, fierce or cajoling ridicule—prevents him becoming stale or stereotyped. His style is fluid, not fixed; he is not long-winded. Other poets of the Franco regime are combative and censorious, but they lack Otero's daring strategies of style. He has none of the dull volubility of Celaya.

Poets cannot serve two masters, art and actuality, and Otero is clearly a satirist, not a historian. He is not necessarily a truthful commentator, even though Spanish critics particularly admire his portrait of Spain. Of course, he writes from a passion inspired by true events, and this has led some to loosely tag his work as *epic* for its communal as opposed to private voice and for its supposed chronicling of events. His satire offers a pervasive sense of history through occasional mention of dates and places, if not events and people, but there is little real topicality. Otero does not give a literary transcript of fact; neither is he backbiting or slanderous. If he could be said to hold a mirror up to life, then the image is limited, simplified, even superficial. Overwhelmingly, Spain is a land of folly and evil. Champions of social poetry, a label kindly devoured by time, boasted of so much testimonial and documentary worth in Otero. However, as forensic writing, the poems provide flimsy evidence to convict. As historical document, they are often so abstract and hyperbolic as to be practically worthless. Choosing to ignore the uniqueness of poetry, those who espouse the documentary fallacy turn the poems into a branch of something that interests them more. Others might argue that his poetry is simply a pack of lies. This statement might be closer to the mark except for the fact that it poses the same problem in antithetical form. Instead of art as historical truth, it implies art to be a form of historical error. Happily, the value of poetry is unaffected by its documentary worth. Creative literature is not identical with historical fact. The poet never transcribes facts as they are; he transcribes them only as he sees them.

Indignation fires Otero's satire. He introduces simplicity where there is none. He portrays a distorted, corrupt world, the perversions of an irrational government which deny Spain her highest potentialities. He throws out mottoes and tags, catchwords and slogans. He throws the picture out of focus by fixing a spotlight on a minor part. He makes sweeping statements, begs the question, admits no middle ground. There is no sense of complexity of mind or morals. He ignores the plain and ancient fact that things labelled bad are always partly good and are perhaps not wholly responsible for their badness. These are the tactics of the skillful debater, as well as the tools of the satirist's trade. They simulate the logic of angry polemic. Durability comes not from whether or not Otero is historically true in his accusations. The political satirist's enduring truth comes from his indignation at human wrongdoing, the conveyed intensity of his moral rage, his literary power to pillory his adversary, and the sense of ultimate goodness.

Unquestionably, a desire to redress the balance overemphasizes the nonfactuality of Otero's poetry. Too narrow a historical focus discounts the poet's powers of selection and invention. It is an old observation that history gives credibility to poetic fiction: because some details are verifiable and trustworthy, then the rest is trustworthy too. If Otero mentions "alángeles y arcángeles se juntan" (alangels and archangels join together) to refer obliquely to Falangists casting in their lots with priests—a valid proposition in the early years at least of the Franco regime—then it appears to follow that his portrayal of wickedness is equally valid. The danger of such false inference is that poetry becomes a subspecies of history, inferior, a pretext rather than a text. Poetry, however, is quintessentially a world of make-believe and imagination. Historical details that do correspond closely with fact are merely an old device used to gain credence for improbable fictions. Quite deliberately, Otero coaxes his readers into taking his fictions literally. The fact that the less alert readily accept his poetic fiction as historical record is, paradoxically, an unconscious compliment to his powers of selection, arrangement, and poetic invention.

Otero, then, is not a historian or a realist; neither is he a preacher. Critics have pointed approvingly to the moral concern of the social poets and have drawn attention to their roots in Machado.[20] Otero certainly aims to influence attitudes and beliefs. Fundamentally he is optimistic: if Spaniards' attention is drawn to folly and evil then they will mend their ways. Man, it can be inferred, is perfectible. However, one difficulty with this utilitarian fallacy, the concern for the relationship between poetry and its audience, is that poetry's highest value becomes didactic. The best poets, it follows, are teachers of good morals. Thus the moral defenders of Otero are similar in their way to the censor. Both measure the poems by an acceptable standard of morality, although the censor judges Otero not to have reached that standard and banishes his books. To refute the censor by suggesting that the moral value of a portrait of sin is cathartic, or to parry Otero's defenders by inquiring whether the defects satirized are universal and as likely to trip up any political order, would only give tacit approval to the assumption that the value of poetry is the improvement of people's character.

The moral defense confers undeniable prestige and power on the poems. Nevertheless, the analyses of Otero's satires suggest that the value of the satires is the literary pleasure they give: the pleasure derived from a well-constructed unity, the pleasure of sound and rhythm, the pleasure of marvelous exaggeration, and perhaps the special Aristotelian pleasure of experiencing pity and fear in poetic form. The satirist is an obstinate, unaccommodating nuisance who hates his country's misdoings and who loves his country. What pleases is his voice, the harsh roar given out by a moral and sensitive animal as a warning that the herd is in danger.

8

A STYLE OF DISSENT

"La stylistique est l'étude de la langue comme art" (Stylistics is the study of language as art).[1] Stylistic analysis is for the most part an inductive process, and surely, we can rise to defining a genre only after we have analyzed the individual styles that are said to compose it. Otero's own statements on composition, suggestive but hardly extensive, simply indicate a broad preference for topics of invention, forms, and ideas of language that do not always fully square with his practice. Certainly, there are some changes in approach that coincide with the appearance of *Pido la paz y la palabra,* but Emilio Alarcos Llorach insists that the basic rhetorical habits continue.[2] Political themes predominate from the mid-fifties through the early seventies, and Otero frequently opts for looser forms and what he calls less-baroque effects. His interview comments are at times superficial, consistent with politically inspired literary journalism.[3] Nevertheless, if Otero's stylistic practices are based on his loosely defined theories, they far exceed the theories in range and subtlety. After all, an author's comments may assist analysis of his style, but they far from fully account for it.

Simply noting the recurrence of rhetorical devices fails to discriminate among their varying functions in a given context.[4] As I have tried to suggest previously, rhetorical effects are inseparable from their meaning in a particular poem. Nevertheless, I now propose to examine some significant details of Otero's style while cautioning the reader not to be seduced by any separate discussion of a feature into ignoring the total imaginative vision of a poem in which it occurs. The simple advantage of this approach is to clearly expose the various planes of literary resource that come into play in the poetry. Any single expressive device is always interwoven with other effects, which gives the poem a flexibility and a richness that, at times, is outstanding.

It is a pity that some readers are upset by Otero's tone, which is gregarious, coercive, and not conciliatory in the least. It is not socially acceptable to speak in this way—defiantly, angrily, slinging words as in battle:

todo
perdido
en la lucha,
día a día
recobrado
a golpes de palabra.
("Patria perdida," *Que trata,* 33)

(everything
lost

in the struggle,
day by day
recovered
with blows from words.)

The expression of resistance in this program poem is interesting; more interesting is the
image of the word as weapon. The satirist incurs the danger of seeming crude because he
reacts so violently to an immediate stimulus. It seems his poems burst directly out of the
heart. Yet an honest man ought to be affronted by injustice, and I have pointed already to
the persona of the satirist as honest Spaniard. For the purposes of explaining his motives in
writing, which is to say, in order to present himself in the most favorable light to support
the aim and mood of his poems, Otero adopts an aggressive tenor. Thus, honest fury and
righteous anger are an appropriate response to felt tyranny. Hence the satirist fulfills both
his moral duties and his poetic function by simulating in his poems the anger he feels in his
heart.

Satire is impolite, since it speaks disagreeable truths. The consciousness and denunciation
of vice demand a fairly continuous mood of outrage, tempered by moments in which Otero
either seeks respite and consolation in emotive scenes of Spain's natural beauty or longs for an
ideal of peace and liberty. This ideal from which Otero judges history will be examined
separately later. However, to express outrage Otero exaggerates, calls on God, digresses, asks
angry questions, exclaims, dwells on powerful pictures of cities and citizens, abounds in
insulting epithets and images. He complains:

Oh patria, árbol de sangre, lóbrega
España.
        ("En castellano," *Pido,* 52)[5]

(Oh my native land, tree of blood, mournful
Spain.)

Madre y madrastra mía,
españa miserable
y hermosa.
("Por venir," *Que trata,* 18)

(Mother and stepmother of mine,
wretched and beautiful
spain.)

In short, the poet selects a certain role for himself to which he fits a certain style. Firmly he
plants himself among men, rejecting the fruitless quest for absolutes of his early poems:

Este es mi sitio. Mi terreno. Campo
de aterrizaje de mis ansias. Cielo
al revés. Es mi sitio y no lo cambio
por ninguno. Caí. No me arrepiento.
        ("Juicio final," *Pido,* 40)

(This is my place. My patch. Landing
ground for my longings. Heaven
upside down. This is my place and I'm not changing it
for another one. I fell down. I don't regret it.)

Such relatively bare statements have clinching force: a powerful movement of angry defiance
is given greater strength by blending elliptical syntax, fresh imagery, and plain diction.

Language, thought, and feeling are indissolubly intertwined: tongue, heart, and head are
interdependent. Ancient and modern critics have argued long that literary style imitates
normal speech in certain emotional states.[6] However, which stylistic factors have literary
significance or which express anger and derision will of course vary from writer to writer
and from poem to poem. Categories cannot be imposed automatically from outside and
clearly are not fixed.[7] Choice of diction, composition of the sentence, and use of schemes and
tropes are, in the end, all tools that can produce beautiful and meaningful forms that will not
come apart.

Satire is subversive; defiance and outrage express themselves in a rhetoric of vituperation.
Otero's diction is markedly impure in the sense of violating the poetic codes of both Modernism and accepted usage. In the first place, he chooses frequently to draw from the register of
low style. He is not averse to moderate swearing, for example: *jodernos, haciéndonos la puñeta,
qué cabrón, qué caray, puto cielo, la mala leche, el culo al aire, este mundo puñetero, esa gran cabronada,
mecachis* (fuck us over; screw us up; what the hell; what the heck; goddam heaven; bitter
fucking bile; arse in the air; this damn world; that big screw-up; shit).[8] By post–Civil War
literary standards this is shocking even if relatively mild. Equally rising are the neologisms,
the most celebrated of which occurs in "Un vaso en la brisa":

Para qué hablar de este hombre cuando hay tantos que esperan
(españahogándose) un poco de luz, nada
más, un vaso de luz
que apague la sed de sus almas.
                              ("Un vaso en la brisa," *Pido,* 56)

(Why bother to talk about this man when there are so many waiting
[chokingonspain] for a drop of light, nothing
more, a glass of light
to quench the thirst of their souls.)

No doubt the popularity of this arresting coinage, a comically violent and brief image, led
Otero to use it as a title in *Que trata de España,* albeit to a not very inspiring poem.[9] Another
form of coinage, using an old word in a new way (technically a trope, anthimeria), can be
pungent, evocative, witty, or memorable. He prefers postsubstantive verbs: *nucleamos, chiri-
cándose, giraldead, desquijotizándote, derrostran, encielan, ayarañando.*[10] At times, other sources of
lexical enrichment are dialectal (*parlan*) or exploit modern acronyms: "En la ONU habla
uno."[11] Sometimes the development of the resources and potentialities of language seems
utterly nonsensical, as at the close of "Plañid así":

y todas a la vez entonen en alta voz
yo por ti, tú por mí, los dos

por todos los que sufren en la tierra despachurrando el contador.
("Plañid así," *Ancia,* 139)[12]

(and let all at the same time intone out loud
me for you, you for me, both of us
for all those who suffer on earth mangling the cash register.)

Yet here, nonsense is just a deliberately absurd response to an absurd censorship. In all of this Otero goes beyond what might be termed accepted poetic usage. Without doubt his language is quite distinct either from the official neoclassicism of the immediate post–Civil War years or from that of the *Generación del '27.*

Nowhere is the tendency of satiric language to draw attention to itself more clear than in the twists and turns Otero gives to commonplace phrases, whether spoken or literary. Carlos Bousoño labels the technique, "ruptura de un sistema formado por una frase hecha" (break in a system formed by a stock phrase) and sees an analogy in the mixing of styles in architecture.[13] Although this may be so, perhaps there is more at work. Examples are numerous, and the technique, as Emilio Alarcos has shown, is a constant from Otero's earliest writing. In "Que cada uno aporte lo que sepa," as noted before, the play on *llamar a filas*—"En 1939 llamaron a misa a los pobres hombres" (In 1939 they called the poor men to mass)—has at least three possible connotations, each grimly ironic. War is as necessary as is the sacrament to renew life; the Church is an accomplice in war; going to war is as routine a matter as going to church.[14] Another example again depends on like-sounding words with differing meaning: "Tachia, los hombres sufren. No tenemos / ni un pedazo de paz con que aplacarles" (Tachia, men suffer. We don't have / even a piece of peace to calm them) ("Paso a paso," *Ancia,* 150). Peace clearly ought to be as common and necessary as bread. In these examples at least, I submit we have examples of pun, strictly paronomasia, although Carlos Bousoño argues that this device is not mentioned in classical rhetoric and goes on to set up his own terminology to explain it.[15]

In a variant type of wordplay, Otero borrows freely from well-known authors but transforms his text in order, as Emilio Alarcos puts it, "hacer chocar contra la locución otra palabra que repite o alude directamente a uno de los elementos constituyentes de aquélla; entonces se destruye el significado de conjunto y se realizan independientemente sus elementos" (to make another word that repeats or alludes directly to one of its elements clash with the phrase; then the overall meaning is destroyed and its elements are realized independently).[16] For example:

arroyo claro,
fuente serena.
(Canción popular)

(clear brook
serene fountain.
[from a popular song])

entrad
a pie desnudo en el arroyo claro

fuente serena de la libertad.
("Árboles abolidos," *Pido*, 66)[17]

(enter
barefoot into the clear brook
serene fountain of liberty.)

En toda la espaciosa y triste España.
(Fray Luis)

(In all our spacious and sad Spain.)

En toda esta espaciosa y triste cárcel.
("Aire libre," *Parler*, 68)[18]

(In all this spacious and sad prison cell.)

Acude, corre, vuela.
(Fray Luis)

(Come, run, fly.)

España no te
aduermas.
Está en peligro, corre,
acude. Vuela
el ala de la noche
junto al ala del día.[19]

(Spain, don't drop off
to sleep
[Man] is in danger, run,
come. The wing of night
is flying beside
the wing of day.)

At times this procedure becomes quite extended, as in "Folia popular," a gloss on a *roman-cerillo*, or in the extravagant interweaving of Quevedo, Heine, Vallejo, and Cervantes in "La muerte de Don Quijote" (*Que trata*, 73, 131–34).[20]

Bousoño declares this phenomenon to be "un intento de hablar un lenguaje colectivo" (an attempt to speak a collective language), using the adjective in a rather specialized sense. Bousoño argues that by adapting familiar phrases and lines from common authors, Otero points to his radical union with other men. The poetry thus becomes an assertion of Ortega's familiar apothegm, "Yo soy yo y mi circunstancia" (I am myself and my circumstance).[21] This account, I think, is farfetched, and neither Alarcos nor Bousoño completely explains the sense of illicit pleasure that some of these smart inventions can give. Alarcos' emphasis in his analysis on the sense of shock and collision does catch the sense of surprise. Nevertheless, I submit that "ruptura de una frase hecha," as well as Otero's coinages and use of mild if titillating swearwords, can all best be grasped by setting them in a more comprehensive theory of humor.

One principle that is at work in coinages, swearing, and "ruptura de una frase hecha" (accepting this terminology for the moment) is distortion. Lexical, stylistic, and literary norms are disregarded and extended so that the reader's horizons are enlarged. Accepted convention is jolted, and part of the pleasure stems from the deformation itself. It seems that the poetic, for the while, is ugly.[22]

Now I think one ought to bear in mind that often novelty and incongruity are not the sole purpose of these effects. Otero aims to surprise and also to attack, to express his outrage at Francoist Spain. In a way he is outwitting not the inner censor, as Freud might have it, but the external censor, the hegemony of Francoist values. When he addresses Spain, "España, hija de padres conocidos" (Spain, daughter of known parents) ("Tierra," *Que trata,* 155), he exposes and at the same time attacks. Here Freud's theory is helpful if it is extended from the sexual to the political. Then we see Otero engaging directly and pleasurably with taboo political themes. Freud argues that hostile and obscene wit is like a denudation of a person of the opposite sex toward whom the joke is directed. The original motive is the pleasure of seeing the sexual displayed.[23] Slightly modifying Freud's formulation, political satire releases political, as opposed to sexual, inhibitions.

Finally, before moving on to Otero's so-called popularism and his use of schemes and tropes to express outrage, it is worth remembering that Freud contends that wit is also a means of absorbing and controlling the anxiety and fear felt in connection with certain themes. Without getting bogged down in Freud's many distinctions, reservations, and definitions, it is broadly conceivable that Otero's explosive flaunting of taboo political themes in an exuberant riot of ingenious invention is simply one way of foisting off the fear and illicit pleasure of speaking about the unconscionable. In short, catharsis, the purging or release of anger and fear through satiric humor, may possibly be the most appropriate metaphor to explain the principle at work in the wordplay.[24]

The tradition of satire is of course lexically permissive, admitting the common, colloquial, obscene, and familiar. Carlos Blanco Aguinaga draws attention in Otero to "un peculiar prosaísmo que tiende al hablar cotidiano" (a characteristic prosaism that leans toward daily speech), although he does not analyze its peculiarities in any depth.[25] Otero himself puts it bluntly: "Escribo como escupo" (I write like I spit), or more diffusely in "Palabra viva y de repente":

Me gustan las palabras de la gente.
Parece que se tocan, que se palpan.
Los libros, no; las páginas se mueven
como fantasmas.

Pero mi gente dice cosas formidables,
que hacen temblar a la gramática.
¡Cuánto del cortar la frase,
cuánta de la voz bordada!
("Palabra viva y de repente," *Que trata,* 42)

(I like people's words.
It seems that you can touch them, feel them.

Not books, no; the pages move
like ghosts.

But my people say tremendous things,
that make grammar shake.
Oh how many clipped phrases,
how many flowery words!)

One critic declares approvingly that "toda la obra del poeta vasco está llena de giros y de figuras retóricas de uso vulgar, de frases proverbiales que la tonifican" (the whole work of this Basque poet is full of expressions and rhetorical figures of popular usage, of proverbial phrases that fortify it).[26] This begs the following questions: of what does Otero's vulgar prosaism consist exactly, whether and in what ways is it poetic, and why should he choose to write this way?

In the first place, it ought to be recognized that Otero's prosaism involves mostly the use in poetry of everyday diction, proverbs, and pithy sayings, an abundance of proper names and toponyms, cusswords, and a syntax that creates an illusion of spontaneity. There are only two qualifications. First, he is by no means a popular writer. His diction is not cropped clear of all esoteric usages and is not readily familiar to the widest reading public. His style is not unobtrusive and, as I hope my earlier analyses illustrate, may become at times quite contrived. Moreover, he often prefers to inject a new vigor into bald and colorless *frases hechas.* Second, the claim to speak plainly—*Parler clair: En castellano,* as the title has it—is only one element of his style and not an obsession. Otero makes a point of emphasizing it because he clearly believes it to be lacking in certain of his literary predecessors who champion a higher level of diction. In one way prosaism attacks the literary canon: it is defiantly impure poetry for the *inmensa mayoría* with antecedents in the *Generación de '98,* especially the direct speech of Unamuno, and in the *cancionero,* as opposed to the cult of Góngora before the Civil War.[27]

Vernacular speech has immediacy and intimacy. One way in which Otero simulates this is through extensive references to people and places. Two anthologies emphasize this familiarity: *Esto no es un libro* and *Poesía con nombres.* Of course, many references are learned and literary, but others carry a local or private resonance: Punta Galea, Aldea del Rey, Barambio, Elanchove, Erandio, Herrera de Pisuerga, Llodio, Luyando, Calle del Carmen, Moncloa, Andrés, Pedro Lorenzana, Nico, Justo Corral, Linda, Loli, Rafael, and so on.[28] Partly, this naming is an attempt to create a sense of community and a shared vision of Spain. Partly, it reflects Otero's enthusiasm for *popularismo,* since place-names are very much a feature of the *romancero,* not to mention Unamuno's poetry. Notwithstanding, in spite of his claim to be "un hombre contra todo el Arte" (a man against all Art) ("Y otro," *Parler,* 136), Otero cites, devotes poems to, or alludes to a pantheon of scarcely popular figures, for example, Alberti, Beethoven, Berceo, Celaya, Éluard, Hikmet, Nora, Quevedo, Unamuno, Velázquez, Zurbarán, Alfonso el Sabio, Baudelaire, Cadalso, Darío, Góngora, Jovellanos, Nietzsche. I conclude from the sheer volume of proper names and the poet's easy reference to them that this is one way he attempts to convey an impression of topicality and familiarity. Name-dropping imitates that intimacy of shared concerns.[29]

Although there may be disagreement as to the exact origin and nature of the *refrán* and *cantar,* there is no doubt as to their status in Otero's poetry.[30] They help create an illusion of unity with the *pueblo* which, in the aftermath of the Spanish Republic, has political as much as aesthetic implications. However, Otero tends to adapt and transform his borrowings no matter what their source. If we recall the climax of "Cartas y poemas a Nazim Hikmet," the ironic pun on *tortas* enlivens the *refrán*, and the popular becomes at once stylized and artistic: "aquí decimos *A falta de pan, buenas son tortas,* se cumplió" (here we say "When there's no bread, the cudgel of life will do," and it's true). Carlos Blanco, in an effort to recruit Otero to the Marxist-Leninist camp, declares that "el verso de Blas de Otero se vuelve llano para hablar, en lo posible, como se hablaría cotidianamente" (Blas de Otero's poetry becomes plain in order to speak, as far as possible, like one speaks every day).[31] This idea is only a half-truth, despite the concessive phrase. Also, behind so much Marxian veneration for the popular there is a hidden assumption, I think, that the untrained voice is somehow more effective than the trained. This view tends to ignore the question of what inventive use Otero makes of such material and the varying effects that it produces in his poetry.[32] He has little of that flatness and artificiality of *Volkstümlichkeit,* that is, partisanship for the socialist cause coupled with a poetic language immediately accessible to the masses. Nonetheless, the recourse to proverbs, proper names, expletives, and common idioms, as well as to popular poetic forms, points to a rejection of *Modernismo,* however unjust, in the name of a politically subversive neopopularism.[33]

The effect of all this, I think, is that the distinction between a high and a low style begins to melt away. The reader is aware of Otero's poetry not so much as fine writing but as writing that has a sublunary vitality and strength. Nowhere is this more noticeable than in the syntax, which has a colloquial freedom that is close to the suppleness and responsive elasticity of everyday speech. Again, this largely is a reaction to inheritance, because the energy of Otero's verse often stems from his rejection of the style of his immediate predecessors, whether of *Modernismo* with its studied beauty or of *garcilasismo* with its faked classicism.

The whole stance of his poetry is aggressive, intolerant, and uncouth. Otero assumes an attitude of cheeky arrogance. "Cierta bronquedad, cierta hirsutez" (A certain coarseness, a certain roughness) sets the tone in the view of Dámaso Alonso, whereas Joaquín González-Muela notes "sintaxis a martillazos, pero bien hecha, nada de chapucerías" (a hammering syntax, but well done, nothing shoddy).[34] Poetic syntax, of course, is bound up with questions of rhythm, metrics, and figures of speech. I wish simply to draw attention to dramatic elements and a sense of colloquy in the poems. These features produce a freshness that reads like inspiration. They also create the impression of shared outrage and assert the poet's attitude of uncompromising intolerance, truculent and splenetic.

Otero admires gesture:

lo más hermoso
son los hombres que parlan a la puerta
de la taberna, sus solemnes manos
que subrayan sus sílabas de tierra.
("Hablamos de las cosas," *Que trata,* 43)[35]

(the most splendid thing
are the men chatting at the door

of the bar, their dignified hands
underlining their syllables of earth.)

He incorporates vivid signals into the poems:

Porque la verdad es que La Habana es la verdad, y hermosa, y valiente, y tiene un sitio así de grande
en mi memoria.

("Morir en Bilbao," *Mientras,* 145)[36]

(Because the truth is that Havana is the truth, and beautiful, and brave, and it has a spot this big in
my memory.)

In fact, urgent questions, exclamations, hesitations, calls to attention create an illusion of
spontaneity.[37] Poetry aspires to a public and communal role; the satirist plays to his audience.
He invites them to take part in an imaginary scene, a grim caricature of the Vietnam War:

¿Qué hacéis por ahí arriba? Pobres diablos, venid
a ver la función: sentaos tras la ametralladora.
Oíd. Vais a morir. No disparar, porque vais a morir de un momento a otro. Todos.
Tirad tirad tirad tirad tirad porque de todos modos vais a morir.

("Una especie de," *Mientras,* 176)

(What are you doing up there? Poor devils, come
and see the event: sit down behind a machine gun.
Listen. You are going to die. Don't shoot, because you are going to die at any moment. All of you.
Fire fire fire fire fire you are all going to die in any case.)

The poems frequently give the impression of talking at somebody or something: "Aquí
tenéis mi voz..." (Here you have my voice...) ("En castellano," *Parler,* 14); "Alzad, / cimas
azules de mi patria, / la voz..." (Raise your voice, / blue peaks of my / homeland...) ("Ni
una palabra," *Pido,* 64); "No esperéis que me dé por vencido..." (Don't expect me to surrender...) ("Un vaso en la brisa," *Pido,* 57); "Hojas sueltas, decidme..." (Loose pages, tell
me...) ("Túmulo de gasoil," *Expresión,* 289); "Bebamos otra jarra. Camarero / más cerveza." (Let's drink another pitcher. Waiter, / more beer.) ("Segunda vez con Gabriel Celaya," *Parler,* 106); "Tenga, un vaso de whisky para usted, y para mí coca-cola..." (Here, a
glass of whisky for you, and Coca-Cola for me...) ("Cuando venga Fidel se dice mucho,"
Expresión, 255). More than just a technique to give immediacy to the poems, one effect is to
establish what Emilio Alarcos terms a "diálogo implícito con la mayoría" (an implicit
dialogue with the majority).[38] Thus, apart from being an intrinsic denial of Juan Ramón's
inmensa minoría, these dramatic touches create the illusion, as it were, of a collective consensus.

It is not irrelevant to view these dramatic effects together with the semblance of conversa-
tion as an attempt to overcome the divisions of the Civil War by restoring a sense of community.[39] On the other hand, by definition consensus holds only for the like-minded. Alarcos'
explanation is adequate insofar as it accounts for poetic function: "Cumplen, pues, un pro-
pósito expresivo estos materiales prósicos, no son un mero peso muerto; son llamadas, apela-

ciones, toques de atención para evitar la distracción" (These prose materials, then, fulfill an expressive intention; they are not merely dead weight, they are summonses, appeals, calls to attention in order to prevent distraction).[40] This explanation accounts solely for aesthetic effects. In addition, bantering and hectoring cheer on the faithful in the clandestine opposition to Franco even though the myth of the many is perhaps only a dream for the few.

To move now from diction and syntax to schemes and tropes: what is most surprising is the relative unimportance of metaphor in Otero's satiric poetry. To be sure, there is a whole metaphoric system to express hope and the ideal by which Spain is to be judged and found wanting. Metaphor abounds as well, of course, in *Ancia* and has been well studied elsewhere.[41] Otero, however, tends not to rely on metaphor to expose the ugly in Spain, to affront the reader's preconceptions and so bring out Spain's vicious state. In this he is radically different from Quevedo. Admittedly, "Un minero," "Libro perdóname," "Aire libre," and "Pato," (*Que trata*, 118, 12; *Parler*, 68–69, 90–91), for example, all use metaphor; but, broadly speaking, the trope is not used to the same degree as the extravagant Quevedo conceit to shatter illusion and bare perversion in all its ugliness. At most, Spain is quite simply in the dark:

Cuando pronuncio sombra, velaría
las letras de mi patria, como a un muerto.
        ("Cuando digo," *Que trata*, 52)

(When I say shadow, I would keep vigil
over the name of my homeland, as over a dead man.)

Sometimes, the image of darkness is scornfully joined with that of the bullfight:

es como si España toda fuese una sola horrorosa plaza
        de toros,
blanca de sol
comido poco a poco por un espantoso abanico
negro.
        ("Pluma que cante," *Parler*, 72)

(it is as if all Spain were a single horrifying bullring,
white with a sun
gradually eaten by a frightening
black fan.)

Pregunto, me pregunto: ¿Qué es España?
¿Una noche emergiendo entre la sangre?
¿Una vieja, horrorosa plaza de toros
de multitud sedienta y hambrienta y sin salida?
        ("España," *Que trata*, 121)

(I ask, I wonder: What is Spain?
A night emerging from blood?
An old, frightening bullring
with a thirsty, hungry crowd and no exit?)

Unpleasant imagery here is part of a technique of moral dissuasion, presenting a distorted and corrupt world. However, the more dense and daring imagery of *Ancia* has been abandoned. Besides, simile softens the shock of metaphor alone.

Oxymora, in the main, are trite and commonplace: "vivos...muertos" (live . . . dead) ("Plano de la ciudad," *Todos*, 104); "puro y terrible" (pure and terrible) ("En el principio," *Pido*, 14); "Españolitos helándose / al sol—no exactamente el de justicia" (little Spaniards / freezing under the sun—not exactly of justice) ("Censoria," *Parler*, 110); "fusil de paz" (gun of peace) ("Recuerdo que en Bilbao," *Poesía con nombres*, 93). Antonomasia, on the other hand, develops with particularly savage effect at the close of "Cuando venga Fidel se dice mucho":

Tenga, un vaso de whisky para usted, y para mí coca-cola,
¡hola, hola! no está mal,
pero será mejor que le ponga un poco de sal
para que se vaya acostumbrando
ya sé yo a qué y casi casi el cuándo.
   ("Cuando venga Fidel se dice mucho," *Expresión*, 255–56)

(Here, a glass of whisky for you, and for me a coca-cola,
hey, hey! it's not bad,
but it would be better to put a bit of salt in it
to begin getting used to
I already know what and almost, almost when.)

The conventional metonymy for things American, Coca-Cola, is sharpened by the surprise threat.

Perhaps Otero plays down imagery because he reacts against the cult of the image among poets of the *Generación del '27* and because he desires to produce a poetry, "moins baroque, moins scintillante mais plus profonde" (less baroque, less scintillating but more profound).[42] Instead of developing tropes, he develops figures of thought or schemes, especially pun and wordplay, to a high degree. Critics have consistently acclaimed his inventiveness in this respect.[43] This is a conscious development corresponding to a will to write for the mythic great majority:

...cerceno
imágenes, retórica
de árbol frondoso o seco,
hablo
para la inmensa mayoría,...
("Impreso prisionero," *Que trata*, 29)

(...I cut out
imagery, the rhetoric
of leafy or dry trees,
I speak
to the great majority,...)

Clearly, Otero holds a commonly modern and erroneous view of rhetoric and reduces the art disparagingly to ornament, but his imagery is not completely eliminated.

Whether all of the satirist's playing with words, recondite or merely flippant, would not be over the heads of a mass audience is questionable. Ricardo Senabre-Sempere, for instance, draws attention to the paradox of what he terms "un creciente hermetismo" (a growing hermeticism) going hand-in-hand with speaking to a wider audience. But let us look at the purpose of the wordplay in the poetry. Here, the same critic was disturbed by the possible deterioration of wordplay into obscurity and nonsense: "El peligro estriba en lo que hasta ahora es un medio de indiscutible eficacia, pueda convertirse en un fin" (The danger lies in what has up to now been an unquestionably effective means becoming an end). He goes on to characterize the wordplay as "juegos de ingenio típicamente barrocos" (typically baroque play of wit) and likens Otero to Quevedo.[44] However, without our querying what precisely are typically baroque effects, Otero does not as a rule use wordplay to enrich extravagant conceits. In this he differs greatly from Quevedo.[45] His wordplay is self-contained.

The theory of wit as release from social or psychic restraint mentioned earlier also helps to account for Otero's verbal games involving figures of thought. Paronomasia, antanaclasis (repetition of a word with a shift of meaning), syllepsis (taking parts of speech together that properly should be separated), polyptoton, alliteration, and irony (strictly a trope) serve to expose and deride. The satirist's anticlericalism appears, for example, in the following:

Libros de misa. Tules. Velos. Velas.
    ("Muy lejos," *Parler,* 66)

(Missals. Shawls. Veils. Candles.)

Pasaron, insomnes,
ángeles viadores y arcángeles aviadores.
("Parábola del sembrador," *Ancia,* 114)

(Sleepless, they went by
viator angels and aviator archangels.)

la casa a oscuras y los curas . . .
. . . .

la Superiora no me quiere dar café con leche
que la echen a la Superiora
que la echen sopas con honda a la Superiora
           ("La casa a oscuras," *Esto,* 118)

the house in the dark and the priests . . .)
. . . .

(Mother Superior doesn't want to give me white coffee
let them throw out Mother Superior
let them send Mother Superior to hell

...ciudad donde nací, turbio regazo

de mi niñez, húmeda de lluvia
y ahumada de curas, . . .
        ("Bilbao," *Expresión,* 291)

(...city where I was born, troubled lap
of my childhood, damp with rain
and smoked up with priests, . . .)

Lo que más me gusta de todo el libro [la Biblia]
        es que tiene erratas.
                ("Retablo," *Esto,* 112)

(What I like most about the whole book [the Bible]
        is that it has errata.)

Torna, por la comida, el hijo pródigo.
                ("Parábola del hijo pródigo," *Ancia,* 114)

(He turns back, the prodigal son, for the food.)

Or, he rides his hobbyhorse of anti-Americanism:

¡Ojo!
Estados Unidos sale
de espadas.
Para defender el oro.
("Oros son triunfos," *Parler,* 48)

(Look!
The United States leads
with clubs.
To defend diamonds.)

tú trotamundos, poeta maldito de la burguesía y de la policía y simplemente de la CIA.
                ("Me complace más que el mar," *Expresión,* 300)

(globetrotter you, a poet cursed by the bourgeoisie and the police and simply by the CIA.)

sin norte, Norteamérica, cayéndose hacia arriba.
        ("Hijos de la tierra," *Redoble,* 57)

(without a north [Lodestar], North America, stumbling upwards.)

Such jesting depends in varying degrees on the discovery of something new and surprising, as in the modification of familiar idioms and literary tag lines. The familiar is rediscovered and takes on a new application. North America navigates without a compass north. The Bible has errata like any other book, and so on. Literarily, the technique depends on economy of means. Intellectually, it depends on the breaking out of well-worn mental paths. The poet jolts the reader out of political ruts. Psychologically, what is in life unendurable changes into the pleasurable experience of humor. Jokes, as is well known, make light of serious situations: laughter makes the unbearable bearable. Humor puts life into perspective. Taken to extremes, this playful spirit in Otero can produce riddles and anagrams.[46]

Carlos Bousoño finds a connection between Otero's technique and the theater of the absurd, as well as the joining of incongruous elements in contemporary painting, sculpture, music, architecture, and fashion, but such farfetched comparisons fail to explain the purpose of the wordplay.[47] As I have suggested, the play is sometimes hostile, concealed aggression, for instance: "indignos dignatarios" (unworthy dignitaries); "estereotipados teletipos mercenarios" (stereotyped mercenary teletypes) ("Amo el Nervión," "El mar suelta un párrafo sobre la inmensa mayoría," *Que trata*, 26, 59). Sometimes it is defensive, a means to laugh off an outrageous predicament: "nos turnaremos, / en tornos de cristal, ante la muerte" (we'll take it in turns, like revolving glass doors, in the face of death) ("Me llamarán," *Pido*, 44); "pasan los días y pasamos" (the days pass and we pass) ("Libro de memorias," *Todos*, 103). However, there is also play simply for its own sake:

Puede suceder que aquí precisamente
se acabe el cabo
      de la calle.
    ("Termina? Nace," *Ancia*, 78)

(It can happen that right here
ends the end
      of the street.)

viene la nieve
            cae
poco
a
copo.
("Un verso rojo alrededor de tu muñeca," *Parler*, 118)

(the snow comes
            it falls
little
by
flake.)

Here we have examples of inoffensive wit delivered with the naiveté, spontaneity, and self-absorption of a child. Once viewed in conjunction with Otero's experiments in free typography, his stream-of-consciousness prose pieces, and his fascination with childhood themes, it may not be too farfetched to say that the purpose of such play is freedom. Unencumbered by conceptual fixity or subordination to reason or ethics, the poet is mentally fresh and awake to new ideas. It is play, breezy and free, not thought, purposeful and calculating. I suggest that this is more than the self-indulgent daydreaming and triviality feared by Senabre, but less than the "deconstruction of the cultural sign-system" proposed by recent defenders of the play spirit in Dadaism.[48] Aesthetics holds a freedom that politics denies.

One of Otero's most notable skills is in modulation of tone: his poetry is indignant and compassionate, playful and serious in turn. To convey emotion, anger and indignation in particular, he depends entirely on the appropriate union of style and satiric attitude. Figures of thought have a major function in arousing feeling and high emotion.[49] Irate questions, it is well known, can forcefully express outrage, and Otero erupts when imaginary interlocutors deride his outspokenness:

¡Escribir lo que ve! ¡habrase visto!
exclaman los hipócritas de enfrente.
¿No ha de haber un espíritu valiente?,
contesto.
¿Nunca se ha de decir lo que se siente?,
insisto.
("No quiero que le tapen la cara con pañuelos," *Que trata,* 44)[50]

(Write about what you see! Have you ever seen such a thing!
exclaim the hypocrites opposite.
Should there not be a brave spirit?
I answer.
Must one never say what one feels?
I insist.)

Here, the interwoven quotations from Quevedo intensify the speaker's indignation. However, over-reliance on dramatic questions, in my view, mars the ending of "Inestable lluvia" (*Que trata,* 151) and fragments "Campañas antiespañolas" (*Que trata,* 154) where it is overdone and verges on bathos. Yet employed judiciously, as in the pair of sonnets "Tierra inerme," questioning conveys indignation:

¿Por qué he nacido en esta tierra? Ruego
una disculpa. Algo, en fin, de comer,
de vivir. Es horrible no saber
andar por esta tierra, aire, mar, fuego

incógnitos. Si a un cojo guía un ciego,
¿qué harán sino caer, caer, caer?
Pero yo he visto y he palpado. Ser
o no ser. Cara o cruz. Trágico juego.
("Tierra inerme," *Que trata,* 155)[51]

(Why was I born in this land? I beg
an apology. At least, something to eat,
to live on. It is horrible not knowing
how to go about this land, air, sea, fire

—all unknown. If a lame man guides a blind man,
what will they do but fall, fall, fall!
But I have seen and touched. To be
or not to be. Heads or tails. A tragic game.)

Questions, therefore, are a distinct feature of the satirist's style. By their phrasing they also induce the audience to make the appropriate response and can be a more effective device than direct assertion.

Another figure commonly designed to arouse emotion is apostrophe. Otero fulminates, with echoes of Garcilaso:

¡Salid corriendo a verlas, hipócritas!
¡Escribid al cielo lo que aquí pasa!
¡Sobornad a vuestros monitores para admirar esto!
                    ("Censoria," *Parler,* 110)

(Run out to see them, you hypocrites!
Write to heaven about what is happening here!
Bribe your officials so they admire this!)

He laments:

Oh piedra hendida. Tú. Piedra de escándalo.
Retrocedida España, . . .
    ("Sobre esta piedra edificaré," *Pido,* 17–18)[52]

(Oh cracked stone. You. Stone of scandal.
Backward Spain, . . .)

By this means the poet simulates indignation, the exclamation forming part of his general denunciation of Francoist Spain. As a patriotic Spaniard he abhors what has happened: everything contradicts his patriotic ideal. He appears as a man living in an age and an environment that can no longer accommodate him.

Less obviously, yet essentially accomplishing the same results, a variety of figures (including parenthesis, hyperbaton, asyndeton, alliteration, and repetitions of one kind or another) assumes roused emotions in the speaker. Otero is well aware of the possibilities of parenthesis, for example, and employs it shamelessly in "Crónica de una juventud" (*Que trata,* 157) to mock his own naiveté while growing up. The parentheses go off on a tangent, commenting, editorializing; and because deviation surprises, the style draws attention to itself. In a similar way, hyperbaton deviates from normal word order. Inspired by readings in Golden Age poetry, Otero rearranges word order to give extraordinary emphasis to the initial and terminal words (metrically or syntactically speaking):

secreta fluye, en soledad, la frase
y se dirige al hombre y se le embraza.
. . . .

... Y por mi voz toman el aire
alas halando hacia la luz, airadas.
            ("Prefacio," *Ancia,* 127)[53]

(secretly flowers, in solitude, the sentence
and is directed to man and grasps him.
. . . .

... And through my voice wings take to the air
pulling toward the light, angry.)

The figure in this prefatory poem is an effective device for highlighting indignation.

The main effect of asyndeton is to produce a hurried rhythm by omitting conjunctions. "¿Qué ocurre?" depends heavily on the scheme to produce an emotional reaction of bewilderment. The modern city is crowded, disorderly, choked:

La calle en crepitante cremallera
desliza coches, autobuses, olas
humanas, deslizadamente solas,
semáforos frutales en la acera.

¿Qué ocurre? ¿qué ciudad de sol y cera
derrite pasos arrastrando colas,
abanicos, periódicos, pianolas
de claxons, turbia gente vocinglera?
        ("¿Qué ocurre?" *Todos*, 110)[54]

(The street with crackling gears
shifts cars, buses, waves
of people, shiftily alone,
fruited traffic lights on sidewalks.

What is happening? What city, sunny and ceral,
melts footsteps dragging in line,
fans, newspapers, pianolas of
car horns, muddled, screaming people?)

Distortion of regular connectives in the sentences symbolizes the distorted feelings of the speaker. He follows the opening stanza, which is enriched by polyptoton ("desliza," "deslizadamente"), imagery and alliteration ("crepitante cremallera"), with a sharp question. Then he follows with anaphora ("¿Qué...," "¿qué"), and then apparently loses control of himself in a string of impressions.[55]

Otero's technique is deliberately exciting, but once grasped, fairly obvious. He can be declamatory on occasion to the point of bombast, indulging too freely in the exclamatory. This tends at times to inflation, and through overemployment can be wearisome. For my taste, some of the political set pieces, such as "Perdurando," "Heroica y sombría," or "El temor y el valor de vivir y morir" (*Que trata*, 17, 19, 168), appear forced and contrived. However, a scrutiny of Otero's feverish mannerisms and willful faults need not blind one to his merits. He writes with a skill that exploits many of the advantages of rhetorical teaching, and it is a reasonable conjecture that his Jesuit formation equipped him well. In Spanish schools, especially those with the more traditional Jesuit curricula, the teaching of rhetoric persisted at least up to the Civil War.[56] Otero is sensational, rhetorical in the modern sense; behind his clever artifice there lies no mystery. He half surprises, half wearies with his dazzling tricks of style, but he can enchant with his impudent beauty. His better poems prove that he can be fiery and well-nigh irresistible.

The style of dissent conveys hatred of all that Francoist Spain represents, but to think of the poems as persuasive arguments is to misinterpret their purpose. The style conveys the most patent of emotions: anger, fury, outrage, in short, indignation at the state of things. Otero translates the rhetorical requirements of indignation and vituperation into poetic terms. There is no pretense of political subtlety. The persona is incorrigibly impudent and incredibly naive. The chief appeal is not intellectual but sensational. If his caustic tongue, witty repartee, and faculty for punning are recognized in all their grim or merry humor, then they cannot be taken seriously as political slogans. The appeal lies less in the political message, if really there is one, than in the poetic attitude.[57] Basically, the satirist is an agitator, a mischievous nuisance. He is no granite-faced political theorist with a detailed blueprint for tomorrow.

Most of us feel an instinctive pleasure in an occasional reversal, an occasional reminder that no human states or institutions are infallible, no human judgments final. In spite of Otero's immense priggishness in a poem such as "Por caridad" (*Parler*, 74–74), for example, or his proud sense of superiority to the established orders, sacred or profane, his final appeal lies in a delusion of freedom. His poems overturn governments, rectify the Church, provide a corrective to the pretentious vanity of the times. They also dissolve events, evade topical issues, throw doubt on the finality of fact. Dissent nourishes a sense of secret spiritual independence of that which would otherwise be the intolerable tyranny of circumstance. The satirist clasps hands, in the end, with the fool who, as Enid Welsford argues, is the "creator not of beauty but of spiritual freedom."[58] The literary satirist, nevertheless, creates a certain beauty of his own. He represents humanity itself, ultimately mysterious in its dignity and absurdity, its weakness and power.

9
SATIRE AND RENEWAL

There are compelling arguments for the origins of satire in primitive fertility rituals. Iambic abuse is an essential feature of the Old Comedy, where the expelling of malign influences with abuse prepares the way for the invocation of good influences. This combination of ridicule and revival, the purging of evil in order to usher in the return of a golden age, may or may not have any real effect on the world. Since Aristophanes, writers have exalted high spirits and an instinctual desire for the renewal of life instead of simply reflecting life as it is.[1] Comedy's happy ending, its sense of harmony and integration, is one form of this mythical thinking. Comedy and satire are kith and kin, and the triumphant endings of *Pido la paz y la palabra, En castellano, Que trata de España,* and *Mientras,* with their promises of a new beginning, fresh happiness, another Spain, all reflect such an underlying convention. With the magical death of the old Spain, pierced mortally by the barbs of satire, and the warding off of threatening spirits with invective, a new Spain can be born. Poetry creates a utopian realm of community, peace, and freedom which history may deny.[2]

It would be misguided to expect an account of historical origins and processes from satire. Gilbert Highet concludes his brisk overview of satire with the observation that all satirists are idealists. Roy Jones, looking at the divorce between ideal and grotesque reality in Quevedo, glumly suggests that "it may be that the choice of a model impossible of attainment expressed, beneath the energy of the writing, an invincible despair of the possibility of change." Elsewhere, Graham Greene notes that "there was always in Evelyn [Waugh] a conflict between the satirist and the romantic. I suppose the satirist is always to some extent a romantic: but he doesn't usually express his romanticism."[3] Idealist, pessimist, romantic dreamer, the satirist most surely is, if judged pragmatically. Yet once Otero's visionary longing appears in the broad context of myth, with origins in seasonal ritual, the underlying pattern of the killing of the old season and the ritual institution of the new emerges. The myth restores, invigorates, and springs from a belief that in Spain there is a constant struggle of opposing powers, and also from a belief that Spaniards can fashion their own happiness, not unaided but dependent on society and on something beyond human society as well.[4]

Otero's myth of a new Spain is more figurative and fanciful than literal and descriptive. Like utopian thought, it is imaginative, less concerned with achieving ends than with visualizing possibilities. On such a mysterious subject, definiteness is neither to be expected nor desired. Otero longs for a unified Spain, for peace, for freedom, for community, for the harmony of man with nature. Whether backward, in the world of the Spanish traditional lyric, or forward toward a Marxian utopia, he strives to recover this imagined paradise. His satire tries to abolish all that might threaten the existence of this dream.[5] His poems of hope aspire to recover an eternal mythical present that others too (Machado, Larra, Jovellanos,

Quevedo, Fray Luis) have periodically renewed through the ritual of writing. Psychologically, the myth is protective and shields the poet from a a terrifying reality. However, by providing a sense of shared community and common (if vague) aims, Otero plays his part in national regeneration, if not in the perennial quest for betterment of the human spirit.[6]

The idea of two Spains also has its roots in the familiar and simple dichotomy between a reactionary and isolationist Spain on the one hand and, on the other, a Spain internationalist and liberal.[7] Publicly Otero throws in his lot with the latter: "hay que escribir a favor del viento pero contracorriente" (one must write with the wind but against the current).[8] Elsewhere, his antithetical presentation of Spain as "madre y madrastra" (mother and stepmother), "bella y doliente patria" (beautiful and suffering homeland) ("Por venir," *Que trata*, 18), "España, espina de mi alma. Uña / y carne de mi alma" (Spain, thorn in my soul. One flesh / and blood with my soul) ("Proal," *Pido*, 48), as well as the grotesque vision of the continuing presence of a Neotorquemada and "gente armada de la Santa Hermandad" (armed men of the Holy Brotherhood) ("Reforma agraria," *Historias*, 143) in Francoist Spain, all preserve this sense of division. The bugaboo of the Black Legend peeks out. Otero pleads for reconciliation, but whether or not unity is to be achieved by the victory of the one Spain oviner the other is at best undecided. Melodic vowel play in "El mar" glimpses a lost unity:

borrad
los años fratricidas
unid
en una sola ola
las soledades de los españoles.
    ("El mar," *Que trata*, 15)[9]

(erase
the fratricidal years
unite
in a single wave
the solitariness of Spaniards.)

A heterodox expectation of an impending kingdom, a division into good and evil, possibly; but for many Spaniards it was a consolation to realize that though they might feel repelled from activity in the political sphere, they yet remained citizens of a larger world in space and time—in the end, remained citizens of a spiritual realm.[10]

This visionary ideal contrasts with the conservative traditionalism, rooted in reactionary and retrospective thinking, of the Nationalists. Otero is more in tune with the poetry of the vanquished, and he echoes the poetic sentiments of the Republic, viewed by one sympathetic commentator as "la manifestación de un pueblo que, entregándose con valor a una guerra que no había provocado, veía acercarse el tiempo en que en España habría más justicia, más fraternidad, y menos desigualdad social, más libertad para todos" (the declaration of a people who, bravely devoting themselves to a war they had not provoked, saw a time drawing near where in Spain there would be more justice, more fraternity, and less social inequality, more freedom for everyone).[11] In turn, such anticipatory and deluded dreaming harmonizes with the so-called "España soñada" (dreamt Spain) of Unamuno and Machado and, at a distance, with the at times rosy aspirations of nineteenth-century Spanish liberals. Otero's earnest concern for liberty, brotherhood, and social equality (often synonymous with unity) links him with a string of liberal predecessors, including Larra, Cadalso, and Jovellanos. This places him on the progressive side of a long and hypothetical struggle between two Spains dating back (as Menéndez y Pidal would have it) to the Punic wars.[12] One school of thought plants Otero firmly in the Bolshevik camp.[13] However, if Otero's strong reaction against a severe, rigorous, official, and demanding Catholicism is at all comparable with French anticlericalism, it is arguable that this reaction leads him to espouse principles that are virtually identical with Christian tenets. The lapsed Jesuit in search of a new faith moves toward mankind "en su contexto histórico y con fuerte aliento de solidaridad. Esto es religión en su sentimiento más noble . . . religión es amor" (in its historical context and with a strong encouragement to solidarity. This is religion in its most noble sense . . . religion is love).[14]

This, of course, is Pauline, but it is pointless to trace sources. Otero is ultimately of his own party. There are many sectarian influences in the poems. He manifests some of the tenets of socialism, others of anarchism, and one—the belief in the perfectibility of mankind—of the liberal, all with imaginative freedom. His strengths as well as his limitations lie in the way he blends several strains of ancient and modern thought and then subordinates them to his own poetic vision. He uses ideas as they suit his poetic purpose. The logic is the logic of revelation, not of political argument. Variants on the themes of liberty, brotherhood, and peace stem from *Cántico espiritual* to the late sonnets, that is, from dawn to twilight of Franco rule.[15] The foundation is a desire to capture and communicate an apprehension of a living hope, a hope found essentially beyond the reach of feeling, imagination, and understanding. There is of course a progression over forty years from messianism to socialism to wistful stoicism. Nonethelesss, the foundations of Otero's world view lie in a quest for the absolute, to be realized here and now, guided by an apocalyptic vision and a not altogether indomitable will.

There are three stages in the development of Otero's apocalyptic imagination: first, a pervasive longing for inner light, then a desire to realize a kingdom of felicity on earth (with increasingly revolutionary expectations) which ends by praising Castro's Cuba as portent of Spain's salvation, and finally, a loss of confidence in a new Spain brought about by means of revolution and, with awareness of his approaching death, a trusting in the human spirit and its unquenchable hope.[16] The poet is the mystic seeking union with divine light:

"En el principio..." Dame
la creación devuelta con mi mano
a aquella luz; y enrame
las puertas de lo arcano
con palabras de fe, libre y humano.
　　　　　("Lyra 4," *Cántico, 26*)

("In the beginning..." Give me
creation to be returned by my hand
to that light; and adorn

the doorway of the arcane
with words of faith, free and human.)

He is a messiah bringing salvation now in this world:

Yo os traigo un alba, hermanos. Surto un agua,
eterna, no, parada ante la casa.
Salid a ver. Venid, bebed. Dejadme
que os unja de agua y luz, bajo la carne.
        ("Canto primero," *Angel,* 49)[17]

(I bring you a dawn, brothers. I provide a water,
not eternal, but paused in front of the house.
Come out and see. Come, drink. Let me
annoint you with water and light, under your flesh.)

And he is a revolutionist inciting struggle:

Dormir, para olvidar
España.

Morir, para perder
España.

Vivir, para labrar
España.

Luchar, para ganar
España.
("Dormir, para olvidar," *Que trata,* 115)

(Sleep, to forget
Spain.

Die, to lose
Spain.

Live, to shape
Spain.

Struggle, to win
Spain.)

Indeed, a long stay in Cuba confirms Otero's faith in the arrival of a New Jerusalem:

Aquí estamos para dar testimonio, para asegurar la puerta madre que ningún mal viento desquiciará, ésa [revolución] que hoy vemos aquí cegada pero que tiene ya su lazarillo popular y antillano.
        ("De playa a playa," *Expresión,* 253)

(Here we are to bear witness, to assure our mother gateway that no evil wind will disturb that [revolution] which we can see here is blinded today but which already has its popular and Antillean guide.)

Revolutionism disappears from the late sonnets. In "Ayer mañana," Otero joins in song with a chorus of preferred poets, from the *cancionero* to Vallejo and stretching into the future, who affirm the human spirit:

La primera palabra está escondida
en la boca del pueblo: el romancero
y el cancionero popular: prefiero
este hontanar con agua reunida.

Luego viene Fray Luis, con recia brida
tirando de su labio verdadero;
y Quevedo, chascando el verso, fiero
látigo relampagueándole la herida.

Y viene Rosalía, estremecida
como niebla en el valle: una campana
tañe en la lontananza, dolorida.

Y Machado. Y Vallejo. Y la ventana
de aquella cárcel de Nazim. La vida
sigue, otra voz resonará mañana...
        ("Ayer mañana," *Todos,* 119)[18]

(The first word is hidden
in the mouth of the people: collections of ballads
and popular song books: I prefer
this spring with refreshed water.

Then Fray Luis comes, with a strong bridle
pulling on his truthful lips;
and Quevedo, cracking his verse, a wild
whip striking lightning in the wound.

And Rosalía comes along, trembling
like mist in the valley: a bell
tolls in the distance, pained.

And Machado. And Vallejo. And the window
in that cell of Nazim. Life
goes on, another voice will ring out tomorrow...)

Although in the later sonnets he has been tempered by experience, Otero still seeks that same inner light of the early poems. "Caminos" is a good example:

Después de tanto andar, paré en el centro
de la vida: miraba los caminos
largos, atrás; los soles diamantinos,
las lunas plateadas, la luz dentro.

Paré y miré... Saliéronme al encuentro
los días y los años: cien destinos
unidos por mis pasos peregrinos,
embridados y ahondados desde adentro.

Cobré más libertad en la llanura,
más libertad sobre la nieve pura,
más libertad bajo el otoño grave.

Y me eché a caminar, ahondando el paso
hacia la luz dorada del ocaso,
mientras cantaba, levemente, un ave.
                    ("Caminos," *Todos,* 127)[19]

(After so much travelling, I stopped in the center
of life: I was looking at the long
roads behind; the glittering suns,
silvery moons, the light within.

I stopped and looked... There came out to meet me
the days and the years: a hundred destinies
united by my pilgrim steps,
restrained and deepened from within.

I gained more freedom on the plain,
more freedom on the pure snow,
more freedom under a grave autumn.

And I began to walk, quickening my pace
toward the golden light of sunset,
while a bird, softly, was singing.)

Despite forebodings, he is ultimately an optimist, but his optimism is no longer based solely on man or political change. Rather, he believes in an absolute that will finally triumph, bringing perfect blessing to man. Salvation now is placed on the far horizon. This creed, of course, is synthetic—messianic, Marxian, and often governed by conventional Christian symbolism. Yet it ennobles his vision by placing the reader in a cosmic drama where transcendental issues come to the fore. The human condition is conceived of nobly, majestically, and pressingly.[20]

Otero's poems on the renewal of Spain are hybrid blooms that emerge from the crossing of many strains. Recurrent imagery of renewal is drawn from nature: trees and plants, the sea, the air, light and dawn. His use of symbols of death and resurrection together with elemental rural imagery has immediate antecedents in the ballads of the Spanish Civil War, but the source of light and air imagery is Christian. Ernst Robert Curtius argues that in messianically or apocalyptically excited periods, faded symbolic figures can be filled with new life.[21] In more general terms, Fernando Díaz-Plaja asserts: "Catholicism is like a second skin which may be torn off but not replaced. The Spaniard lives as a Catholic even when he is a revolutionary."[22] To be sure, Otero gives himself to atheism with the zeal of a convert and becomes "un Torquemada vuelto del revés" (a Torquemada turned inside out).[23] Nobody could claim that he is a consistently or deeply religious poet, but he is a poet who has drunk deeply at the wells of Holy Scripture. Bible and prayerbook nourished his developing mind and are more formative than usually acknowledged. Singing psalms, saying prayers, listening to Bible stories, he absorbed their values and symbolic cosmology, comparing them with life around him.[24]

Air is a symbol of spaciousness, deliverance, freedom, and wholeness, a traditional metaphor for the Holy Spirit, although the use of Christian imagery does not of course imply a Christian meaning.[25] Certainly, in the early poems a traditional meaning is explicit. "El viento de Dios" heralds the divine presence and brings comfort and inner peace:

Aquí te siento yo, aquí me llenas
con tu aire de adentro y tus campanas.
  ("El viento de Dios," *Cántico,* 14)[26]

(Here I feel you, here you fill me
with your inside air and your bells.)

Un nuevo aire se abre. Y se recuesta
el alma, a la ventana de lo bello
con son de flores e intuída fiesta.
      ("Nocturno," *Cántico,* 44)[27]

(A fresh air is beginning. And the soul
leans, at the window of everything beautiful
with a sound of flowers and sensed celebration.)

However, although Otero consistently works within the most obvious and conventional imagery, what is striking is the varied use he makes of his inheritance of Christian symbol. In "MXCLV" he links cosmic symbolism with the prevailing political order:

Se ha parado el aire.

En seco,
el Ebro. El pulso.
El Dauro.

Oremus. El aire lleva
dieciseis años parado.
("MXCLV," *Parler,* 38)[28]

(The wind has ceased.

The Ebro,
dried up. The pulse.
The river Dauro.

Let us pray. Fresh winds
have ceased for sixteen years.)

In the prose poem "El aire," the image is self-explanatory: "El aire es la imagen de la libertad, sin estatuas tramposas ni antorchas trasnochadas" (Air is the image of freedom, without fraudulent statues or torches ablaze all night) (*Expresión,* 286).[29] In short, Otero employs cosmic imagery to set cosmic sanctions against the Franco government.

Literary symbol is richer than its compacted meanings. Otero enriches the symbol of air, for example, by associating it with García Lorca:

Mas no hay paz todavía
no podrá haberla en tanto tus huesos no resuciten
en la tumba de la luna,
donde tú, niño terriblemente serio,
después de expulsar a los astronautas de tu *Poeta en Nueva York,*

te asomas a la ventana abierta del aire
y ves
un niño comiendo naranjas
un segador segando
y a todos los que aquí estamos intentando borrar la sangre
y escribir con tu sonrisa escandalosa
rodeada de banderas blancas
verdaderamente blancas
verdaderamente rojas
verdaderamente verdaderas.[30]

(But there is still no peace
there can be none as long as your bones do not come alive
in the tomb of the moon,
where you, terribly serious little boy,
after kicking the astronauts out of your *Poet in New York,*

lean out of your window open to the fresh air
and see
a little boy eating oranges
a reaper reaping
and all of us who are here trying to wipe away the blood
and to write with your scandalous smile
surrounded by white flags
truly white
truly red
truly true.)

In this long period shaped by the force of feelings, Otero interweaves the image with a gloss on Lorca's "Si muero," a pageant of revolutionary vengeance, and a salute to the Red Flag. In a previous homage to Machado, the symbol blends with vegetative and light imagery. It also forms the conclusion to the varied and comprehensive design of "Cuándo será que España." Here, breeze image and wordplay move the poem from a key of outrage to one of sure hope:

¿Cuándo será que España
se ponga en pie, camine
hacia los horizontes
abiertos, aterrice
de su cielo teológico
y pise tierra firme
y labore y prosiga
su labor y edifique
una casa con amplias
ventanas, y en la linde
del tejado,
brille un ramo de oliva
que la brisa, alta, brice?
("Cuándo será que España," *Que trata,* 114)[31]

(When will it be that Spain
stands on its feet, walks
toward open
horizons, comes down
from its theological heaven
and steps on solid ground
and works and presses on
with her work and builds
a house with wide
windows and, on the edge
of the rooftop,
waves an olive branch
which the breeze, on high, sways?)

To my mind, however, the most successful effects appear when simple imagery is simply renovated within a simple poetic form, as in the *villancico,* "Canción quince":

Ramo de oliva, vamos
a verdear el aire,
que todo sea ramos
de olivos en el aire.

Defendemos la tierra
roja que vigilamos.
Que todo sea ramos
de olivos en el aire.

Puestos en pie de paz,
unidos, laboramos.
Ramo de oliva, vamos
a verdear el aire.

A verdear el aire.
Que todo sea ramos
de olivos en el aire.
("Canción quince," *Que trata,* 176)[32]

(Olive branch, let's
make the air green,
let everything be olive
branches in the air.

We defend the red
earth that we watch over.
Let everything be olive
branches in the air.

On a peace footing,
united, we are working.
Olive branch,
Let's make the air green.

Make the air green,
let everything be olive
branches in the air.)

Here, little is more.

   Sea imagery in Otero is also varied. The sea is traditionally a symbol of death, violence, and disorder; but it can suggest the infinity of passion, the divine, and (severed from Christian meaning) freedom and hope.[33] Otero associates the sea with the triumph of a new and populist Spain. Anger and struggle are leitmotifs in the sea imagery: "las anchas olas rabiosas" (the wide angry waves); "olas de rabia" (waves of anger); "el mar revolviéndome con rabia" (the sea tossing me angrily); "airado mar de los acantilados" (angry sea by the cliffs); "predico con olas / que imponen pánico a los ricos" (I preach with waves / that put the rich to panic).[34]

   "La va buscando" is an allegory of the two Spains:

"...España sobre todas es adelantada et más que todas preciada por lealtad. ¡Ay España!, non ha lengua nin ingenio que pueda contar tu bien.
   Pues este reino tan noble...fue derramado et astragado en una arremesa por desaveniencia de los de la tierra que tornaron sus espadas en sí mismos unos contra otros...; et perdieron í todos, ca todas las ciudades de España fueron presas..."

                                        Alfonso X El Sabio, *Primera Crónica General de España.*

Dos espumas frente a frente.
Una verde y otra negra.
Lo que la verde pujaba,
lo remejía la negra.
La verde reverdecía.
Rompe, furiosa, la negra.

Dos Españas frente a frente.

Al tiempo del guerrear,
al tiempo del guerrear,
se perdió la verdadera.

> *Aquí yace*
> *media España.*
> *Murió de la otra media.*
> ("La va buscando," *Parler,* 30–33)

("...Spain is especially advanced and prized more than other nations for her loyalty. Alas, Spain! There is no tongue or talent that can tell of your well being.

Then this most noble kingdom...was wasted and ruined in quarrels caused by rifts between those in the land who turned their swords against each other...; and everyone lost in this because the cities of Spain were taken captive...")

Two foaming waves face to face.
One green and the other black.
What the green one pushes up,
the black one shakes about.
The green one comes to life again.
Furiously the black one breaks its force.

Two Spains face to face.

When it was time to wage war,
when it was time to wage war,
the true one lost.

"Here lies
half of Spain.
Killed by the other half.")

The quotations from Larra and the *PCG,* if somewhat heavyhanded, give a sense of historical credibility to this mythical combat. They also confirm the persistent appeal of a myth of renewal. In part, Otero's originality lies in his association of the new world with the new community of the *inmensa mayoría.* "Advertencia a España (Coral)" closes with a blend of sea and resurrection images:

No estoy solo, mi pobre patria sola,
asida a un clavo ardiente. Estás conmigo,
mira qué inmensa mar nos acompaña.

¡Ay mísera de ti! ¡Ay española
ola lejana! ¡Sálvame contigo,
somos millones para una España!
("Advertencia a España [Coral]," *Que trata,* 165)

(I am not alone, oh my poor, lonely country,
clutching a burning nail. You are with me,
look what an immense sea accompanies us.

Oh, you wretched thing! Oh, far-off
Spanish wave! Save me with you,
we are millions favoring one Spain!)

Whether this is the unity of the like-minded or whether the new Spain would be born out of violence as was the old, the point is that the poems represent mythic thinking: for the primitive mind, true meaning lies outside of time. Since present suffering and the ordeal of fighting the Black Legend of Spain are given a metahistorical meaning, the pain is tolerable. Moreover, the precise nature of the new does not matter. The sonnet "Año muerto, año nuevo" sets the old against the new, darkness against light, land against sea:

Otro año más. España en sombra. Espesa
sombra en los hombros. Luz de hipocresía
en la frente. Luz yerta. Sombra fría.
Tierra agrietada. Mar. Cielo que pesa.

Si esta es mi patria, mi vergüenza es esa
desde el Cantábrico hasta Andalucía.
Olas de rabia. Tierra de maría
santísima, miradla: hambrienta y presa.

Entré en mi casa; vi que amancillada
mi propia juventud yacía inerte;
amancillada, pero no vencida.

Inerte, nunca desesperanzada.
Otro año más camino de la muerte,
hasta que irrumpa España a nueva vida.
("Año muerto, año nuevo," *Que trata,* 183)[35]

(Another year. Spain in darkness. A heavy
shadow on our backs. The light of hypocrisy
on our brow. Frozen light. Cold shadow.
Cracked land. Sea. Heaven that weighs heavily.

If this is my fatherland, my shame stretches
from the Bay of Biscay to Andalusia.
Waves of fury. The land of Holy
Mary, look at it: hungry and captive.

I went into my house; I saw that sullied
my own youth was lying lifeless;
sullied but not overcome.

Inert, never completely deprived of hope.
Another year on the road to death,
until Spain bursts into new life.)

Here is a vision of a new community, a sense of combat and scorn for the enemy, but above all the sonnet provides a new modulation to the Quevedo sonnet, which was pure *desengaño,* and seeks a replenishment of life and nation.

Precisely how new life is to be created is, of course, a mystery. Life renews itself periodically, and in mythic thought "the mystery of the inexhaustible appearance of life is bound up with the rhythmical renewal of the cosmos."[36] In Otero the origins of vegetative imagery are clearly sacramental:

¡Oh Sembrador del ansia; oh Sembrador de anhelo,
que nos duele y es dulce, que adolece y nos cura!
Aquí tenéis, en haz de horizontes, mi suelo

para la vid hermosa, para la espiga pura.
El surco es como un árbol donde tender el vuelo,
con ramas infinitas, doliéndose de altura.
                    ("Cántico espiritual," *Cántico,* 9)

(Oh Sower of yearning; oh Sower of longing,
that pains and is so sweet, hurts and cures us!
Here you have, in a sheaf of horizons, my ground

for the beautiful vine, for the pure ear of grain.
The furrow is like a tree from which to spread one's wings,
with infinite branches, aching from the height.)

Later, Machado becomes an immediate source of inspiration:

Primavera en Castilla.

Flores azules, azulejos,
amapolas,
tomillo, espliego, salvia.

La cigüeña dormita
en lo alto de la torre.

Entre los leves álamos
pasa, sereno, el Duero.

Primavera en Castilla.
Salvia, tomillo, espliego.
("Cuando los trigos encañan," *Que trata,* 93)[37]

(Spring in Castile.

Blue flowers, ornamental tiles,
poppies,
thyme, lavender, sage.

The stork naps
high up on the tower.

Between the slight poplars
the river Duero goes by, serene.

Spring in Castile.
Sage, thyme, lavender.)

Sometimes the rebirth ritual is associated with a proto-Marxian new world. The old Spain will be sacrificed for the resurrection of the new, symbolized by a blend of the images of wheat and industrial worker:

Pasan días. España
parece dormida,
pero un pulso, una rabia
tercamente palpita,
puja debajo de
los trigos de Castilla,
golpea por los puentes
del Duero, descamisa
el pecho, lucha, canta,
entra en las herrerías,
en los viejos talleres
armados de pericia,
asciende por los álamos
esbeltos,
ladea la cabeza
junto a unos cerros, trepa
el vasto Guadarrama:
oscila cima a cima,
se derrama en el cielo
azul, clava la vista
en el mar y amenaza
con olas descautivas.
("Descamisadamente ibérico," *Que trata*, 116)[38]

(Days go by. Spain
seems asleep,
but a pulse, an anger
throbs stubbornly,
pushes beneath
the Castilian wheat fields,
beats against the bridges of the river
Duero, unbuttons
its shirt, struggles, sings,
goes into the ironworks,
and into the old factories
stocked with skills,
rises up through the graceful
poplars,
tilts its head
by some hills, climbs
the vast Guadarrama range:
swings from peak to peak,
overflows into the blue
sky, fixes its gaze
on the sea and threatens
with waves unleashed.)

Thus poetically the regeneration of nature testifies to the coming of the kingdom of the *inmensa mayoría.* Onto the ancient image of wheat rising to fruitfulness Otero grafts two messianic motifs: the prophetic role of the worker and the final battle between good and evil.[39]

Unconventionally, Otero applies the conventional image of the Tree of Life to Spain:

Oh patria, árbol de sangre, lóbrega
España.

Abramos juntos
el último capullo del futuro.
        ("En castellano," *Pido,* 52)

(Oh native land, tree of blood, mournful
Spain.

Let us open
together the last bud of the future.)

The hope that Spaniards will collectively forge new life for Spain vindicates present suffering. Moreover, the budding promise of a second coming, with its implied resurrection of the just, ensures the legitimate victory of the anonymous, plural agents of renewal. Elsewhere in *Que trata de España* the just are identified sentimentally as landless Spanish peasants, their shoeless feet symbolic of a state of grace and their glorious future once more symbolized by budding leaves. In fact, trees are variously associated in Otero with the new day, light and clarity, peace, freedom, and—*olmo, encina,* and *álamo,* of course—with Machado.[40] One of the more felicitous expressions of this desire for renewal is "Cantar de amigo," the conclusion to *Parler clair: En castellano:*

Quiero escribir de día.

De cara al hombre de la calle,
y qué
terrible si no se parase.

Quiero escribir de día.

De cara al hombre que no sabe
leer,
y ver que no escribo en balde.

Quiero escribir de día.

De los álamos tengo envidia,
de ver como los menea el aire.
...1959]
("Cantar de amigo," *Parler,* 138)[41]

(I want to write by daylight.

Face to face with the man in the street,
but how
terrible if he didn't stop.

I want to write by daylight.

Face to face with the man who doesn't know how
to read,
and see that I do not write in vain.

I want to write by daylight.

Oh, how I envy the poplars' freedom,
when I see them swaying in the wind.
...1959])

The traditional *estribillo* gives poignancy to the poet's hope.

This longing for a lost world where only the good will rule finds expression not only in the apocalyptic symbolism but also in the lyrical evocations of an idyllic life in nature. "Orozco" presents landscape as sacred space, the idealization now of a lost paradise of childhood. The poem records memories of Spain by Otero in Russia. The verb forms trace the processes of recollection, and Otero recalls his Basque adolescence, until the anticlimax at the close. The abundance of nouns and adjectives makes this regional picture vivid:

> Heuskara, ialgi adi kanpora! Heuskara,
> habil mundu guzira!
> > Etxepare'k.
> Gazte-sail Kementsua goraño ba-dadi
> izozpetik eguzkik yare dik Euzkadi!
> > Lizardi: Biotz-Begietan

El valle
se tendía al pie del Gorbea,
daba la vuelta alrededor
de Santa Marina,
ascendía
hacia Barambio, doblaba
hasta la línea del ferrocarril
en Llodio,
valle delineado por la lluvia
incesante, liviana,
dando molde, en el lodo,
a las lentas ruedas de las carretas
tiradas por rojos bueyes,
tras la blusa negra o rayada
del aldeano con boina,
pequeña patria mía
cielo de nata
sobre los verdes helechos,
la hirsuta zarzamora,

el grave roble, los castaños
de fruncida sombra,
las rápidas laderas de pinares.

He aquí el puente
junto a la plaza del Ayuntamiento;
piedras del río
que mis pies treceañeros
traspusieron, frontón
en que tendí, diariamente, los músculos
de muchacho,
aires de mis campos
y són del tamboril,
           atardeceres
en las tradicionales romerías
de Ibarra, Murueta,
Luyando, mediodía
en el huerto
de la abuela,
luz de agosto irisando los cerezos,
pintando los manzanos, puliendo
el fresco peral,
patria mía pequeña,
escribo junto al Kremlin,
retengo las lágrimas y, por todo
lo que he sufrido y vivido,
soy feliz.

        ("Orozco," *Que trata,* 21–22)

        (Basques, go forth! Basques
        travel the earth!
                    Etxepare'k.
        By the time he is a young man, the sun
        will have freed the Basques from the power of ice!
                Lizardi: Biotz-Begietan

The valley
stretched out at the foot of Gorbea,
turned right around
Santa Marina,
rose up
toward Barambio, turned
at the railway tracks
in Llodio,
a valley marked out by the rain,
unceasing, fickle,
giving shape, in the mud,
to the slow wheels of the carts
drawn by red oxen,
behind the black striped shirt
of the villager with his beret,
oh, my little homeland,

with a creamy sky
above the green ferns,
bristly blackberry
weighty oak tree, chestnut trees
with their wrinkled shade,
and swift slopes of pine groves.

Here is the bridge
next to the town hall square;
river pebbles
which my thirteen-year-old feet
kicked about, the fronton wall
where I tested, daily, my muscles
of a boy
the songs of my country fields
and the sound of the tambourine,
          dusky evenings
on traditional outings
to Ibarra, Murueta,
Luyando, midday
in grandma's
back garden,
August light making the cherry trees shimmer,
painting the apple trees, polishing
the cooling pear tree,
my little homeland,
I am writing beside the Kremlin,
holding back my tears and, for all
I have suffered and lived through,
I am happy.)

The geography is local, not regional, and the poet knows this area intimately. He looks down the valley and traces its convolutions with flexible imperfects skirting past well-known local landmarks. As if the railway were an intrusion of the outside world into this pictur-esque provincial paradise, there is a pause at the mention of Llodio: he has extended his gaze sufficiently. The territory has been mapped out, and Otero now enlarges the picture with close-ups of the human and natural landscape. Participles move the poem gently from an affective geography to a picture of a Basque laborer. Rain is the catalyst for the transition, moving down the valley to the waggoner. Imperceptibly the poem imitates, in its winding, unhurried development, the processes of memory.

   The idealized description of the old order of rustic life is subordinate to the local geogra-phy, grammatically at least, but equally important. The force of the common nouns ("ruedas," "carretas," "bueyes," "blusa," "aldeano," "boina") matches the homely famil-iarity evoked by the catalogue of place-names. Here we have a Basque worker. Otero presents him proudly, almost as a bare caricature, a tableau offered to the goddess Labor. The poem's first part closes with an evocation of natural surroundings that recalls Unamuno and Machado (ll. 16–22). A simple exclamation of love ("pequeña patria mía") sums up the response to the landscape, and the poem now celebrates the plants and trees. The eye first looks upward to the pure heavens, metaphorically "cielo de nata," and then falls on fern, blackberry, oak, chestnut, and pine. The stylized innocence of the scene is evoked by the simplicity of the adjectives, ranging from a common "verdes" to the naive personifications "grave roble" and "castaños / de fruncida sombra."

The second part places the poet in the landscape (ll. 23–40), and the shift of focus signaled by "He aquí" triggers childhood memories, deliberately summoned up by preterites. However, beginning with the hexasyllabic couplet "aires de mis campos / y son del tamboril," verb forms are omitted and the poem moves unobtrusively to a world in which time is felt simply as the timeless cycle of day and season (ll. 30–40). The tone is relaxed, without being slack or uninventive, as Otero evokes the local geography of religious festivals and the blooming fruit trees of his grandmother's orchard. Nature is bountiful provider for a world as self-sufficient as it is innocent. Then, with "patria mía pequeña"—a variant of the earlier exclamation—"Orozco" draws quickly to its end. With a surprise, the present comes to the fore as the poet reveals that he looks back from the Kremlin on this blissful image of the landscape. Recollection has led to the recognition, in spite of adversity, of the restorative power of the landscape. From awareness of the past comes discovery of identity, since the transcendent power of the landscape prevents lachrymose self-pity and permits personality and destiny to take on shape, meaning, and value (ll. 42–45). Ironically, he writes from the land of agricultural collectivism.

Otero presents a landscape of the mind. By artful selection of details he projects a picture that, though rooted in geographical reality, is finally symbolic and transcendental. This accounts for those songs and lyric fragments evoking Spain in the section "Geografía e historia" of *Que trata de España*, for example. The landscape becomes a symbol of tranquillity and permanence: man is absent. The images shut out for the while the modern world, and there is a sense of being alive to an immortal beauty. For Otero, as for the Generation of 1898, the Spanish landscape can be a consistent, pure, and uncontaminated reality. In "Canción once," for example:

Crepúsculo y aurora.
Puentes de Zamora.

El alba
se enreda entre los troncos
de los álamos verdes,
orillados de oro.

Puentes de Zamora.

De oro del poniente
tienes la frente roja;
la brisa cabecea,
cecea entre las hojas.

Crepúsculo y aurora.
Puentes de Zamora.
("Canción once," *Que trata,* 104)

(Dusk and dawn.
Bridges of Zamora.

Daybreak
is tangled in the trunks
of the young poplars,
trimmed with gold.

Bridges of Zamora.

From sunset's gold
your brow is reddened;
the breeze shakes,
lisps between the leaves.

Dusk and dawn.
Bridges of Zamora.)

Otero popularizes this larger world in space and time by using the forms of the traditional lyric and a traditionally Christian source of imagery. However, this consciousness of a realm that draws meaning not just from the present but from what transcends the present is, for all the championing of the mythic *inmensa mayoría*, intellectually aristocratic.

One way the poet broadens his popular appeal is by recourse, as has been noted, to the simplest of imagery. The preferred image, more frequent than air, sea, vegetative, or landscape symbolism, is light. Whether pure light, sunshine, or dawn, the coming age is visualized as one of transcendent and infallible clarity.[42] At first, light is part of what Erika Lorenz calls "eine unendliche Sehnsucht nach Gott" (an endless yearning for God).[43] Later, light imagery is separated from the possibility of any strictly Catholic intention and is put to a combative social purpose. Sometimes we detect it in a line of mere description, "caudal humano / hacia otra luz" (a human flow / toward another light) ("Fidelidad," *Pido*, 75), and sometimes in a flight of fancy, "entre la luz con un cuchillo / brillante, ¡ay de mi España!" (let the light come in with a shining / knife, oh my wretched Spain!) ("Soledad tengo de ti," *Parler*, 56). More elaborate in its imagery is the longing expressed in "Un vaso en la brisa":

Para qué hablar de este hombre cuando hay tantos que esperan
(españahogándose) un poco de luz, nada
más, un vaso de luz
que apague la sed de sus almas.
                              ("Un vaso en la brisa," *Pido*, 56)

(What's the use of speaking about this man when there are so many hoping
[chokingonspain] for a little light, nothing
more, a glass of light
to quench the thirst in their souls.)

Light bathes the memory of Antonio Machado and Joaquín Costa and, more daringly, is linked with communist emblems of redemption.[44] Otero's use of imagery clearly is creative rather than innovative: he often cheats Christian expectations to produce shock.

The imagery of renewal comes from common poetic stock. He revives the conventional image of the sun, a common Christian symbol of the divine, by linking it with a Marxian myth of the end of this age and the coming of a kingdom of justice for all. This is the case, for instance, in "Todavía," where the imagery is singularly naked and powerful. Here the metrical pause in the first line of the refrain increases expectation:

Mañana
brillará España.

(Mañana
de borrasca y ventisca.)

Campos de Castilla,
Galicia, Andalucía.

(Mañana
de cielo rojo y sol.)

Campesino, minero,
tejedor, forjador.

Mañana
brillará España.
("Todavía," *Que trata,* 96)[45]

(Tomorrow
Spain will shine.

[Tomorrow
with squalls and blizzards.]

Country fields of Castile,
Galicia, Andalusia.

[Tomorrow
with a red sky and sunshine.]

Peasant, miner,
weaver, blacksmith.

Tomorrow
Spain will shine.)

The form and strength of the poem derive partly from the active image of light, but Otero departs from the traditional symbol and its characteristic evocation of divine justice. Redemption will not be effected entirely from without through a divine principle of order and light. Spaniards are not to be passive spectators and astonished beneficiaries of some remote performance. They are not quite innocent bystanders: they, or rather the chosen workers, will lead their redeemed into the new community as surely as the sun will rise. Hence, traditional symbolism is recast to give sanction for the chosen and an explanation for the triumph of the *inmensa mayoría* over the past. The close of the elegy for Miguel Hernández presents new Spaniards forging a new Spain. The transcendent image of the sun is now merely ornamental:

Así, noche tras noche, sucumbiste
en medio de una España negra y triste:
como el toro en la plaza, como el toro.

La juventud de hoy, la de mañana,
forja otro cielo rojo, audaz, sonoro,
con un rayo de sol en la ventana.
("1939–1942," *Que trata,* 138)[46]

(Like this, night after night, you succumbed
in the midst of a black and sad Spain:
like the bull in the ring, like the bull.

The youth of today, of tomorrow,
is forging a different sky—red, bold, echoing,
with a ray of sunshine at the window.)

Increasingly, Otero experiments with more esoteric and private apocalyptic symbolism.

Light imagery invests the familiar with dignity and meaning. Otero rings the changes on dawn imagery, for example, in "No te aduermas," "Con un cuchillo brillante," or "Antedía" (*Que trata,* 95, 99, 170). They are relatively stylized poems that derive their expectation of a new Spain from an apocalyptic expectation of dawn. At the close of "Ultimas noticias," dawn is linked with Judgment Day in a melodramatic flourish:

Amanecer, sin músicas, ha sucedido. Cerrad los ojos. Alzadlos. Los hijos de la tierra, erguidos, por dentro, avanzan hacia el salón damasco de la aurora.
("Ultimas noticias," *Parler,* 114)[47]

(Dawn, without fanfare, has happened. Close your eyes. Look up. The children of this land, upright, bold, are advancing toward the damask salon of dawn.)

Earlier in this prose piece, however, there is a sobering hint that the new day will come only with the concerted effort of all Spaniards: "Porque amanecer, tanto como amanecer, es mucho pedir, posiblemente. Todos tenemos que trabajar, juntarnos" (Because dawn, as such, is much to ask for, possibly. We all have to work, join together). There is little practical idea of what the new day will bring. The coming age is conceived of as pure light. Poetry provides simply one way of apprehending its power and truth.[48]

This is not to say that Otero affirms an imagined new world that is totally amorphous and diaphanous. Often the poems do appeal to commonplaces of Enlightenment and Spanish liberal thought, namely liberty, peace, and brotherhood. Such broad moral appeals are as much a transparent indictment of Francoist Spain as they are a vision of the good society. Yet this strongly ethical and idealistic song is colored in the sixties by the strains of liturgical socialism. Not only will the good society embrace some sort of communitarian spirit that is mystically embodied in the *inmensa mayoría*, but also the workers will assume a role of central importance:

Nuestro destino está
"en las manos de los que aran la tierra,
de los que cavan la viña,
de los que plantan el naranjo,
de los que pastorean la cabaña,
de los que arrancan el mineral,
de los que forjan el hierro,...
     ("Doble llave," *Que trata*, 144–45)[49]

(Our fate is
"in the hands of those who plough the earth,
of those who hoe the vineyards,
of those who plant the orange tree,
of those who shepherd the flock,
of those who extract ore,
of those who forge iron,...)

However, it is notable that Otero speaks of the sovereign people in terms of religious devotion, since his litany affirms the redemptive possibilities of their political power. Mystically, the advent of a worker society will attain for Spain a lost purity and unity.[50]

The theme of ritual renewal constantly reappears. Indeed, the poet's testament in *Mientras* claims this fundamentally serious purpose for his work:

> he acercado a los ojos la línea
> desaliñada, enderezándola y limitándola
> entre márgenes navegables

DEJO UNAS LÍNEAS Y UN PAPEL EN BLANCO.
Líneas que quiero quiebren la desesperanza.
Líneas que quiero despejen la serenidad.
Líneas que balanceen el reposo.
Líneas sobrias
como el pan.
Transparentes como el agua.
Cuando me lean dentro de treinta años,
de setenta años,
que estas líneas no arañen los ojos,
que colmen las manos de amor,
que serenen el mañana.
           ("Serenen," *Mientras*, 41–45)

> (I have brought the slovenly line [of the
> horizon] closer to our eyes, straightening it
> and fixing it between navigable shores

I am leaving a few lines and a blank sheet of paper.
Lines that I wish would break despair.

Lines that I wish would clarify serenity.
Lines that may lull our rest.
Lines sober
as bread.
Transparent like water.
Should they read me in thirty years,
in seventy years,
may these lines not scratch their eyes,
may they fill their hands to overflowing with love,
may they calm the future.)

Such pronouncements about authorial functions must take into account the satiric convention that allows the satirist to seek approval by denoting his honest purpose. The satirist
must have an audience, real or imagined, that shares his commitment to those moral standards by which he judges the world. But Otero's claims to a serious purpose need to be
assessed in their literary context. Here, the incantatory tone of the anaphora with which they
are expressed, as well as the petitionary form and abstract content, suggests that Otero's
vision extends beyond politics to a dream of spiritual regeneration and collective salvation.[51]

The hope of regeneration presides over the entire body of Otero's work, from *Cántico
espiritual* to the late poems, "poesía abierta a toda forma y todo fondo y todo cristo"
(poetry open to all forms, all contents, all gods) ("Oigan la historia 1," *Mientras,* 54). In the
satires, Otero pits his wits and moral authority against perceived evil. His attacks depend on
a commitment to ethical norms and a utopian view of a better Spain which are given
expression in the poems. In a post–Civil War world bereft of unifying symbols and searching
for beliefs, poetry consciously formulates a vision of a people on its march toward an ideal
and different future. In other cultural contexts such a role might seem grandiose or an odd
legacy of Romantic sensibility. In Spain, Otero overcomes postwar malaise and alienation
with his commitment to poetic censure of vice and folly, his belief in the vatic function of the
poet, and his enlargement of poetry to include the theme of national renewal. The utopian
impulse has had an indispensable role in the intellectual tradition of liberalism. Satire, however, has for even longer had the privilege of enjoying freedom from restrictions. It has also
long been impotent to exert practical influence on social and political life.

10

CONCLUSION

This book rejects the proposition that the literary critic's best approach to Otero is to study the historical, social, and political circumstances from which the poems come. By accounting for the poems in terms of apocalyptic satire, I have been concerned less with specific sources than with underlying literary conventions. The chapters on the figure of the satirist and the topics and techniques of the satires develop a simple thesis that the poet's enduring appeal depends on literary effects and that the task of the critic is to elucidate the poet's art. This poetry will survive its topicality because of literary inventiveness, not because of the justice of Otero's indictment or the accuracy of historical particulars, of which there are in any case so few. The rhetorical analyses of individual poems show Otero's literary powers.

The moral aim of the poems is to turn Spain from vice to virtue. Yet in order to persuade the reader to resist injustice, more is required than that injustice appear cruel or unpleasant. Spain must appear absurd, and startlingly so, a grotesque anomaly. Otero's creative imagination presents a picture of Spain deformed. As Edward Rosenheim so cogently argues for Swift, "a manifest fiction of some kind is indispensable to the satirist's art," and furthermore, "the depth and permanence of the satirist's appeal depends quite directly upon the nature of the fiction." [1] Through the poetic world he creates and, arguably, the moral truth it contains, the individuality of Otero's genius will assure him a permanent fame against all the feeble echoes and falsetto voices of his contemporaries. In the exuberant riot of wordplay, the quest after something novel, startling, shocking, leads far away from reality into extravagances of ingenuity which can, at times, carry the poet away in the sheer exuberance of his style. More self-criticism would have spared much that fatigues: senseless bombast, weary elaboration of the same idea, too ingenious cleverness, overly subtle borrowings. [2] Notwithstanding, I think I have shown that there is a wealth of memorable compositions that undeniably demonstrate a superlative poetic talent.

The acuteness of his ear and his sharp rhetorical manipulations create an image of Spain both bitter and beautiful. In short, Otero strives to arouse disgust for Spain's present and to inspire hope for the future. Tension comes from the contrast between murderous imprecation on the one hand and, on the other, poignant longing for a paradisial Spain of unique beauty, delight, and ethical consciousness.[3] Aesthetic pleasure comes from the exercise of insult and panegyric, the rhetoric of praise and blame. Thus I have proposed that ridicule and outrage are balanced by a therapeutic ideal. The satiric impulse is corrosive, but also humane.

There is much still to be done. We have no definitive edition, and the much-heralded *Hojas de Madrid* has not appeared. Critical interest continues, especially in Spain and fortunately without homage to fashionable Franco-American literary panjandrums. However, Otero's debts and influences, his spiritual affinities with Machado, the '98, and Spanish liberalism, the effects of Catholicism on his writing, Biblical influences and the Jesuit theme of "sweet tears," the transformations of Marxian doctrine, the nature of his populism, a definitive biography, and a detailed study of his approach to metrics and prosody or to valediction, elegy, and epigram all demand varying degrees of attention. Edith Kern's formulation from Bakhtin of carnivalesque justice and James Iffland's study of the grotesque in Quevedo suggest fruitful approaches. The distinctions among satire, parody, burlesque, and the moral poems need to be drawn more closely, as well as the differences and continuities among early, middle, and late Otero. It is too soon to write a literary history of the day before yesterday, but it might be possible to consider Otero in the context of Spanish Romanticism as defined by Donald Shaw and Richard Cardwell. At a distance, Otero certainly seems assured of his place as a major poet of a Silver Age.

It is possible to become too solemn about Otero's achievement. The poetry insists on a moral order to which Spain must conform that possesses a tonic value beyond the reach of outworn *garcilasismo* and that links Otero with Republican Spain (and with a post–Francoist Spain more socialist than Azaña had ever imagined). "Otero cree, como creía Machado, en la España del mañana en que la justicia, la libertad y la paz sean reales, vividas por el pueblo" (Otero believes, as Machado believed, in the Spain of tomorrow in which justice, liberty, and peace were real, lived by the people), as José Luis Cano affirms.[4] In fact, the roots are to be found even deeper, in Costa and Giner, "espiritualistas, inspirados en una concepción del hombre y la sociedad que, por mediación de Krause, heredan del idealismo alemán" (spiritualists, inspired by a conception of man and society that, through Krause, they inherit from German idealism).[5] Thus, Otero's voice bears constant and fascinating testimony to the indestructible continuity of the human spirit. Spain's past can be emended; literature can make man good.

The political implications are explicit, of course, but a poet in politics succeeds by imagination and by values beyond the realm of politics.[6] Otero shows more regard for literary convention than for historical truth. His is not an ordinary political ambition: it is through poetry that it is realized. Otero makes Spain into what he wants her to become, creating an image consonant with his aspirations. Readers at large may not so much listen to his doctrine as be amused by his wit. What counts in the end is not his being earnest, but his being entertaining in his earnestness. Insofar as Otero successfully addresses himself to mankind, his place will be secure on Parnassus.

NOTES

Notes for Chapter 1: Introduction

1. See, for example, Víctor Garcia de la Concha, *La poesía española de posguerra: teoría e historia de sus movimientos*; Fanny Rubio, *Las revistas poéticas españolas (1939–1975)*; Francisco Ribes, ed., *Antología consultada de la joven poesía española*; José María Castellet, ed., *Veinte años de poesía española: antología (1939–1959)* and *Nueve novísimos poetas españoles*; Leopoldo de Luis, ed., *Poesía española contemporánea Poesía social. Antología (1939–1964)*; Jaime Ferrán and D. Testa, eds., *Spanish Writers of 1936*. See Johannes Lechner, *El compromiso en la poesía española del siglo XX*, vol. 2.

2. See, for example, María de Gracia Ifach, ed., *Cuatro poetas de hoy: José Luis Hidalgo, Gabriel Celaya, Blas de Otero, José Hierro*; Philip W. Silver, "New Spanish Poetry: The Rodríguez-Brines Generation"; J. García Hortelano, ed., *El grupo poético de los años 50*; Andrew Debicki, *Poetry of Discovery: The Spanish Generation of 1956–71*. However, Eleanor Wright, *The Poetry of Protest under Franco*, is a useful introductory survey.

3. See Carlos Blanco Aguinaga, Julio Rodríguez-Puértolas, and Iris Zavala, *Historia social de la literatura española*, 3 vols.; María Luisa Muñiz, "Poeticeskaia trilogia Blasa de Otero *Rec idet ob Ispanii*"; Elias L. Rivers, "Hispanism Now in the United States," *Ideologies and Literature* 4 (1983): 81–87; and Jean Franco, "Trends and Priorities for Research on Latin American Literature," *Ideologies and Literature* 4 (1983): 107–20.

4. See the seminal article of Donald L. Shaw, "Towards the Understanding of Spanish Romanticism"; Richard A. Cardwell, "The Persistence of Romantic Thought in Spain"; Lilian Furst, *Romanticism* (London: Methuen, 1969). Otero, incidentally, relished his readings of Espronceda, Larra, Rilke, and Rimbaud.

5. Rosalie L. Colie, *The Resources of Kind: Genre Theory in the Renaissance*, ed. Barbara K. Lewalski.

6. Blas de Otero, *Ancia (Angel fieramente humano. Redoble de conciencia); Pido la paz y la palabra; Parler clair: En castellano; Que trata de España; Expresión y reunión: a modo de antología (1941–1969); Mientras; Historias fingidas y verdaderas; Verso y prosa; Todos mis sonetos*. Unless noted, first editions are cited.

7. J. M. Cohen, "Since the Civil War: New Currents in Spanish Poetry"; Silver, "New Spanish Poetry"; John Butt, *Writers and Politics in Modern Spain*; G. G. Brown, *Literary History of Spain: The Twentieth Century* (London: Ernest Benn, 1972). Debicki, *Poetry of Discovery*, 1–6, is ambivalent.

8. Dámaso Alonso, "Poesía arraigada y poesía desarraigada," *Poetas españoles contemporáneos*; Max Aub, *La poesía española contemporánea* and *Una nueva poesía española (1950–1955)*; Emilio Alarcos Llorach, *La poesía de Blas de Otero*; J. González-Muela, "Un hombre de nuestro tiempo: Blas de Otero"; José María Alín, "Blas de Otero y la poesía tradicional"; Blas de Otero, *Expresión y reunión*, ed. Sabina de la Cruz; Itziar Zapiaín and Ramón Iglesias, *Aproximación a la poesía de Blas de Otero*.

9. Ribes, *Antología consultada*; Sergio Vilar, *Arte y libertad: encuesta estre los intelectuales y artistas españoles*; Antonio Núñez, "Encuentro con Blas de Otero"; Claude Couffon, "Rencontre avec Blas de Otero." See also Emilio de la Torre, *José Hierro: poeta de testimonio*. Wright, *Poetry of Protest*, provides a comprehensive overview.

10. The literary discussion of Spanish identity is a persistent topic: see Pedro Lain Entralgo, *La generación de '98* and *España como problema*; Dolores Franco, *España como preocupación*; Segundo Serrano Poncela, "La preocupación por España," *Antonio Machado: su mundo y su obra* (Buenos Aires: Losada, 1954), 157–207; José Luis Cano, ed., *El tema de España en la poesía española contemporánea*; Blas de Otero, *País (Antología 1955–1970)*, ed. José Luis Cano; Sumner M. Greenfield, ed., *La generación de 1898 ante España: Antología de literatura de temas nacionales y universales* (Lincoln, Neb.: Society of Spanish and Spanish American Studies, 1981). At a distance, see Julio Rodríguez-Puértolas, *Poesía de protesta en la edad media castellana*. However, for a defiantly contrary stance, note J. M. Blecua, *Los pájaros en la poesía española: antología* (Madrid: Editorial Hispánica, 1943).

11. Francis Cairns, *Generic Composition in Greek and Roman Poetry* (Edinburgh: Edinburgh University Press, 1972), 31–33, offers a salutary blast at the limitations of the Romantic sensibility. See also Lionel Trilling, *Sincerity and Authenticity* (Harvard: Harvard University Press, 1971).

12. George Lincoln Hendrickson, "Satura tota nostra est," *Classical Philology* 22 (1927): 46–60.

13. Manuel Rodrigues Lapa, *Cantigas d'escarnho e de mal dizer*.

14. Kenneth R. Scholberg, *Algunos aspectos de la sátira en el siglo XVI*, 9. The approach is essentially the same in Scholberg, *Sátira e invectiva en la España medieval*.

15. Robert Jammes, *Études sur l'oeuvre poétique de Don Luis de Góngora y Argote*; R. M. Price, ed., *An Anthology of Quevedo's Poetry*. Jammes places satirical and burlesque poetry under the title "Le poète rebèle."

16. Alastair Fowler, *Kinds of Literature: An Introduction to the Theory of Genres and Modes*, 110. "Concepts of Genre" and "Historic Kinds," 37–74, provide an overview of the pitfalls that beset categorical generic definitions and argue against essential, definitive elements in favor of family resemblances.

17. Fowler, *Kinds of Literature*, 110; Geoffrey Grigson, ed., *The Oxford Book of Satirical Verse* (Oxford: Oxford University Press, 1980), v.

18. Edward W. Rosenheim points to the rhetorical bases of satire, then goes on to distinguish persuasive from punitive satire in "The Satiric Spectrum," *Swift and the Satirist's Art*, 1–34. James R. Sutherland, *English Satire*, 5, asserts that the art of the satirist is the art of persuasion.

19. Michael Coffey, *Roman Satire*, 11–23.

20. Grigson, *Oxford Book of Satirical Verse*, v. John Peter, *Complaint and Satire in Early English Literature*, draws fine distinctions, whereas Sutherland, *English Satire*, 23–43, and Rosenheim, *Swift*, 109–12, emphasize the roots of modern satire in invective. Gerald Robert Owst, *Literature and the Pulpit in Medieval England* (1933; reprint, Oxford: B. Blackwell, 1961), outlines the medieval background in the declamations of friars and priests.

21. Edward A. Bloom and Lillian D. Bloom, *Satire's Persuasive Voice*, stress the importance of the ideal by which the satirist judges the world, although Mary Clair Randolph, "The Structural Design of the Formal Verse Satire," *Philological Quarterly* 21 (1942): 368–84, establishes satire's fundamental structural opposition of the ideal and the actual. See Robert C. Elliott, *The Shape of Utopia: Studies in a Literary Genre* (Chicago: University of Chicago Press, 1970).

22. Juan López-Morillas, "Antonio Machado: ética y poesía"; José Olivio Jiménez, *La presencia de Antonio Machado en la poesía española de posguerra* (Lincoln, Neb.: Society of Spanish and Spanish American Studies, 1983).

Notes for Chapter 2: The Satirist

1. Jaime Gil de Biedma, *Diario del artista seriamente enfermo*, 153.

2. Otero, *Esto no es un libro*, 5, cited hereafter in the text as *Esto*. Compare Miguel de Unamuno, *Cancionero: diario poético*, ed. Federico de Onís (Buenos Aires: Losada, 1953), 216: "Walt Whitman, tú que dijiste: / esto no es libro, es un hombre; / esto no es hombre, es el mundo / de Dios a que pongo nombre" (Walt Whitman, you who said: / this is not a book, it is a man; / this is not a man, it is the world / of God to which I give a name).

3. Antonio Núñez, "Encuentro con Blas de Otero," 1.

4. Rosemond Tuve, *Elizabethan and Metaphysical Imagery: Renaissance Poetic and Twentieth Century Critics* (1947; reprint, Chicago: University of Chicago Press, 1965), 189.

5. Aristotle, *The 'Art' of Rhetoric*, trans. John Henry Freeze (1926; reprint, London: William Heinemann, 1967), I.ii.4.

6. Robert C. Elliott, *The Power of Satire: Magic, Ritual, Art*, 3–99.

7. Otero, "Lo eterno," *Angel fieramente humano*, 13, cited hereafter in the text as *Angel*. "Lo eterno" is entitled "La tierra" in Otero, *Ancia*, 54, cited hereafter in the text as *Ancia*.

8. "Aren en paz," *Redoble de conciencia*, 59–60, cited hereafter in the text as *Redoble*. See the close study of the burlesquing of Juan Ramón in "Aren en paz": Nelson R. Orringer, "La espada y el arado: una refutación lírica de Juan Ramón por Blas de Otero," *Inti* 1 (November 1974): 12–19.

9. Marina Mayoral, *Poesía española contemporánea: análisis de textos* (Madrid: Gredos, 1973), 231–42, suggests the New Testament roots of the language. Renato Poggioli, *The Theory of the Avant Garde*, 65–68, offers perceptive remarks on the agonistic sacrifice.

10. Otero, "Un vaso en la brisa," *Pido la paz y la palabra*, 56, cited hereafter in the text as *Pido*. Compare the Christ imagery in Otero's "Ecce homo," *Ancia*, 52, or "Oigan la historia," *Mientras*, 54.

11. Otero, "que nadie me veía," *Mientras*, 81, cited hereafter in the text as *Mientras*. This poem is entitled "Ultima noche en Cuba" in *Todos mis sonetos*, cited hereafter in the text as *Todos*. This blending of the motifs of spiritual redemption and secular liberation, as well as an uncompromising moral fervor, echoes a dominant chord in Spanish anarchism. See Gerald Brenan, *The Spanish Labyrinth* (1950; reprint, Cambridge: Cambridge University Press, 1971), 188–97; Raymond Carr, *Spain 1808–1939* (Oxford: Clarendon Press, 1966), 440–47.

12. Otero, "Ruando," *Parler clair: En castellano*, 76, cited hereafter in the text as *Parler*.

13. Edmund L. King, "Blas de Otero: The Past and the Present of 'The Eternal,'" in *Spanish Writers of 1936*, ed. Jaime Ferrán and D. Testa, 125–33, offers a perceptive discussion of variants of the epigraph, "A la inmensa mayoría."

14. Otero, "Impreso prisionero," *Que trata de España*, 29, cited hereafter in the text as *Que trata*. In Claude Couffon, "Rencontre avec Blas de Otero," Otero solemnly discusses his progress from individual to universal subjects, but "Dicen-digo," *Parler*, 24, offers a lighter self-assessment. "Español de pura bestia" echoes Vallejo's "Salutación angélica," and Otero's debts are briefly discussed by José Angel Valente in *Las Palabras de la tribu*, 158–60.

15. Otero, *Historias fingidas y verdaderas*, 183–84, cited hereafter in the text as *Historias*. Carlos Blanco Aguinaga,

"El mundo entre ceja y ceja: releyendo a Blas de Otero," 180–96, seeks to square Otero's aesthetics in *Historias* with Marxist-Leninist certainties. As a satirist, however, Otero identifies and condemns vice rather than persuades to dialectical materialist or other virtues, and the skill with which he wields his verbal bludgeon, not moral crusading, is what delights in the end.

16. Compare "La vida," *Que trata*, 35.

17. Compare the censored version in Otero, *Expresión y reunión: a modo de antología (1941–1969)*, 147–49, cited hereafter in the text as *Expresión*.

18. Compare Renato Poggioli, *The Oaten Flute: Essays on Pastoral Poetry and the Pastoral Ideal*, 1–41.

19. Compare Otero, "Muy lejos," *Pido*, 25–27, and "Bilbao," *Expresión*, 291–92; Emilio Alarcos Llorach, "Al margen de Blas de Otero."

20. See Unamuno, *Cancionero*, 39, and *Que trata*, 11.

21. Otero, "Y así quisiera la obra," in Francisco Ribes, ed., *Antología consultada de la joven poesía española*, 180.

22. José María Alín, "Blas de Otero y la poesía tradicional," selectively documents Otero's cultured stylization of the popular.

23. See the close of Jorge Guillén's 1974 homage to Blas de Otero: "Hombre y poeta dicen / con una sola voz: no miento" (The man and the poet say / with a single voice: I do not lie).

24. See also Elliott, *Power of Satire*, under the word *magic*.

25. Compare Otero's birthday poem of a year later, "Historia de mi vida," *Todos*, 97.

Notes for Chapter 3: The Satires, Hypocrisy

1. Kenneth Burke, *The Philosophy of Literary Form* (Baton Rouge: Louisiana State University Press, 1941), 231–32, argues that conditions are more favorable to satire under censorship than under liberalism.

2. Critics have asserted but not studied Quevedo's influence on Otero, for example, Emilio Alarcos Llorach, *La poesía de Blas de Otero*, 25: "En cuanto a la expresión es probablemente Quevedo el más cercano a Otero" (As far as expression is concerned, Quevedo is probably the closest to Otero).

3. Robert C. Elliott, *The Power of Satire: Magic, Ritual, Art*, 271–72, sees synecdoche as one source of the satirist's ancient magical power.

4. Carlos Blanco Aguinaga, "El mundo entre ceja y ceja: releyendo a Blas de Otero," 154–56, underlines the absence of the Civil War but dates the second and third stanzas inconsistently as 1916–1936, willfully restricts stanza three to being a critique of the Spanish bourgeoisie, and clumsily handles the use of pronouns in the poem. José M. González, *Poesía española de posguerra (Celaya, Otero, Hierro: 1950–1960)*, 84, argues for "fuegos japoneses" signalling the bombing of Pearl Harbor. Carlos Bousoño, "Un ensayo de estilística explicativa (ruptura de un sistema formado por una frase hecha)," 73–75 et passim, despite neo-rhetorical pirouettes, sensitively examines a relevant aspect of Otero's wit.

5. Alfonso Rangel Guerra, "La poesía de Blas de Otero," 288–89, judges the poem one of Otero's best, although he overlooks the grim humor and exaggerates the importance of Nerudian *enumeración caótica*.

6. Emilio Alarcos Llorach, "Al margen de Blas de Otero," 122–24, adduces the poem as evidence of censorship, but though it may be tempting to exaggerate the importance of "el grito ahogado por la mordaza" (the cry stilled by the gag), this fails to take into account that the theme of silence is often simply a figure, aposiopesis or paraleipsis. José R. Marra López, "Una nueva generación poética," points to the echoes of Vallejo.

7. Otero, [Muy Lejos], *Pido*, 25–27, exhibits a facsimile of the holograph.

8. Otero sets "Por caridad" among lighter pieces in *Esto*, 89–90.

9. See also *Expresión* pp. 215–16. Alarcos, "Al margen de Blas de Otero," 136–41, offers suggestive comments on the formative influence of Bilbao.

10. See Otero, "Hagamos que el soneto se extienda," *Todos*, 133. Although "Un minero" is omitted from this anthology, metrics and arrangement suggest perhaps an aborted sonnet.

11. Aristotle, *Rhetoric*, III.ix.8.

12. This is the assessment of French anticlericalism by Theodor Zeldin, "Religion and Anticlericalism," *France 1848–1945* (Oxford: Clarendon Press, 1973–1977), 2: 218–75.

Notes for Chapter 4: The Satires, Woman

1. Ernst Robert Curtius, *European Literature and the Latin Middle Ages*, trans. Willard R. Trask (1948; reprint, New York: Harper & Row, 1953), 125, 155n, 240n, stresses a vein of misogynistic writing in early modern Europe; Amy Richlin, *The Garden of Priapus* (New Haven: Yale University Press, 1983), documents its ancient origins. See also Amédée Mas, *La Caricature de la femme, du mariage, et de l'amour dans l'oeuvre de Quevedo*; Kenneth R. Scholberg, *Sátira e invectiva en la España medieval* and *Algunos aspectos de la sátira en el siglo XVI*. Scholberg lumps all under the label of misogyny, whereas R. M. Price simply states that "the satire of women is very

ancient . . . we cannot speculate on personal motives" (Francisco Gómez de Quevedo y Villegas, *Los sueños*, ed. R. M. Price [London: Grant and Cutler, 1983], 72). Otero had a fair reputation as a womanizer, and, moreover, his love poetry has been characterized as "eine unendliche Sehnsucht nach Gott" (an endless yearning for God) by Erika Lorenz, *Der metaphorische Kosmos der modernen spanischen Lyrik*, 176.

2. The poems are possibly a loose parody of García Lorca, "La Lola" and "Amparo," from the section "Dos muchachas" in *Poema del cante jondo*, although La Lola figures in Manuel and Antonio Machado's play, *La Lola se va a los puertos*, and is a figure of popular tradition and song.

3. Sabina de la Cruz notes "el juego gongorino de 'Mira' y 'Venus' " (the Gongorine play in "Mira" and "Venus") in her introduction to *Expresión y reunión*, by Blas de Otero, 16.

4. On Otero's sonneteering, see Sabina de la Cruz, "Los sonetos de Blas de Otero," introduction to *Todos mis sonetos*, by Blas de Otero, xi–xxiii, and José Luis Cano, "Blas de Otero y el soneto heterodoxo," in *Blas de Otero: Study of a Poet*, ed. Carlos Mellizo and Louise Salstad, 11–18.

5. Whimsical encomia are an ancient form of intellectual gymnastics. A. S. Pease, "Things without Honour," *Classical Philology* 21 (1926): 27–43, asserts their influence through the sixteenth century and beyond. Whether swayed by Golden Age literary models, legal training, or Jesuit schooling, Otero's approach is within the bounds of a long-established rhetorical tradition. See François Charmot, *La pédagogie des Jésuites: ses principes, son actualité* (Paris: Spes, 1943).

6. Overviews are provided by Joaquín González-Muela, "Un hombre de nuestro tiempo: Blas de Otero"; Emilio Alarcos Llorach, *La poesía de Blas de Otero*; Moraima de Semprún Donahue, *Blas de Otero en su poesía*; and Itziar Zapiaín and Ramón Iglesias, *Aproximación a la poesía de Blas de Otero*. Cruz, introduction to *Expresión*, 16, singles out "Venus."

7. Robert C. Elliott, *The Power of Satire: Magic, Ritual, Art*, argues the connection of satire with primitive forces; see also Fred Norris Robinson, "Satirists and Enchanters in Early Irish Literature," in *Studies in the History of Religions Presented to Crawford Howell Toy*, ed. D. G. Lyon and G. F. Moore (New York: Macmillan, 1912), 95–130; Mary Claire Randolph, "Celtic Smiths and Satirists: Partners in Sorcery," *English Literary History* 8 (1941): 184–97; E.G.V. Knox, *The Mechanism of Satire*; Gilbert Highet, *The Anatomy of Satire*.

8. Highet, "Diatribe," *Anatomy of Satire*, 24–66, gives a general survey. See also Niall Rudd, *The Satires of Horace* (1966; reprint, Berkeley: University of California Press, 1982), under "The Diatribes" chapters.

9. Some have taken offense to the reading of these poems at an academic conference, believing, I think impracticably, that only socially and morally good poems should appear in public. Unwillingness to accept the literary kind perhaps makes it difficult to draw the distinctions of earlier critics between "salty joking, mordant satire, pungent malediction, and foul ugliness." See Alastair Fowler, *Kinds of Literature: An Introduction to the Theory of Genres and Modes*, 138; James Iffland, *Quevedo and the Grotesque*, and " 'Antivalues' in the Burlesque Poetry of Góngora and Quevedo," *Neophilologus* 63 (1989): 220–37. Perhaps, like Quevedo, Otero is more derisive in his mockery because he is so caught up in what he reacts against.

10. Carlos Blanco Aguinaga, "El mundo entre ceja y ceja: releyendo a Blas de Otero," 168, claims this to be one of the most outstanding poems in the collection. Literary value here depends on accepting a particular notion of the good life. Poetry is merely the symptom of something else.

11. Selections of *Hojas de Madrid* (inédito) appear in *Expresión*, 287–308.

Notes for Chapter 5: The Satires, World of Art

1. See, for example, Emilio Alarcos Llorach, *La poesía de Blas de Otero*; José María Alín, "Blas de Otero y la poesía tradicional"; José Luis Cano, "Blas de Otero y el soneto heterodoxo"; José Olivio Jiménez, *La presencia de Antonio Machado en la poesía española de posguerra*; Marina Mayoral, "Blas de Otero: Canto primero," *Poesía española contemporánea: análisis de textos*; José Angel Valente, *Las palabras de la tribu*.

2. Otero, "Lira 4," *Cántico espiritual*, 25, cited hereafter in the text as *Cántico*.

3. See Edmund L. King, "Blas de Otero: The Past and the Present of 'The Eternal' "; Alfredo Carballo Picazo, "Sobre unos versos de Blas de Otero," *Homenaje universitario a Dámaso Alonso*, 253–64. Antonio Núñez, "Encuentro con Blas de Otero," presents Otero's reflexive comments on his audience.

4. Nelson R. Orringer, "La espada y el arado: una refutación lírica de Juan Ramón por Blas de Otero," examines an Otero parody of Juan Ramón. However, Aurora de Albornoz, "Blas de Otero, hoy, mañana," underlines an abiding interest in Juan Ramón, "lo consideraba uno de sus maestros" (he considered him one of his masters). See also Juan Cano Ballesta, *La poesía española entre pureza y revolución, 1930–1936*.

5. John Butt, *Writers and Politics in Modern Spain*, 44–47, perceives an "intense, almost religious humanism" that is procommunist and finds little of merit.

6. Emilio Alarcos Llorach, "Al margen de Blas de Otero," 127–34, offers a close analysis.

7. See the seminal remarks of Juan López-Morillas, "Antonio Machado: ética y poética," *Hacia el '98: literatura, sociedad, ideología*, 255–69.

8. José María Alin, "Blas de Otero y la poesía tradicional," cursorily surveys Otero's debts, but a close study of imitations and appropriations remains to be done.

9. Cited in Alin, "Blas de Otero y la poesía tradicional," 283.

10. See also "El ballet," *Que trata,* 175. This, of course, is the Modernist world of correspondences.

11. See Lope de Vega, *Poesía selecta,* ed. Antonio Carreño (Madrid: Cátedra, 1984), 587–88.

12. Antonio Machado, "Problemas de la lírica," in *Obras: Poesía y prosa,* ed. Aurora de Albornoz and Guillermo de Torre (Buenos Aires: Losada, 1964), 714.

13. Sabina de la Cruz, "Los sonetos de Blas de Otero," and Cano, "Blas de Otero," begin to map the territory, but a full-scale study is yet to be done.

14. The Barcelona edition contains 67 poems; the Paris edition 147 poems. Such encounters with the censor gave Otero a certain *succès de scandale,* but there is no automatic correlation between political notoriety and poetic achievement.

Notes for Chapter 6: The Satires, The Times

1. Emilio Miro, "La poesía prohibida de Blas de Otero y Gabriel Celaya," celebrates the publication in Spain of *En castellano* and *Que trata de España;* María Luisa Muñiz, "El poeta y la patria en la trilogía de Blas de Otero *Que trata de España,*" argues the stylistic consequences of censorship. What is notable is the extent of "exiled" publications in Paris, Mexico, Cuba, Russia, and Argentina. See Manuel Luis Abellán, *Censura y creación literaria en España (1939–1976)* (Barcelona: Península, 1980).

2. This poem forms part of a much-heralded but never published collection entitled *Hojas de Madrid (Mientras,* 287–308).

3. Otero, "Francisco de Quevedo," *País,* 86.

4. Entitled "Grandes almacenes" in *Todos,* 88.

5. Available texts of Otero's late poems are charged with moralizing commonplaces. Marina Mayoral, "Blas de Otero: Canto primero," notes early biblical echoes, but the poet's Catholic formation has more extensive effects. His complaint on the times is essentially medieval, although the motif of "O tempora, o mores" is ancient; see Ernst Robert Curtius, *European Literature and the Latin Middle Ages,* trans. Willard R. Trask (1948; reprint, New York: Harper & Row, 1953), 94–98.

6. The motif of the all-seeing poet frequently appears, although in the unedited collection of *Hojas de Madrid,* from which this poem is excerpted, Otero is probably influenced by Rimbaud.

7. The image has caught the poet's imagination and appears in differing contexts. See "Provincia de Segovia" and "¿Qué ocurre?" *Todos,* 109–10.

8. See Emilio Alarcos Llorach, "Algunas configuraciones imaginativas," *La poesía de Blas de Otero,* 71–82; Moraima de Semprún Donahue, *Blas de Otero en su poesía,* 115–51; Mercedes Clarasó, "Sea Imagery in the Poetry of Blas de Otero," in *Blas de Otero: Study of a Poet,* ed. Carlos Mellizo and Louise Salstad, 41–52.

9. "Blas de Otero, con los ojos abiertos," *Reseña* 91 (January 1976): 17, cited in Joaquín Galán, *Blas de Otero, palabras para un pueblo: tres vías de conocimiento,* 115. Compare: " . . . el poema es un ente estético . . . la calidad estética es insoslayable" (. . . the poem is an aesthetic entity . . . aesthetic quality is unavoidable) (Antonio Núñez, "Encuentro con Blas de Otero," 1).

Notes for Chapter 7: The Satires, Tyranny

1. Gilbert Cannan, *Satire,* 9–10. The lineage is ascribed by Heinrich Heine.

2. See John Butt, *Writers and Politics in Modern Spain,* 46: " 'MXCLV' is unintelligible to the reader without some Latin and arithmetic."

3. See the 1969 censored variant:

¿Hablar en castellano? Parler claire [*sic*].
Buscar españa en el desierto
de un oasis de sílabas.
Silencio.
Y más silencio. Y voluntad de vida
a contra viento y contra tiempo.
                    (*Expresión,* 149)

Speak Castilian Spanish? Speak freely.
Seek Spain in the desert
of an oasis of syllables.
Silence

And more silence. And with a will to live
against the wind and against time.

4. Reprinted in *Que trata,* 128.

5. José Olivio Jiménez, *La presencia de Antonio Machado en la poesía española de posguerra,* passes over the theme of Cain and Abel, but the continuity with Unamuno and Machado is unmistakable, as is the traditional moral framework.

6. See E. H. Gombrich, "The Experiment of Caricature," *Art and Illusion,* 330–58.

7. Job 42:6. Compare: "…me resigno a ser ceniza, solitaria ceniza húmeda de lágrimas" (…I resign myself to being ashes, solitary ashes moist with tears) ("Cap. 10 Lib II," *Ancia,* 70).•

8. On the theme of silence in Otero, see Emilio Alarcos Llorach's "Al margen de Blas de Otero," and note José Luis Cano: "Su callar grave tenía mas fuerza a veces que su hablar" (His serious silence had more force at times than his speaking) ("En la muerte de Blas de Otero," 7).

9. Compare José Angel Valente:

Estábamos remotos
chupando caramelos,
con tantas estampitas y retratos
con tanto ir y venir y tanta cólera,
tanta predicación y tantos muertos
y tanta infancia irremediable.

("Tiempo de guerra," *Punto Cero* [Barcelona: Barral, 1972], 193)

We were far away
sucking caramels
with so many little holy pictures and portraits
with so much coming and going and so much anger,
so much preaching and so many dead
and so much irreparable infancy.

10. On the popularity of the Eiffel Tower among poets in the twenties, see C. B. Morris, *A Generation of Spanish Poets* (Cambridge: Cambridge University Press, 1969), 85.

11. Alarcos, "Al margen," 134–36, offers a close analysis of the sound effects in the poem.

12. See Unamuno's *romances,* with their lines composed only of place-names, for example *Cancionero,* nos. 271, 274. They are, as Pedro Salinas affirms, neither narrative nor dramatic ("El romancismo en el siglo XX," *Ensayos de literatura hispánica* [Madrid: Aguilar, 1961], 310–41).

13. J. M. Caballero Bonald compares Otero passingly with Unamuno and plays up panegyric: "Otero es un peregrino de España, que la ha caminado trocha a trocha, buscándole su entraña. Su poesía está llena de alusiones, de concretas citas geográficas que cobran, dentro del peculiar tono expresivo del poeta una dimensión de elegíaco rendimiento" (Otero is a wanderer of Spain, who has walked path by path, seeking her heart. His poetry is full of allusions, of concrete geographical references that gather, within the peculiar expressive tone of the poet, a dimension of elegiac surrender) ("Vigencia de la poesía de Blas de Otero," 122).

14. See Otero, "Reforma agraria," *Historias,* 143.

15. "Diecinueve cegadores años" marks 1958 as the date of composition.

16. The poem is glossed by Carlos Blanco Aguinaga, "El mundo entre ceja y ceja: releyendo a Blas de Otero," 175–76. See also the valuable article by Ricardo Senabre-Sempere, "Modelos y transformaciones en la poesía de Blas de Otero," which elucidates the image of "echarme en tu regazo . . . tragar agua de mar" (35–36).

17. For the theme of liberty, see also "El aeroplano de papel" and "Con la espalda," *Todos,* III, 118.

18. Carlos Blanco Aguinaga, Julio Rodríguez-Puértolas, and Iris Zavala, eds., *Historia social de la literatura española,* 1:143–44, cite the *zéjel* of "Tres morillas."

19. The prose squibs, "Reforma agraria" and "Desterrados," *Historias,* 143–45, echo the social theme of rural migration.

20. For example see José María Castellet, ed., *Veinte años de poesía española antologia (1939–1959);* Juan López-Morillas, "Antonio Machado: ética y poesía"; Jiménez, *La presencia de Antonio Machado.*

Notes for Chapter 8: A Style of Dissent

1. W. Meyer Luebke, as quoted in Stephen Ullmann, *Language and Style* (Oxford: Oxford University Press, 1964), 99.

2. Emilio Alarcos Llorach, *La poesía de Blas de Otero,* 154.

3. For example, see Claude Couffon, "Rencontre avec Blas de Otero," and Antonio Núñez, "Encuentro con Blas de Otero."

4. René Wellek, "Closing Statement from the Viewpoint of Literary Criticism," in Thomas A. Sebeok, ed., *Style and Language* (Cambridge, Mass.: M.I.T. Press, 1960), 408–19.

5. Entitled "Vencer juntos" in Otero, *Hacia la inmensa mayoría*, 106–7; "Otro tiempo" in Francisco Ribes, ed., *Antología consultada de la joven poesía española*, 194–95, and in Dario Puccini, ed., *Romancero de la résistance espagnole* (Paris: Maspéro, 1962), 294–95. Max Aub, *La poesía española contemporánea*, points to variants.

6. See Brian Vickers, *Classical Rhetoric and English Poetry* (London: Cambridge University Press, 1970), 86–124, for succinct comments on rhetoric and psychology in Aristotle, Quintilian, and later theorists; or see the useful primer of W. Rhys Roberts, *Greek Rhetoric and Literary Criticism* (New York: Cooper Square, 1963).

7. See Amado Alonso, "The Stylistic Interpretation of Literary Texts," *Modern Language Notes* 57 (1942): 789–96; Vickers, *Classical Rhetoric*; and Ullmann, *Language and Style*.

8. Otero, *Expresión*, 289, 255, *Parler*, 26, 106, *Ancia*, 123, *País*, 85, *Mientras*, 74, 183, *Todos*, 133. See also the use of archaisms to shock in "Hija de Yago," *Pido*, 19–20.

9. See "Españahogándose," *Que trata*, 33.

10. Otero, *Pido*, 20, *Parler*, 82, 108, *Que trata*, 156, 158, *Todos*, 101, *Mientras*, 25. Note prefix invention too: *superexplotados* (*Todos*, 108) and *extradisuelva* (*Poesía con nombres*, 33).

11. Otero, *Todos*, 125, *Expresión*, 300. See also the incorporation of a found dialect letter, "Una carta," *Que trata*, 146–49.

12. See the closure in the Buenos Aires edition: "sin que les haga caso Dios" (*Hacia*, 80). Note also "y voluntad de vida / a contra viento y contra tiempo" ("Impreso prisionero," *Expresión*, 149) versus "a contradictadura y contra tiempo" (*Que trata*, 29).

13. Carlos Bousoño, "Un ensayo de estilística explicativa." See also Alarcos, *La poesía de Blas de Otero*, 88–96.

14. A fourth connotation is that church attendance became a measure of one's adherence to the regime. Crudely put, one had to go to mass to avoid being accused of being a Red. Moraima de Semprún Donahue, *Blas de Otero en su poesía*, 175, clarifies the wordplay, although her general account of *frases hechas* follows Alarcos.

15. Bousoño, "Un ensayo de estilística explicativa." He examines the technique at length in *Teoría de la expresión poética*. Taxonomy can become the bugbear of rhetoricians. Whereas I recognize that paronomasia is not at play in all of Bousoño's Otero exhibits, I resist novel terms where suitable traditional labels exist.

16. Alarcos, *La poesía de Blas de Otero*, 90, speaks strictly of idioms but argues that literary references undergo "parecida transformación y revaloración" (a similar transformation and revaluation) (97). J. M. Caballero Bonald, "Vigencia de la poesía de Blas de Otero," acknowledges early the power of the technique.

17. See also *Parler*, 104; José María Castellet, ed., *Un cuarto de siglo de poesía española (1939–1964)*, 289; Emilio Alarcos Llorach, "Secuencia sintáctica y secuencia rítmica," *Elementos formales en la lírica actual*; Bousoño, "Un ensayo de estilística explicativa," 77.

18. Otero, "Aire libre," *Parler*, 68, cited in Bousoño, "Un ensayo."

19. Otero, "En el nombre de España, paz," *Pido*, 68, cited in Bousoño, ibid. See also José María Alín, "Blas de Otero y la poesía tradicional." Gordon Williams, *Tradition and Originality in Roman Poetry* (Oxford: Oxford University Press, 1968), particularly chapter 11, "Thought and Expression: Language and Style," is a superb study of imitation, or the ways in which poets conscious of an identifiable tradition (variously interpreted) achieve originality of their own.

20. See Alín, "Blas de Otero y la poesía tradicional," 282–83. Donahue, *Blas de Otero en su poesía*, 182–83, asserts but gives no evidence for the "genial maestría" and "valor extraordinario" of "La muerte de Don Quijote," which is simply quoted.

21. Bousoño, "Un ensayo de estilística explicativa," 79–81.

22. One school of thought holds that the ludicrous is a form of ugliness. See, for example, Aristotle, *The Poetics*, trans. W. Hamilton Fyfe (1932; reprint, London: William Heinemann, 1960), 18–19; James Iffland, "Theories of the Grotesque and the Applicability to the Problem of the Grotesque in Quevedo," *Quevedo and the Grotesque*, 2:17–60.

23. See Sigmund Freud, *Wit and its Relation to the Unconscious*, trans. A. A. Brill (London: Kegan Paul, 1922), especially chapter three. See also the stimulating if brief commentary in D. H. Monro, *Argument of Laughter* (Carlton: Melbourne University Press, 1951), 182–200.

24. Eric Bentley, "Farce," draws attention to Gilbert Murray's thesis of the close similarity between Aristotle and Freud, in Robert W. Corrigan, ed., *Comedy: Meaning and Form*, 2d ed. (San Francisco: Chandler, 1981), 279–303. Compare *Symposium*, 223D, where Socrates argues that the arts of comedy and tragedy are equal. María Luisa Muñiz, "Poeticeskaia trilogia Blasa de Otero Rech' idet ob Ispanii," holds the bleak view that Otero's voice is deliberately muffled in order to outwit Fascist censorship.

25. Carlos Blanco Aguinaga, "El mundo entre ceja y ceja: releyendo a Blas de Otero," 158. Blanco underestimates the degree to which Otero demands the imaginative cooperation of the reader. He mixes styles, parodies,

forms, and it is questionable whether his literary references are part of a truly shared culture or of private erudition. Otero appears to speak man to man, but his candor can easily be exaggerated. For an elastic interpretation of "lo cotidiano" in Otero, see Antonio Molina, ed., *Antología de la poesía cotidiana* (Madrid: Alfaguara, 1966), 297–316.

26. Caballero Bonald, "Vigencia de la poesía," 121.

27. I recognize the impishness of these labels and use them loosely as convenient shorthand. Attempts to define pure and impure poetry seem neat but are really more confusing than helpful; see Juan Cano Ballesta, *La poesía española entre pureza y revolución, 1930–1936*; Gustav Siebenmann, *Los estilos poéticos en España desde 1900*; Johannes Lechner, *El compromiso en la poesía española del siglo XX*, 2 vols. (Leiden: Universitaire Pers Leiden, 1968–75). For "popular poetry," Luis Cernuda, "Poesía popular," *Bulletin of Spanish Studies* 18 (1941): 161–73, and Eric Proll, "*Popularismo y barroquismo* in the poetry of Rafael Alberti," *Bulletin of Spanish Studies* 19 (1942): 59–83, capture the spirit of the term.

28. *Que trata de España* has an index of both names and places. David Bary, "Sobre el nombrar poético en la poesía española contemporánea," *Papeles de Son Armadans* 44 (1967): 161–89, contains perceptive insights.

29. Bary, ibid., considers naming to be a rejection of Modernism and the building of a lost sense of community. Nonetheless, Aurora de Albornoz, "Blas de Otero, hoy, mañana," 6, cautions against applying labels as if they were precise and exclusive definitions:

Aquella temporada—1968, verano—un libro le acompañaba a todas partes: era la *La Tercera Antología* de Juan Ramón. Porque . . . , sí, a Juan Ramón Jiménez lo había admirado siempre; lo consideraba uno de sus maestros. Recuerdo que esto me dijo más de una vez en esos días.

(At that time, the summer of 1968, one book went with him everywhere: it was *The Third Anthology* of Juan Ramón. Because . . . , that's the way it was, he had always admired Juan Ramón Jiménez; he considered him one of his masters. I remember he told me this more than once at that time.)

And this was at the height of fashion for the putative *poesía social.*

30. See Louis Combet, "Proverbes et poésie populaire," *Recherches sur le Refranero Castillan* (Paris: Les Belles Lettres, 1971), 49–55. Alarcos, Donahue, and Caballero Bonald all laud Otero's originality in using proverbs, surely a stylization of the popular.

31. Blanco, "El mundo entre ceja y ceja," 177. With its question-begging, superficiality, and blunt assertions, Otero's style is deliberately "unpoetical," but not therefore to be deplored. What matters, I think, is less the source of word and phrase than their treatment in the poetry. It is easy to talk too much about subject matter; what makes a poet is the more intangible quality of style.

32. Gerald G. Brown, *A Literary History of Spain: The Twentieth Century* (London: Benn, 1972), and John Butt, *Writers and Politics in Modern Spain*, contain unsympathetic appraisals of Otero. Geoffrey Ribbans, "Modern Spanish Literature," in Peter E. Russell, ed., *Spain: A Companion to Spanish Studies* (London: Methuen, 1973), offers a more balanced judgment. Siebenmann observes in Otero "la inaparente literaridad de los versos antiliterarios" (the unapparent literariness of antiliterary lines) (*Los estilos poéticos*, 469).

33. The term is Siebenmann's, *Los estilos poéticos*, 327, and he cautiously notes "huellas de un acercamiento a la tradición popular" (traces of an approach to popular tradition). See also Dámaso Alonso, "Escila y Caribdis de la literatura española," *Ensayos sobre poesía española* (Buenos Aires: Revista de Occidente, 1946); Arnold Hottinger, *Das volkstümliche Element in der modernen spanischen Lyrik.* Much Marxian ink has been spilled inconclusively in trying to determine the correct proletarian style; even conventional labels are not watertight or exactly helpful. Distinctive features of "popularism" can be found in the hardly political poetry of the *Generación del '27*. Quite simply, I argue that Otero's style exemplifies a rhetoric of indignation. This sufficiently accounts for the poetry without having to subscribe to a specious political view of poetic diction.

34. Dámaso Alonso, "Poesía arraigada y poesía desarraigada," 367; Joaquín González-Muela, "Un hombre de nuestro tiempo: Blas de Otero," 138.

35. See also Otero, "Trozos de patria," in "Escrito para," *Papeles de Son Armadans* 72 (1974): 260: "Entramos en un café donde unos hombres sin rostro hablaban con las manos llenas de sangre" (We went into a cafe where some faceless men were talking with their hands covered in blood).

36. The written style is perhaps influenced by Otero's public declamation of his poems. *Historias fingidas y verdaderas* shows his fascination with the power of electronic media to disseminate poetry.

37. See Alarcos, *La poesía de Blas de Otero*, 133–38.

38. Ibid., 137.

39. See Paul Ilie, *Literature and Inner Exile: Authoritarian Spain 1939–1975* (Baltimore: Johns Hopkins University Press, 1980), particularly "Alienation and Exilic Homology," 47–58, and "Clandestinity and Marginality," 93–113.

40. Alarcos, *La poesía de Blas de Otero*, 136.

41. Donahue's survey of imagery, *Blas de Otero en su poesía*, 115–51, is separated from the account of style and is quite impressionistic. Alarcos, *La poesía de Blas de Oteros*, 60–82, remains the standard account.

42. Couffon, "Rencontre avec Blas de Otero," 21.

43. See Ricardo Senabre-Sempere, "Juegos retóricos en la poesía de Blas de Otero"; also, Bousoño, Donahue, Cano. Alarcos signals (with shades of Juan Ramón) "la mayor desnudez de la expresión" (increased bareness of expression) after the mid-fifties (*La poesía de Blas de Otero*, 154).

44. Senabre, "Juegos retóricos," 148, 150.

45. See Dámaso Alonso, "El desgarrón afectivo en la poesía de Quevedo," *Poesía española* (Madrid: Gredos, 1952), 531–43; Alexander A. Parker, "La 'agudeza' en algunos sonetos de Quevedo," in *Estudios dedicados a Menéndez Pidal*, vol. 3 (Madrid: Consejo Superior de Investigaciones Clentíficas, 1952), 345–60; Arthur Terry, "Quevedo and the Metaphysical Conceit," *Bulletin of Hispanic Studies* 35 (1958): 211–22; and especially, Parker's important study of seventeenth-century wit in *Polyphemus and Galatea: A Study in the Interpretation of a Baroque Poem*. Unlike the wit of Quevedo, Otero's wit is not organic. However, as I try to show, it is functional and not purely decorative.

46. See Senabre, "Juegos retóricos," 149–50, for discussion of "Caniguer" (*Parler*, 126–29, an anagram of Guernica) and of the riddle "La solución mañana" (*Que trata*, 75).

47. Bousoño, "Un ensayo de estilística explicativa," 81–84.

48. Senabre, "Juegos retóricos," 150; Stephen C. Foster and Rudolf E. Kuenzli, eds., *Dada Spectrum: The Dialectics of Revolt* (Madison: University of Wisconsin Press, 1979), 65. See also Sigmund Freud, *Creative Writers and Daydreaming*, trans. J. Strachey (London: Kegan Paul, 1959).

49. See Vickers, *Classical Rhetoric*, and Quintilian, *Institutio Oratoria*, trans. H. E. Butler, 4 vols. (1920–22; reprint, London: William Heinemann, 1966), 3:358–59.

50. See Senabre, "Modelos y transformaciones," on Otero's borrowings. Note Christopher Maurer's reading, " 'Defeated by the Age': On Ambiguity in Quevedo's 'Miré los muros de la patria mía,' " *Hispanic Review* 54 (1986): 427–42.

51. See also "(Viene de la página 1936)," "Cuándo será que España," *Que trata*, 56, 114; Phyllis Turnbull, "La frase interrogativa en la poesía contemporánea," *Boletín de la Real Academia Española* 43 (1963): 473–605.

52. See the sarcastic apostrophe, "Santiago, y cierra, España" in "Hija de Yago," *Pido*, 20.

53. See also Parker, *Polyphemus*, 87–89.

54. See Quintilian, *Institutio*, 3:476–77.

55. See also "Entre papeles y realidades," "(Viene de la página 1936)," "Del árbol que creció en un espejo," "Avanzando, cayendo, y avanzando," "Vámonos al campo," and "Tierra inerme," *Que trata*, 36, 56, 70, 76, 127, 155–56; *Expresión*, 293–94; Alarcos, *La poesía de Blas de Otero*, 110–21, 139ff.

56. See F. Charmot, *La pédagogie des Jésuites: ses principes, son actualité*; Charles Sears Baldwin, *Medieval Rhetoric and Poetic to 1400* (New York: Macmillan, 1928), 26; Harry Caplan, *Of Eloquence: Studies in Ancient and Mediaeval Rhetoric* (Ithaca: Cornell University Press, 1970), 217, 239ff. L. Martz, *The Poetry of Meditation* (New Haven: Yale University Press, 1954), contains a perceptive account of the Ignatian technique of meditation which is applicable to the religious sonnets of *Ancia*.

57. Note, however, the thorough and indispensable study of sociopolitical issues by Eleanor Wright, *The Poetry of Protest Under Franco* (London: Tamesis, 1986).

58. Enid Welsford, *The Fool*. For the relationship between satire and irrational forces, popular festivals, primitive religion, and magical concepts, Robert C. Elliott, *The Power of Satire: Magic, Ritual, Art*, is the standard study. The elemental power of inchoate comedy, however, is not enough to advance it beyond what can be found anywhere at any time. Otero succeeds, I have suggested, because he is able to rise above his ancient foundations.

Notes for Chapter 9: Satire and Renewal

1. Robert C. Elliott, *The Power of Satire: Magic, Ritual, Art*, 4–5. Francis Macdonald Cornford, *The Origin of Attic Comedy* (London: E. Arnold, 1914), argues that comedy is the ritual representation of the triumph of the new year over the old, but note the corrective comments of K. J. Dover, "Greek Comedy," in Maurice Platnauer, ed., *Fifty Years of Classical Scholarship* (Oxford: Basil Blackwell, 1954), 112–13; Richard F. Hardin, " 'Ritual' in Recent Criticism: The Elusive Sense of Community," *PMLA* 98 (October 1983): 846–62; and John Herrington, *Poetry into Drama* (Berkeley: University of California Press, 1985). E. H. Gombrich, "The Experiment of Caricature," underlines the driving out of evil with laughter. See also the readable primer by L. J. Potts, *Comedy*, and compare René Bouvier, *Quevedo: Homme du Diable, Homme de Dieu* (Paris: Champion, 1929), 192–204.

2. See Mircea Eliade, *The Myth of the Eternal Return* (New York: Pantheon, 1954); Theodor H. Gaster, *Thespis* (New York: Schuman, 1950); Leo Salingar, "The Wheel of Fortune," in *Shakespeare and the Traditions of Comedy* (Cambridge: Cambridge University Press, 1974), 129–56; Robert C. Elliott, *The Shape of Utopia: Studies in a Literary Genre* (Chicago: University of Chicago Press, 1970); Mikhail Bakhtin, *Rabelais and His World*, trans.

Helene Iswolsky; Mahadev Apte, *Humor and Laughter: An Anthropological Approach*. In Francoist Spain, the value of laughter lies partly in its victory over fear.

3. Roy Jones, *A Literary History of Spain: Golden Age Poetry and Prose* (London: Ernest Benn, 1971), 191; Graham Greene, *Ways of Escape* (New York: Simon and Schuster, 1980), 267.

4. See H. and H. A. Frankfort, eds., *Before Philosophy* (Baltimore: Penguin, 1974); G. W. Trompf, *The Idea of Historical Recurrence in Western Thought* (Berkeley: California University Press, 1979), a dense account of classical, Christian, and Renaissance views of historical change; James H. Billington, *Fire in the Minds of Men: Origins of the Revolutionary Faith* (New York: Basic Books, 1980).

5. See Otero's note on "un ideal positivo . . . cual un futuro ya presente" (a positive ideal . . . like an already present future) in Francisco Ribes, ed., *Antología consultada de la joven poesía española*, 179–80. See Potts, *Comedy*, 154: "Great satirists are of course more than merely angry, bitter, or disappointed men; they are usually baffled idealists. They compare life as it is with life as they would have it to be; and being unable to reconcile the two, they attack that which is less clear to them." Also, Mircea Eliade, "The Yearning for Paradise in Primitive Tradition," *Daedalus* 88 (Spring 1959): 255–67; Northrop Frye, "Varieties of Literary Utopias."

6. See Jerome Bruner, "Myth and Identity," *Daedalus* 88 (Spring 1959): 350; Judith Shklar, "The Political Theory of Utopia: From Melancholy to Nostalgia," *Daedalus* 94 (Spring 1965): 367–81; Sylvia Thrupp, ed., *Millenial Dreams in Action* (The Hague: Mouton, 1962); Frank E. and Fritzie P. Manuel, *Utopian Thought in the Western World*.

7. See Henry Kamen, *La Inquisición española* (1967; reprint, Madrid: Grijalbo, 1985), 319ff.; Carr, *Spain 1808–1939* (1966; reprint, Oxford: Clarendon, 1970).

8. Otero, "Y así quisiera la obra," in Ribes, ed., *Antología consultada*, 180.

9. See Mercedes Clarasó, "Sea Imagery in the Poetry of Blas de Otero."

10. This vision of freedom accounts for Otero's restless wanderings, according to José Luis Cano, "En la muerte de Blas de Otero."

11. Johannes Lechner, *El compromiso en la poesía española del siglo XX*, 1:152.

12. Ramón Menéndez y Pidal, *The Spaniards in Their History*, trans. W. Starkie (1947; reprint, New York: Norton, 1966), 102–43. See also Claudio Sánchez Albornoz, *España: un enigma histórico* (Buenos Aires: Sudamericana, 1956); H. Juretschke, *El origen doctrinal y génesis del romanticismo español* (Madrid: Ateneo, 1954); Vicente Llorens, *Liberales y románticos: una emigración española en Inglaterra 1823–1834*, 2d ed. (Madrid: Castalia, 1968); Aurora de Albornoz, "Huella unamuniana en la visión de España de AM," *Unamuno y Machado, La presencia de Miguel de Unamuno en Antonio Machado* (Madrid: Gredos, 1968), 111–225. For another view, see Julián Juderías, *La leyenda negra* (1914; reprint, Barcelona: Araluce, 1943).

13. Carlos Blanco Aguinaga, Julio Rodríguez-Puértolas, and Iris Zavala, eds., *Historia social de la literatura española*; Carlos Blanco Aguinaga, "El mundo entre ceja y ceja."

14. Leopoldo de Luis, ed., *Poesía española contemporánea 1939–64. Poesía religiosa* (Madrid: Alfaguara, 1969). See Theodor Zeldin, *France 1848–1945* (Oxford: Clarendon Press, 1977), 2:1031.

15. See Emilio Alarcos Llorach, "La poesía de Blas de Otero." See also M. H. Abrams, "Politics of Vision," *Natural Supernaturalism: Tradition and Revolution in Romantic Literature* (New York: Norton, 1971), 358–72. The influence of Heine and Rilke has not been addressed by critics.

16. Alarcos, "La poesía de Blas de Otero," 3, suggests four stages: "desde la fe ingenua inicial, pasando por la duda, hasta la nueva fe, templada al final por cierto escepticismo nostálgico" (from an initial ingenuous faith, passing through doubt, to a new faith, tempered in the end by a certain nostalgic skepticism). See Evelyne Martin Hernández, " 'A la inmensa mayoría': Les 'voix' de l'absolu dans Blas de Otero," *Iris* (Montpellier) 4 1984: 121–29.

17. Later editions omit the author's note: "Este poema es una llamada a la sinceridad. No excluye lo trascendente" (This poem is a call to sincerity. It does not exclude the transcendent) (*Parler* 50).

18. See Alarcos, "La poesía de Blas de Otero," 5.

19. Ibid., 8, notes echoes from Otero poems of the forties.

20. See Pedro Laín Entralgo, "La esperanza en la poesía española actual," *La espera y la esperanza: Historia y teoría del esperar humano*, 456–67.

21. Ernst Robert Curtius, *European Literature and the Latin Middle Ages*, trans. Willard R. Trask (1948; reprint, New York: Harper & Row, 1953), 104; Lechner, *El compromiso*, vol 1, 175–76, stresses the elemental rural imagery of death and resurrection in Civil War ballads.

22. Fernando Díaz-Plaja, *The Spaniard and the Seven Deadly Sins*, trans. J. I. Palmer (New York: Scribner, 1967), 39. Américo Castro, *The Spaniards* (Berkeley: University of California Press, 1971), chapters 9 & 14, following Brenan, argues the religious character of anarchist and utopian struggles. Shklar, "The Political Theory of Utopia," 376, suggests that political millenialism feeds religious longings that traditional religions cannot satisfy.

23. Luis Romero, "Evocación de Blas de Otero," in Carlos Mellizo and Louise Salstad, eds., *Blas de Otero: Study of a Poet,* 82.

24. Emilio Alarcos Llorach has pointed to the pervasiveness of religious icons in Otero's Bilbao house (private letter), but a definitive biography has still to be written.

25. See Abrams, *Natural Supernaturalism,* on secularization of Christian ideas (65–70) and on the quasi-religious post-Romantic vision of hope (409–62).

26. See also "Amiga de la luz," *Cántico,* 45.

27. Moraima de Semprún Donahue, *Blas de Otero en su poesía,* 123–28, breezily covers air imagery.

28. Otero, "MXCLV," *Parler clair: en castellano,* 38–39. Blanco, "El mundo entre ceja y ceja," 168, counts the poem among "los mas notables poemas del libro" (the most remarkable poems in the book). See also "Se ha parado el aire," *Que trata,* 73.

29. See Otero, "Cuando digo," *Que trata,* 52: "Cuando escribo aire libre, mar abierto / traduzco libertad (hipocresía / política)" (When I write open air, open sea / I translate liberty [political / hypocrisy]). See also, "El aire," *Todos,* 108.

30. Otero, "Recuerdo que en Bilbao," *Poesía con nombres,* 93–94, declaimed at the Lorca homage at Fuentevaqueros. Ricardo Senabre-Sempere, "Modelos y transformaciones . . . ," 30–32, sketches Otero's debts to Lorca. See Cano, "En la muerte," 7: "Pero ¿de dónde sacaba fuerzas su cuerpo enfermo para gritar 'libertad y amnistía' en aquel homenaje inolvidable a Federico en Fuentevaqueros, en junio de 1976?" (But, from where did he get the strength in his sick body to shout "liberty and amnesty" in that unforgettable homage to Federico at Fuentevaqueros, in June 1976?). Interestingly, Machado also espoused the cause of amnesty in 1918, according to Manuel Tuñon de Lara, "Antonio Machado y la superación del '98," in José Carlos-Mainer, ed., *Modernismo y 98* (Barcelona: Crítica, 1980), 421.

31. See the winnowing wind of "Hombre en desgracia," *Ancia,* 73, and "Penúltima palabra," *Mientras,* 158, and also "Collioure, 1959," *Que trata,* 169.

32. See John G. Cummins, ed., *The Spanish Traditional Lyric* (Oxford: Pergamon Press, 1977), 19–22.

33. See Erika Lorenz, *Der metaphorische Kosmos der modernen Spanischen Lyrik,* 7–52; Donahue, *Blas de Otero en su poesía,* 116–23; Clarasó, "Sea Imagery," and Gustavo Correa, "El simbolismo del mar en la poesía española del siglo XX."

34. *Que Trata,* 30, 183, 59, 25, 59. Clarasó, "Sea Imagery," 41, equates the raging sea with "the long awaited revolt against the forces of oppression." See Gaster, *Thespis,* on ritual combat and the rites of invigoration (20–27) and on sea imagery in the psalms, where victory over raging waters is characteristic of divine power (77–81).

35. See Mircea Eliade, *The Myth of the Eternal Return,* trans. Willard R. Trask (New York: Pantheon, 1954) and Philip Wheelwright, *The Burning Fountain: A Study in the Language of Symbolism* (Bloomington: University of Indiana Press, 1954), 155–69. Note, however, the revaluation of Quevedo by Christopher Maurer, " 'Defeated by the Age': On Ambiguity in Quevedo's 'Miré los muros de la patria mía,' " *Hispanic Review* 54 (1986): 427–42.

36. Mircea Eliade, *The Sacred and The Profane: The Nature of Religion,* trans. Willard Trask (New York: Harcourt, Brace, Jovanovich, 1959), 148.

37. See Segundo Serrano Poncela, *Antonio Machado: su mundo y su obra* (Buenos Aires: Losada, 1954), 175–87.

38. See Donahue, *Blas de Otero en su poesía,* 53. See also, for symbolism of buried corn, Maud Bodkin, *Archetypal Patterns in Poetry* (Oxford: Oxford University Press, 1934), 270ff.

39. See Bodkin, *Archetypal Patterns,* 206–7.

40. See, for example, "Arboles abolidos," *Pido,* 66, and "Canción primera," "Noche en Castilla," "Cuándo será que España," "Libertad real," *Que trata,* 89, 90, 114, 143.

41. See Cummins, *Spanish Traditional Lyric,* 72, 144–45; Margit Frenk Alatorre, "Glosas de tipo popular en la antigua lírica," *Estudios sobre lírica antigua* (Madrid: Castalia, 1978), 267–308; José Romeu Figueras, " 'De los álamos vengo, madre,' " *Studia philológica: homenaje ofrecido a Dámaso Alonso por sus amigos y discípulos con ocasión a su 60 aniversario* (Madrid: Gredos, 1963), 3:277–86.

42. Alarcos, *La poesía de Blas de Otero,* 65–66; Mircea Eliade, "Sacredness of nature and cosmic religion," *The Sacred and The Profane*; Philip Wheelwright, *Metaphor and Reality* (Bloomington: University of Indiana Press, 1962), 111–28; Lorenz, *Der metaphorische Kosmos,* 123, 155ff.; Janet Martin Soskice, *Metaphor and Religious Language* (Oxford: Clarendon Press, 1985). This idea is an ancient formulation, see Bruno Snell, *Discovery of the Mind* (Cambridge Mass.: Harvard University Press, 1953), 62: "the good appears again and again as an object of glittering beauty. The divine is radiant and luminous."

43. Lorenz, *Der metaphorische Kosmos,* 176. Early Otero work sees poetic creation as reflection of divine light, see *Cántico,* 26.

44. See "In memoriam," "Libertad real," and "Canción veinte," *Que trata,* 137, 143, 185; "Que nadie me veía," *Mientras,* 81.

45. See Paul Tillich, "The Religious Symbol in Symbolism," *Symbolism in Religion and Literature,* ed. Rollo May (New York: Braziller, 1960), 78. See also: "irrumpa / justiciero el sol" (let the sun / burst forth with justice) ("Hace frío. El pico," *Que trata,* 109) and "sé / que mañana / hará sol, será de todos España" (I know / that tomorrow / the sun will shine, it will belong to everyone Spain) ("Atardece. El cielo," *Que trata,* 110).

46. Compare Otero's experimentation with the motif in "Bilbao," *Expresión,* 291–92.

47. See H. T. Rowley, *The Growth of the Old Testament* (1950; reprint, New York: Harper & Row, 1963), 92, and E. M. Wilson, in Arthur T. Hatto, ed., *Eos: An Enquiry into the Theme of Lovers' Meetings and Partings at Dawn in Poetry* (The Hague: Mouton, 1965), 299–343.

48. See "Indemne," *Mientras,* 135–40, on the consolatory peace and constant miracle of dawn; and note José Luis Cano's judgment of *Mientras*: "Es una palabra de esperanza muy cargada de acento temporal" (It is a world of hope very heavily loaded with a temporal accent) (*Insula,* 8).

49. See also Zapiaín and Iglesias, *Aproximación,* 187–204.

50. See Steven Lukes, "Marxism and Utopianism," in Peter Alexander and Roger Gill, eds., *Utopias,* 153–67.

51. Compare Elías Díaz, "F. de los Ríos: la conciencia del socialismo español," *Revista de Occidente* 2 (1980), 93–108, and Juan López-Mory, "Francisco Giner y la redención nacional," *Sistema,* 33 (1981): 39–49.

Notes for Chapter 10: Conclusion

1. Edward W. Rosenheim, *Swift and the Satirist's Art,* 105, 174ff.

2. See Sabina de la Cruz, introduction to Otero, *Expresión,* on methods of composition.

3. See José Luis Cano, Prologue to *País*; Emilio Miró, "España, tierra y palabra en la poesía de Blas de Otero."

4. Otero, *País,* ed. José Luis Cano, 15.

5. Juan López-Morillas, "Francisco Giner y la redención nacional," 47.

6. See Lionel Trilling, *The Liberal Imagination: Essays on Literature and Society* (New York: Viking, 1950).

Selected Bibliography

Works by Blas de Otero

Otero, Blas de. *Cántico espiritual*. San Sebastián: Cuadernos del Grupo Alea, 1942.

———. "Poesías en Burgos." *Escorial* 12 (August 1943): 221–24.

———. *Angel fieramente humano*. Madrid: Insula, 1950.

———. *Redoble de conciencia*. Barcelona: Instituto de Estudios Hispánicos, 1951.

———. *Pido la paz y la palabra*. Torrelavega: Cantalapiedra, 1955.

———. *Ancia (Angel fieramente humano, Redoble de conciencia)* Barcelona: Alberto Puig Editor, 1958.

———. *Parler clair: En castellano*. Translated by Claude Couffon. Paris: Seghers, 1959.

———. *Angel fieramente humano: Redoble de conciencia*. 1950, 1951. Reprint. Buenos Aires: Losada, 1960.

———. *Con la inmensa mayoría (Pido la paz y la palabra, En castellano)*. 1955, 1959. Reprint. Buenos Aires: Losada, 1960.

———. *En castellano*. México: Universidad Nacional Autónoma de México, 1960.

———. *Hacia la inmensa mayoría (Angel fieramente humano, Redoble de conciencia, Pido la paz y la palabra, En castellano)*. Reprint. Buenos Aires: Losada, 1962.

———. *Esto no es un libro*. Río Piedras: Universidad de Puerto Rico, 1963.

———. *Que trata de España*. Barcelona: Editorial RM, [1964].

———. *Que trata de España*. Paris: Ruedo Ibérico, 1964.

———. *Que trata de España (Pido la paz y la palabra, En castellano, Que trata de España)*. La Habana: Editora Nacional de Cuba, 1964.

———. "Donde se habla de las flores silvestres" (three poems). *Casa de las Américas* 41 (March-April 1967): 76–79.

———. "Homenaje a Jose Martí." *Insula* 260–61 (July-August 1968): 2.

———. *Expresión y reunión: a modo de antología (1941–1969)*. Madrid: Alfaguara, 1969.

———. *Mientras*. Zaragoza: Javalambre, 1970.

———. *Ancia*. 1958. Madrid: Visor, 1971.

———. *Historias fingidas y verdaderas*. Madrid: Alfaguara 1971.

———. *País (Antología 1955–1970)*. Edited by José Luis Cano. Madrid: Plaza y Janés, 1971.

———. "Beso verso." *Insula* 332–33 (July-August 1974): 4.

———. "Escrito para." *Papeles de Son Armadans* 72 (March 1974): 252–64.

———. *Verso y prosa*. Madrid: Cátedra, 1974.

———. *Pido la paz y la palabra*. 2d ed. Barcelona: Lumen, 1975.

———. *Verso y prosa*. Reprint. Madrid: Cátedra, 1976.

———. *En castellano*. 2d ed. Barcelona: Lumen, 1977.

———. *Poesía con nombres*. Madrid: Alianza, 1977.

———. *Que trata de España*. 1964. Reprint. Madrid: Visor, 1977.

———. *Todos mis sonetos*. Madrid: Turner, 1977.

———. "Escucho las palabras." *Insula* 374–75 (January-February 1978): 5.

———. *Historias fingidas y verdaderas*. Edited by Sabina de la Cruz. Madrid: Alianza, 1980.

———. *Expresión y reunión: (a modo de antología)*. 1969. Edited by Sabina de la Cruz. Madrid: Alianza, 1981.

Secondary Sources

Alarcos Llorach, Emilio. *La poesía de Blas de Otero*. Oviedo: Universidad de Oviedo, 1956. 2d ed. Salamanca: Anaya, 1966.

———. *Elementos formales en la lírica actual*. Santander: Universidad Internacional Menéndez y Pelayo, 1967.

————. "Al margen de Blas de Otero." *Papeles de Son Armadans* 85 (May-June y: 121–46.

————. "La poesía de Blas de Otero." In *Blas de Otero: Study of a Poet,* edited by Carlos Mellizo and Louise Salstad, 1–10. Laramie: University of Wyoming, 1980.

Albornoz, Aurora de. "Blas de Otero, hoy, mañana." *Insula* 392–93 (1979): 6.

Alcántara, Manuel. "La incorporación de la frase hecha en la poesía española." *Revista de Archivos, Bibliotecas y Museos* 63 (1957): 223–50.

Aleixandre, Vicente. "Blas de Otero entre los demás." *Los encuentros,* 1268–70. Madrid: Guadarrama, 1958.

Alexander, Peter, and Roger Gill, eds. *Utopias.* London: Duckworth, 1984.

Alin, José María. "Blas de Otero y la poesía tradicional." *Archivium* (Oviedo) 15 (1967): 275–89.

Alonso, Dámaso. "Poesía arraigada y poesía desarraigada." *Poetas españoles contemporáneos. 1952,* 345–58. 3d ed. Madrid: Gredos, 1965.

Ambrozio, Leonilda. "Palabra y silencio en *Verso y prosa* de Blas de Otero." *Ibero-amerikanisches Archiv* 10 (1984): 1–12.

Anderson, William S. *Essays on Roman Satire.* Princeton, N.J.: Princeton University Press, 1982.

Apte, Mahadev. *Humor and Laughter: An Anthropological Approach.* Ithaca: Cornell University Press, 1985.

Aub, Max. *La poesía española contemporánea.* México: Imprenta universitaria, 1954.

————. *Una nueva poesía española (1950–1955).* México: Imprenta universitaria, 1957.

Bakhtin, Mikhail. *Rabelais and His World (Tvorchestvo Fransua Rable).* Translated by Helene Iswolsky. Cambridge, Mass.: M.I.T. Press, 1968. Reprint. Bloomington: Indiana University Press, 1984.

Barral, Carlos. *Años de penitencia.* Madrid: Alianza, 1975.

————. *Los años sin excusa: Memorias II.* Barcelona: Barral, 1978.

Bary, David. "Sobre el nombrar poético en la poesía española contemporánea." *Papeles de Son Armadans* 44 (February 1967): 161–89.

————. "De Serrano-Plaja a Gabriel Celaya: apuntes sobre el tema del trabajo en la poesía española contemporánea." *Papeles de Son Armadans* 60 (March 1971): 241–64.

Battló, José, ed. *Antología de la nueva poesía española.* Madrid: El Bardo, 1968.

Blanco Aguinaga, Carlos. "El mundo entre ceja y ceja: releyendo a Blas de Otero." *Papeles de Son Armadans* 85 (May-June 1977): 147–96.

Blanco Aguinaga, Carlos, Julio Rodríguez-Puértolas, and Iris Zavala, eds. *Historia social de la literatura española.* 3 vols. Madrid: Castalia, 1978.

Bleiberg, Germán. Review of *Angel fieramente humano. Insula* 54 (June 1950): 4–5.

Bloom, Edward A., and Lillian D. Bloom. *Satire's Persuasive Voice.* Ithaca: Cornell University Press, 1979.

Bousoño, Carlos. "Un ensayo de estilística explicativa (ruptura de un sistema formado por una frase hecha)." *Homenaje universitario a Dámaso Alonso,* 69–84. Madrid: Gredos, 1970.

————. *Teoría de la expresión poética.* 1966. Reprint. Madrid: Gredos, 1976.

Butt, John. *Writers and Politics in Modern Spain.* London: Hodder and Stoughton, 1978.

Caballero Bonald, J. M. "Vigencia de la poesía de Blas de Otero." *Papeles de Son Armadans* 1 (1956): 118–22.

Cairns, Francis. *Generic Composition in Greek and Roman Poetry.* Edinburgh: Edinburgh University Press, 1972.

Cannan, Gilbert. *Satire.* New York: Doran, 1919.

Cano, José Luis. "Una antología consultada." *Cuadernos hispanoamericanos* 38 (February 1953): 245–47.

————. *Antología de la nueva poesía española.* Madrid: Gredos, 1958. 3d ed., 1968.

————. *El tema de España en la poesía española contemporánea.* Madrid: Revista de Occidente, 1964.

————. Review of *Mientras* and *Historias fingidas y verdaderas. Insula* 292 (March 1971): 8–9.

————. Review of *Todos mis sonetos. Insula* 370 (September 1977): 8–9.

————. "En la muerte de Blas de Otero." *Insula* 392–93 (July-August 1979): 7.

————. "Blas de Otero y el soneto heterodoxo." In *Blas de Otero: Study of a Poet,* edited by Carlos Mellizo and Louise Salstad, 11–17. Laramie: University of Wyoming, 1980.

Cano Ballesta, Juan. *La poesía española entre pureza y revolución, 1930–1936.* Madrid: Gredos, 1972.

Carballo Picazo, Alfredo. "Sobre unos versos de Blas de Otero." *Homenaje universitario a Dámaso Alonso,* 253–64. Madrid: Gredos, 1970.

Cardwell, Richard A. "The Persistence of Romantic Thought in Spain." *Modern Language Review* 65 (1970): 803–12.

Castellet, José María, ed. *Veinte años de poesía española: antología (1939–1959).* Barcelona: Seix Barral, 1960.

————. *Un cuarto de siglo de poesía española (1939–1964).* Barcelona: Seix Barral, 1965.

————. *Nueve novísimos poetas españoles.* Barcelona: Barral, 1970.

Celaya, Gabriel. *Exploración de la poesía.* Barcelona: Seix Barral, 1964.

Charmot, François. *La pédagogie des Jésuites: ses principes, son actualité.* Paris: Spes, 1943.

Ciplijauskaité, Biruté. *El poeta y la poesía: del romanticismo a la poesía social.* Madrid: Insula, 1966.

————. "Sobre la estructura del poema en Blas de Otero." In *Blas de Otero: Study of a Poet,* edited by Carlos Mellizo and Louise Salstad, 19–28. Laramie: University of Wyoming, 1980.

Clarasó, Mercedes. "Sea Imagery in the Poetry of Blas de Otero." In *Blas de Otero: Study of a Poet,* edited by Carlos Mellizo and Louise Salstad, 41–52. Laramie: University of Wyoming, 1980.

Coffey, Michael. *Roman Satire.* London: Methuen, 1976.

Cohen, J. M. "Since the Civil War: New Currents in Spanish Poetry." *Encounter* 12 (February 1959): 44–53.

Colie, Rosalie L. *The Resources of Kind: Genre Theory in the Renaissance.* Edited by Barbara K. Lewalski. Berkeley: University of California Press, 1973.

Correa, Gustavo. "El simbolismo del mar en la poesía española del siglo XX." *Revista Hispánica Moderna* 32 (1966): 62–86.

————. "Temporality and Commitment in Spanish Poetry after 1936." *Ventures* (Spring 1970): 33–36.

————. *Antología de la poesía española (1900–1980).* 2 vols. Madrid: Gredos, 1980.

Corrigan, Robert W., ed. *Comedy: Meaning and Form.* San Francisco: Chandler Publishing Company, 1965.

Couffon, Claude. "Rencontre avec Blas de Otero." *Les Lettres Nouvelles* (25 March 1959): 20–21.

Crémer, Victoriano. "Un cuestionario sobre poesía social y de la otra." *Poesía española* 11 (November 1952): 1–5.

Cruz, Sabina de la. "Los sonetos de Blas de Otero." Introduction to Otero, *Todos mis sonetos,* xi–xxiii. Madrid: Turner, 1977.

————. "Blas de Otero en su adolescencia madrileña (1927–1932)." *Insula* 449 (April 1984): 4.

Daydí-Tolson, Santiago. *The Post–Civil War Spanish Poets.* Boston: Twayne, 1983.

Debicki, Andrew. *Poetry of Discovery: The Spanish Generation of 1956–71.* Lexington: University Press of Kentucky, 1982.

Dietrich, Anton. "Literatur unter Franco: Spaniens jüngste Dichtung zwischen Hoffnung und Kommerzialiserung." *Wort und Warheit* 15 (February 1960): 101–16.

Donahue, Moraima de Semprún. *Blas de Otero en su poesía.* Chapel Hill: University of North Carolina, Department of Romance Languages, 1977.

————. "Otero, el labrador de la palabra." *Papeles de Son Armadans* 245–46 (May-June 1977): 219–32.

Donaldson, Ian. *The World Upside Down: Comedy from Johnson to Fielding.* Oxford: Oxford University Press, 1970.

Duff, J. Wight. *Roman Satire: Its Outlook on Social Life.* Berkeley: University of California Press, 1936.

Eastman, Max. *The Enjoyment of Laughter.* New York: Simon and Schuster, 1936.

Eco, Umberto. "The Frames of Comic Freedom." In *Carnival,* edited by Thomas A. Sebeok, 1–10. Berlin, N.Y. and Amsterdam: Mouton, 1984.

Elliott, Robert C. *The Power of Satire: Magic, Ritual, Art.* Princeton, N.J.: Princeton University Press, 1960.

————. "The Definition of Satire." *Yearbook of Comparative and General Literature* 11 (1962): 19–23.

————. *España canta a Cuba.* Paris: Ruedo Ibérico, 1962.

Farrel, Allan P. *The Jesuit Code of Liberal Education: Development and Scope of the Ratio Studiorum.* Milwaukee: Bruce Publishing Co., 1938.

Ferrán, Jaime, and D. Testa, eds. *Spanish Writers of 1936.* London: Tamesis, 1973.

Fowler, Alastair. *Kinds of Literature: An Introduction to the Theory of Genres and Modes.* Cambridge, Mass.: Harvard University Press, 1982.

Franco, Dolores. *España como preocupación.* 1944. 2d ed. Madrid: Guadarrama, 1960.

Frye, Northrop. "The Nature of Satire." *University of Toronto Quarterly* 14 (October 1944): 75–89.

————. "Varieties of Literary Utopias." *Daedalus* 94 (Spring 1965): 323–47.

Galán, Joaquín. *Blas de Otero, palabras para un pueblo: tres vías de conocimiento.* Barcelona: Ambito, 1978.

García de la Concha, Víctor. "Espadaña. Biografía de una revista de poesía y crítica." *Cuadernos hispanoamericanos* 236 (August 1969): 380–97.

————. *La poesía española de posguerra: teoría e historia de sus movimientos.* Madrid: Prensa Española, 1973.

García Hortelano, J., ed. *El grupo poético de los años 50.* Madrid: Taurus, 1978.

García Sánchez, J., and Fernando Millán, eds. *La escritura en libertad*. Madrid: Alianza, 1975.

Garciasol, Ramón de. "Notas sobre la nueva poesía española 1939–1969." *Revista nacional de cultura* (Caracas) 19 (May-June 1959): 48–64.

———. "Poesía y pueblo." *Insula* 200–201 (July-August 1963): 6.

Gil de Biedma, Jaime. *Diario del artista seriamente enfermo*. Barcelona: Lumen, 1974.

———. *El pie de la letra: ensayos 1955–1979*. Barcelona: Crítica, 1980.

Gimferrer, Pere. "Notas parciales sobre poesía española de posguerra." In *Treinta años de literatura en España*, edited by Salvador Clotas and Pere Gimferrer, 91–108. Barcelona: Kairos, 1971.

Gombrich, E. H. "The Experiment of Caricature." *Art and Illusion*, 330–58. 1960. Reprint. Princeton, N.J.: Princeton University Press, 1969.

González, Angel. "¿Que es el social-realismo?" *Poesía española* 22 (October 1953): 1–8.

———, ed. *Gabriel Celaya: Poesía*. Madrid: Alianza, 1977.

González, José M. *Poesía española de posguerra (Celaya, Otero, Hierro: 1950–1960)*. Madrid: Edi-6, 1982.

González-Martin, J. P. *Poesía hispánica 1939–1969: estudio y antología*. Barcelona: El Bardo, 1970.

González-Muela, Joaquín. "Un hombre de nuestro tiempo: Blas de Otero." *Revista Hispánica Moderna* 29 (April 1963): 133–39.

———. *La nueva poesía española*. Madrid: Alcalá, 1973.

———. *Gramática de la poesía*. Barcelona: Planeta, 1976.

González Rodas, Pablo, ed. *Gloria Fuertes, Historia de Gloria*. Madrid: Cátedra, 1980.

Goytisolo, Juan. "Para una literatura nacional popular." *Insula* 146 (January 1959): 6.

Grande, Félix. *Apuntes sobre poesía española de posguerra*. Madrid: Taurus, 1970.

Grant, Helen F. "The World Upside-Down." In *Studies in Spanish Literature of the Golden Age presented to E. M. Wilson*, edited by R. O. Jones, 103–35. London: Tamesis, 1973.

Green, Otis H. "A Hispanist's Thoughts on [Gilbert Highet's] *The Anatomy of Satire*." *Romance Philology* 17 (August 1963): 123–33.

Guereña, Jacinto Luis. "La alentadora poesía de Blas de Otero." *Nueva Estafeta* 14 (1980): 66–70.

Guillén, Claudio. *Literature as System: Essays Toward the Theory of Literary History*. Princeton, N.J.: Princeton University Press, 1971.

Gullón, Ricardo. Review of *Angel fieramente humano. Cuadernos hispanoamericanos* 15 (May-June 1950): 591–92.

Gurewitch, Morton. *Comedy: The Irrational Vision*. Ithaca: Cornell University Press, 1975.

Hernández, Evelyne Martin. "'A la inmensa mayoría': Les 'voix' de l'absolu dans Blas de Otero." *Iris* (Montpellier) 4 (1984): 121–29.

Herrero, Javier. *Los orígenes del pensamiento reaccionario español*. Madrid: Cuadernos para el Diálogo, 1971.

Hierro, José. "Poesía pura, Poesía práctica." *Insula* 13 (November 1957): 1, 4.

———. "Poésie espagnole d'aujourd'hui." *La Table Ronde* 145 (1960): 111–15.

———. "La huella de Rubén en los poetas de la posguerra española." *Cuadernos hispanoamericanos* 212–13 (August-September 1967): 347–67.

Highet, Gilbert. *The Anatomy of Satire*. Princeton, N.J.: Princeton University Press, 1962.

Hodgart, Matthew J. C. *Satire*. New York: McGraw Hill, 1969.

Hottinger, Arnold. *Das volkstümliche Element in der modernen spanischen Lyrik*. Zurich: Atlantis Verlag, 1962.

Howard, Richard. Review of *Twenty Poems of Blas de Otero. Poetry* 107 (February 1966): 339–40.

Ifach, María de Gracia, ed. *Cuatro poetas de hoy: José Luis Hidalgo, Gabriel Celaya, Blas de Otero, José Hierro*. Madrid: Taurus, 1960.

Iffland, James. *Quevedo and the Grotesque*. 2 vols. London: Tamesis, 1978–1982.

Ilie, Paul. "The Disguises of Protest: Contemporary Spanish Poetry." *Michigan Quarterly Review* 10 (Winter 1971): 38–48.

———. "The Poetry of Social Protest: A Review Article." *Hispanic Review* 41 (1973): 78–87.

Inman Fox, E. "La poesía 'social' y la tradición simbolista." *La torre* 64 (1969): 47–62.

Izquierdo Arroyo, J. M. "En torno al silencio de dios en la poesía de Blas de Otero." *Estudios* 27 (1971): 411–74.

Jammes, Robert. *Études sur l'oeuvre poétique de Don Luis de Góngora y Argote*. Bordeaux: Institut d'études ibériques et ibéroamericaines, 1967.

Jiménez, José Olivio. "Medio siglo de poesía española." *Hispania* 50 (1967): 931–46.

———. "Nueva poesía española 1960–1970." *Insula* 288 (November 1970): 1, 2, 13.

————. *Diez años de poesía española (1960–1970).* Madrid: Insula, 1972.

————. *La presencia de Antonio Machado en la poesía española de posguerra.* Lincoln, Neb.: Society of Spanish and Spanish-American Studies, 1983.

Jiménez Martos, Luis. *Informe sobre poesía española (siglo XX).* Madrid: Editora Nacional, 1976.

Kern, Edith. *The Absolute Comic.* New York: Columbia University Press, 1980.

Kernan, Alvin B. *The Cankered Muse: Satire of the English Renaissance.* New Haven: Yale University Press, 1959.

King, Edmund L. "Blas de Otero: The Past and the Present of 'The Eternal.'" In *Spanish Writers of 1936,* edited by Jaime Ferrán and D. Testa, 125–133. London: Tamesis, 1973.

Knoche, Ulrich. *Roman Satire.* Translated by E. S. Ramage. 1949. Reprint. Bloomington: Indiana University Press, 1975.

Knox, E.G.V. *The Mechanism of Satire.* Cambridge: Cambridge University Press, 1951.

Laín Entralgo, Pedro. *La generación de '98.* Madrid: Diana, 1945.

————. *España como problema.* 1948. Reprint. Madrid: Aguilar, 1962.

————. *La espera y la esperanza: Historia y teoría del esperar humano.* Madrid: Revista de Occidente, 1962.

Leacock, Stephen. *Humor: Its Theory and Technique.* New York: Dodd, Mead, 1935.

Le Bigot, Claude. "El lenguaje poético de Blas de Otero en 'Pido la paz y la palabra.'" *Les Langues Néo-Latines* 79 (1985): 55–69.

Lechner, Johannes. *El compromiso en la poesía española del siglo XX.* 2 vols. Leyden: Universitaire Pers Leiden, 1968–1975.

Leiva, Raul. "Blas de Otero, conciencia poética de España." *Cuadernos americanos* 31 (1972): 209–24.

Levin, Harry. "The Wages of Satire." *Literature and Society: Selected Papers from the English Institute,* 1–14. Baltimore: Johns Hopkins University Press, 1980.

Ley, Charles David. *Spanish Poetry Since 1939.* Washington, D.C.: Catholic University Press, 1962.

López Anglada, Luis. *Panorama poético español 1939–1964.* Madrid: Editora Nacional, 1965.

López-Morillas, Juan. "Antonio Machado: ética y poesía." *Insula* 256 (March 1968): 1, 12.

————. *Hacia el '98: literatura, sociedad, ideología.* Barcelona: Ariel, 1972.

————. "Francisco Giner y la redención nacional." *Sistema* 33 (1979): 39–49.

Lorenz, Erika. *Der metaphorische Kosmos der modernen spanischen Lyrik (1936–1956).* Hamburg: Cram, De Gruyter, & Co., 1961.

Luis, Leopoldo de, ed. *Poesía española contemporánea Poesía social: antología (1939–1968).* 2d ed. Madrid: Alfaguara, 1969.

————. "La poesía social, otra vez." *Insula* 247 (June 1967): 4.

————. Review of *Expresión y reunión. Papeles de Son Armadans* 55 (March 1970): 313–17.

————. Review of *País. Revista de Occidente* (June 1972), 378–81.

Mainer, José-Carlos. *Falange y literatura: antología y estudio.* Barcelona: Labor, 1971.

Manuel, Frank E., and Fritzie P. Manuel. *Utopian Thought in the Western World.* Cambridge, Mass.: Harvard University Press, 1979.

Marichal, Juan. "El drama histórico del liberalismo español." *Cuadernos americanos* 12 (1953): 161–74.

Marín, Diego. *Poesía paisajística española 1940–1970: estudio y antología.* London: Tamesis, 1977.

Marra-López, José. "Una nueva generación poética." *Insula* 221 (April 1965): 5.

Mas, Amédée. *La Caricature de la femme, du mariage, et de l'amour dans l'oeuvre de Quevedo.* Paris: Ediciones Hispanoamericanas, 1957.

Mayoral, Marina. "Blas de Otero: canto primero." *Poesía española contemporánea: análisis de textos,* 231–42. Madrid: Gredos, 1973.

Mellizo, Carlos, and Louise Salstad, eds. *Blas de Otero: Study of a Poet.* Laramie: Department of Modern and Classical Languages, University of Wyoming, 1980.

Millán, Rafael. "O inconformismo na poesía espanhola de após-guerra." *Cadernos brasileiros* 2 (1960): 57–63.

Mir, Miguel. *Historia interna, documentada de la Compañía de Jesús.* 2 vols. Madrid: Ratés Martín, 1913.

Miró, Emilio. "La obra de tres poetas: Celaya, Otero, Caballero, Bonald." *Insula* 282 (May 1970): 6–7.

————. Review of *País. Insula* 305 (April 1972): 6–7.

————. Review of *Verso y prosa. Insula* 329 (April 1974): 6–7.

————. "La poesía prohibida de Blas de Otero y Gabriel Celaya." *Insula* 380–81 (July-August 1978): 10.

————. "España, tierra y palabra en la poesía de Blas de Otero." *Cuadernos hispanoamericanos* 356 (1980): 274–97.

————. "La poesía desde 1936." In *Historia de la literatura española. El siglo XX,* edited by J. M. Díez-Borque, 327–89. Madrid: Taurus, 1980.

————. "La palabra libre y creadora de Blas de Otero." *Insula* 419 (October 1981): 6–7.

Muecke, Douglas. *The Compass of Irony.* London: Methuen, 1969.

Muñiz, María Luisa. "Poeticeskaia trilogia Blasa de Otero *Rech' idet ob Ispanii.*" *Vestnik Leningradskogo Universiteta. Istorii, Iazyka, Literatury* 14 (1969): 81–92.

————. "El poeta y la patria en la trilogía de Blas de Otero *Que trata de España*" (translated from Russian). *Estudios ofrecidos a Emilio Alarcos Llorach,* vol. 2, 401–13. Oviedo: Universidad de Oviedo, 1977.

Navarro Tomás, Tomás. *Métrica española: Reseña histórica descriptiva.* New York: Las Américas, 1966.

Nolting-Hauf, Ilse. *Visión, sátira y agudeza en los sueños de Quevedo.* Madrid: Gredos, 1974.

Núñez, Antonio. "Encuentro con Blas de Otero." *Insula* 259 (June 1958): 1, 3–4.

Orringer, Nelson R. "La espada y el arado: una refutación lírica de Juan Ramón por Blas de Otero." *Inti* 1 (November 1974): 12–19.

Parker, Alexander A. *Polyphemus and Galatea: A Study in the Interpretation of a Baroque Poem.* Austin: University of Texas Press, 1977.

Paulson, Ronald. *The Fictions of Satire.* Baltimore: Johns Hopkins University Press, 1967.

————. *Satire: Modern Essays in Criticism.* Englewood Cliffs, N.J.: Prentice Hall, 1971.

Payne, Stanley. *Falange: A History of Spanish Fascism.* Stanford, Calif.: Stanford University Press, 1961.

————. *Spanish Catholicism.* Madison: University of Wisconsin Press, 1984.

Peter, John. *Complaint and Satire in Early English Literature.* Oxford: Clarendon Press, 1956.

Peyregne, Françoise. "Blas de Otero, poeta de la oralidad." *Iris* (Montpellier) 5 (1985): 115–32.

Poggioli, Renato. *The Theory of the Avant Garde.* Cambridge, Mass.: Harvard University Press, 1968.

————. *The Oaten Flute: Essays on Pastoral Poetry and the Pastoral Ideal.* Cambridge, Mass.: Harvard University Press, 1975.

Potts, Abbie Findlay. *The Elegiac Mode: Poetic Form in Wordsworth and Other Elegists.* Ithaca: Cornell University Press, 1967.

Potts, L. J. *Comedy.* London: Hutchkinson, 1948.

Predmore, Michael. *Una España joven en la poesía de Antonio Machado.* Madrid: Insula, 1981.

Price, R. M., ed. *An Anthology of Quevedo's Poetry.* Manchester: Manchester University Press, 1969.

Pring-Mill, R.D.F. "Nature and Function of Spanish American *poesía de compromiso.*" *Bulletin of the Society for Latin American Studies* (Glasgow) 31 (1979): 4–21.

Quevedo y Villegas, Francisco de. *Obra poética.* Edited by José Manuel Blecua. Barcelona: Planeta, 1963.

————. *Poesía varia.* Edited by James O. Crosby. Madrid: Cátedra, 1981.

Rangel Guerra, Alfonso. "La poesía de Blas de Otero." *Humanitas* 2 (1961): 269–98.

Rawson, Claude, ed. *English Satire and the Satiric Tradition.* Oxford: Blackwell, 1984.

Ribes, Francisco, ed. *Antología consultada de la joven poesía española.* Valencia: Distribuciones Mares, 1952.

Rodrigues Lapa, Manuel. *Cantigas d'escarnho e de mal dizer.* Vigo: Galaxia, 1965.

————. *Liçoes de literatura portuguesa: época medieval.* 6th ed. Coimbra: Coimbra editora, 1966.

Rodríguez-Alcalde, Leopoldo. *Vida y sentido de la poesía actual.* Madrid: Editora Nacional, 1956.

Rodríguez-Puértolas, Julio. *Poesía de protesta en la edad media castellana: historia y antología.* Madrid: Gredos, 1968.

————. "Blas de Otero o la voz de España." *Norte* 10 (May-June 1969): 45–52.

Rosenheim, Edward W. *Swift and the Satirist's Art.* Chicago: University of Chicago Press, 1963.

Rubio, Fanny. *Las revistas poéticas españolas (1939–1975).* Madrid: Turner, 1976.

————. "Teoría y polémica en la poesía española de posguerra." *Cuadernos hispanoamericanos* 361–62 (July-August 1980): 199–214.

Salvador, Gregorio. "Cuarto tiempo de una metáfora: en torno a un soneto de Blas de Otero." *Homenaje al Dr. Emilio Alarcos García.* Valladolid: Universidad de Valladolid, 1965–67.

Scholberg, Kenneth R. *Sátira e invectiva en la España medieval.* Madrid: Gredos, 1971.

————. *Algunos aspectos de la sátira en el siglo XVI.* Frankfurt: Peter Lang, 1979.

Seidel, Michael. *Satiric Inheritance, Rabelais to Sterne.* Princeton, N.J.: Princeton University Press, 1979.

Senabre-Sempere, Ricardo. "Juegos retóricos en la poesía de Blas de Otero." *Papeles de Son Armadans* 125 (1966): 137–51.

———. "Modelos y transformaciones en la poesía de Blas de Otero." In *Blas de Otero: Study of a Poet,* edited by Carlos Mellizo and Louise Salstad, 29–39. Laramie: University of Wyoming, 1980.

Shaw, Donald L. "Towards the Understanding of Spanish Romanticism." *Modern Language Review* 58 (1963): 190–95.

Siebenmann, Gustav. *Los estilos poéticos en España desde 1900.* Madrid: Gredos, 1973.

Silver, Philip W. "New Spanish Poetry: the Rodríguez-Brines Generation." *Books Abroad* 42 (1968): 211–14.

———. "Blas de Otero en la cruz de las palabras," *La casa de Anteo: Ensayos de poética hispana* (Madrid: Taurus, 1985), 191–219.

Spallone, Gianni. "Un Sonetto *Sin riberas* di Blas de Otero." *Studi Ispanici* (Pisa: Giadini Editori, 1984): 124–40.

Stewart, Susan. *Nonsense: Aspects of Intertextuality in Folklore and Literature.* Baltimore: Johns Hopkins University Press, 1979.

Stixrude, David. "La espontaneidad en los poemas de *Ancia.*" *Papeles de Son Armadans* 254–55 (May-June 1977): 273–95.

Sutherland, James R. *English Satire.* 1958. Reprint. Cambridge: Cambridge University Press, 1967.

Torre, Emilio de la. *José Hierro: poeta de testimonio.* Madrid: Porrua Turanzas, 1983.

Torre, Guillermo de. "Contemporary Spanish Poetry." *Texas Quarterly* 4 (Spring 1961): 55–78.

Uceda, Julio. "La traición de los poetas sociales." *Insula* 242 (January 1967): 1, 12.

Ulam, Adam. "Socialism and Utopia." *Daedalus* 94 (Spring 1965): 382–400.

Valente, José Angel. *Las Palabras de la tribu.* Madrid: Siglo Veintiuno, 1971.

Vilar, Sergio. *Arte y libertad: encuesta entre los intelectuales y artistas españoles.* New York: Las Américas, 1963.

Welsford, Enid. *The Fool: His Social and Literary History.* London: Faber and Faber, 1935.

Worcester, David. *The Art of Satire.* Cambridge, Mass.: Harvard University Press, 1940.

Wright, Eleanor. *The Poetry of Protest Under Franco.* London: Tamesis, 1986.

Yndurain, Domingo, ed. *Historia y crítica de la literatura española. Epoca contemporánea: 1939–1980.* Barcelona: Crítica, 1980.

Zapiaín, Itziar, and Ramón Iglesias. *Aproximación a la poesía de Blas de Otero.* Madrid: Narcea, 1983.

Zardoya, Concha. "El poeta político (En torno a España)." *Cuadernos americanos* 206 (1976): 139–273.

Index of Works by Otero

INDEX